INSPIRE / PLAN / DISCOVER / EXPERIENCE

COSTA RICA

COSTA RICA

CONTENTS

DISCOVER 6

FIELD GUIDE 54

EXPERIENCE 100

NEED TO KNOW 246

Left: A tiny red-eyed tree frog emerging from a wet leaf
Previous page: Picturesque vista of the majestic Arenal Volcano
Front cover: The stunning Catarata del Toro waterfall during sunset

DISCOVER

The crescent-shaped coves of Parque Nacional Manuel Antonio

WELCOME TO
COSTA RICA

Diminutive Costa Rica packs an enormous punch, with a culture as rich and vibrant as its incredible biodiversity. Add wildlife galore, an idyllic climate, and friendly locals, and you've got the ideal destination. Whatever your dream trip to Costa Rica includes, this DK Eyewitness travel guide is the perfect companion.

1 A boldly colored toucan perching on a branch.

2 Wooden stairs leading down to the base of a waterfall in the rainforest.

3 A team running the rapids on the Río Sarapíqui.

4 The stunning beach at Manuel Antonio.

Straddling the Mesoamerican isthmus between North and South America, this little nation's magnificent biodiversity is justifiably the country's main attraction, and unsurprisingly Costa Rica's forte is ecotourism. There's an endless choice of nature activities and lodges, and visitors have so many ways to answer the call of the wild. Join a guided night tour of the jungle to spy the elusive jaguar. Volunteer to help sea turtle hatchlings make it to the waves or release treacle-slow sloths back into the canopy.

Its cities and villages are equally enticing. San José, the capital, is carving out its place as one of Central America's hippest cities, with buzzing craft breweries, world-class museums, and a lively foodie scene. Westward, Liberia is a laid-back gateway to Costa Rica's *sabanero* (cowboy)

culture. Embracing the Tico (Costa Rican) gospel of *pura vida* (pure life), beachy yoga retreats along the Nicoya Peninsula are all zen, while fun-loving Pavones, to the south, is a surfers' paradise. Over the coffee-estate-strewn central highlands is the alluring blend of white sands and turquoise waters, indigenous culture and delicious cuisine of the Caribbean coast.

With so many different things to discover, it's hard to know where to start. We've broken the country down into easily navigable chapters, with detailed itineraries, expert local knowledge, and colorful, comprehensive maps to help you plan the perfect visit. However long your stay, this DK Eyewitness travel guide will ensure that you see the very best of Costa Rica. Enjoy the book, and enjoy Costa Rica. *¡Pura vida!*

REASONS TO LOVE
COSTA RICA

Its scenery is spectacular. There's wildlife galore. It's peaceful and easy to get around. Ask any Costa Rican and you'll hear a different reason why they love their country. Here, we pick some of our favorites.

1 PURA VIDA

"*Pura vida*" (literally "pure life") is more than a Costa Rican phrase – it's a relaxed, no-stress philosophy of life, and one reason Ticos (Costa Ricans) have been named among the world's happiest people.

BEACH LIFE 2

Costa Rica's palm-fringed beaches, running the length of both coastlines, are perfect for recharging. Some of the finest are on the Nicoya Peninsula *(p154)* and south of Puerto Viejo de Talamanca *(p223)*.

3 TURTLE CONSERVATION

The sight of an *arribada* (mass arrival) of sea turtles crawling up Costa Rica's beaches is pure magic. Go to Tortuguero *(p218)* or Nosara *(p188)* to patrol nesting sites and help tiny hatchlings back to sea.

WEALTH OF WILDLIFE 4

Slow-moving sloths, raucous green macaws, leaping humpback whales, incurious iguanas – bring your binoculars to get face-to-face with Costa Rica's legendary wildlife *(p54)*.

WHITE-WATER RAFTING 5

With fantastic rapids tumbling down steep slopes amid stunning natural beauty, Costa Rica offers world-class rapids across the country. Pack your paddle and head straight for Sarapiquí *(p206)* and the Pacuare River to test your skills on everything from half-day trips to multiday excursions.

THE GRANO DE ORO 6

Start every day with a rich dark brew from the *grano de oro*, the nation's golden bean. Coffee lovers, make a beeline for the Central Highlands to savor the full bean-to-cup experience.

SCUBA DIVING 7
The crystal-clear waters off both sides of Costa Rica teem with sealife and ship-wrecks. Head to Gandoca-Manzanillo (*p222*) and Isla del Coco (*p236*) for the best dives.

**EXTRAORDINARY 8
NATURAL BEAUTY**
From conical Volcán Arenal (*p202*) to the mist-shrouded cloud forest of Monteverde (*p172*) to Corcovado's (*p234*) bottle-green rainforest, Costa Rica is full of inspiring scenery.

9 INDIGENOUS CULTURE
Indigenous peoples make up only a fraction of the population, but they've had a huge impact on the country. Community-run tours provide an insight into their heritages.

10 SURFERS' PARADISE

Catch perfect point and beach breaks off Playa Negra in the Caribbean and Witch's Rock at Pacific-coast Santa Rosa *(p178)* year-round – surf them both in the same day, if you want to.

FIVE A DAY 11

Roadside market stalls and beachfront pop-ups burst with the bounty of fruit yielded by the country's fertile hills. Try local favorites, such as guanábana, maracuya and carambola, blended into a refreshing *batido* (fresh fruit shake).

PEÑAS AND TERTULIAS 12

Costa Rica's lively artistic and literary scene is best expressed in *peñas* and *tertulias* (artistic gatherings). Get involved in one of these arty salons or get-togethers of like-minded people in cultural hotspot San José *(p102)*.

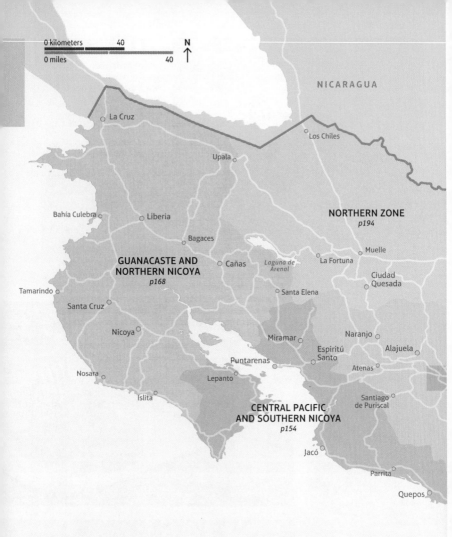

EXPLORE
COSTA RICA

This guide divides Costa Rica into seven colour-coded sightseeing areas, as shown on the map. Find out more about each area on the following pages.

CENTRAL AMERICA AND THE CARIBBEAN

USA

Atlantic
Ocean

BAHAMAS

MEXICO

CUBA

HAITI

PUERTO
RICO

BELIZE
GUATEMALA
EL SALVADOR
HONDURAS
NICARAGUA

JAMAICA

Caribbean Sea

COSTA RICA
PANAMA

VENEZUELA

Pacific
Ocean

COLOMBIA

Barra del
Colorado

Puerto Viejo
de Sarapiquí

Tortuguero

Guápiles

THE CARIBBEAN
p212

Siquirres

Matina

Puerto Limón

SAN JOSÉ
p102

Turrialba

Cartago

CENTRAL HIGHLANDS
p126

Santa María
de Dota

Puerto Viejo
de Talamanca

*Caribbean
Sea*

San Isidro
de El General

Almirante

Dominical

Buenos
Aires

Palmar

Potrero Grande

SOUTHERN ZONE
p226

San Vito

PANAMA

Golfito

La Concepcion

Puerto
Jiménez

David

GETTING TO KNOW
COSTA RICA

Dominated by craggy mountains, gouged by verdant valleys, and hugged by white beaches and turquoise seas, Costa Rica's epic beauty is matched only by its abundant wildlife. Lush coffee estates rule the interior, ringed by laid-back villages and national parks offering unrivaled chances for adventuring.

PAGE 102

SAN JOSÉ

Nestled at 3,800 feet (1,150 m) between the rugged Talamanca Mountains and a chain of volcanoes to the north, the capital city – affectionately known by Costa Ricans as "Chepe" – enjoys a splendid setting and an idyllic climate. San José's magnificent Teatro Nacional and pre-Columbian gold and jade museums add to its attraction. Its architecture bears little trace of its early history, but what it lacks in grandeur it makes up for in an exciting foodie scene and a frenetic nightlife. Located in the heart of Costa Rica, San José is an ideal base for hub-and-spoke touring.

Best for
Buzzy nightlife, contemporary culture

Home to
Teatro Nacional, Museo del Oro Precolumbino, Centro Costarricense de Ciencias y Cultura

Experience
Joining a tertulia, or arty salon, to meet like-minded people

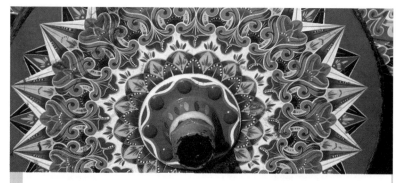

CENTRAL HIGHLANDS

Simmering volcanoes dominate the landscape of the Central Highlands as they tower over the country's central plateau – a broad valley that extends around San José. The climate is always mild, even in the height of summer. With steep slopes corduroyed by coffee fields and higher up by emerald forest, the region offers stunning drives along curving mountain roads and through picturesque villages whose farmers' markets and ancient fiestas call siren songs to anyone who passes.

Best for
Coffee, curving mountain passes, cooler climes

Home to
Monumento Nacional Guayabo, Orosí Valley, Basílica de Nuestra Senora de los Angeles

Experience
Sipping freshly roasted coffee at the finca *where the beans were harvested*

CENTRAL PACIFIC AND SOUTHERN NICOYA

Sun-drenched, forest-fringed beaches line the flank of this rugged region. To the west, Malpaís's wild beauty takes the full brunt of the Pacific, while the effortlessly cool bars of laid-back Monezuma make it a favorite with backpackers. Cut inland and find hiking trails alongside rivers where crocodiles lurk beneath the current. Farther south, lively surfing towns give way to glorious Parque Nacional Manuel Antonio.

Best for
Beach life and surf spots

Home to
Nacional Parque Manuel Antonio

Experience
Traveling up the Río Tárcoles to see crocodiles from the safety of a launch

→

PAGE 168

GUANACASTE AND NORTHERN NICOYA

In the driest of Costa Rica's regions, come to discover dramatic landscapes, gorgeous beaches, and diverse cultures. The handsome city of Liberia is rich in *sabanero* (cowboy) heritage, while farther south, in dusty Guaitíl, you'll find exquisite *artes decorativas* produced by Indigenous Chorotega potters. Easygoing Playas del Coco and Tamarindo on the coral-rimmed west coast are scuba diving and surf hubs. When it's time to relax, turn east to the therapeutic thermal mud pools of Miravalles.

Best for
Cultural insights and national parks

Home to
Parque Nacional Rincón de la Vieja, Monteverde and Santa Elena

Experience
Soaking in the thermal mud pools of Las Hornillas, on Miravalles Volcano

PAGE 194

NORTHERN ZONE

The rolling flatland of the north is quilted in pastureland, fragrant fruit fields, and dense, humid rainforest. To the west, La Fortuna is most people's stopping point before exploring the majestic Volcán Arenal. Stay a while – here there are caves to dive down, rivers to raft over, and bridal paths to mosey along. Eastward, aerial trams whiz through the canopy, while visitors on the ground wade through wetland looking for jaguars. The town of Puerto Viejo de Sarapiquí is the jump-off point for epic whitewater rafting trips and rainforest adventures.

Best for
Volcanic landscapes, canopy tours

Home to
Laguna de Arenal

Experience
Gazing over rainforest to Arenal, hundreds of feet above the ground in Mistico Arenal Hanging Bridges Park

THE CARIBBEAN

PAGE 212

The Caribbean coast is incredibly diverse in terms of cultures, cuisines, landscapes, and wildlife. Its jewel is the Parque Nacional Tortuguero – an important nesting ground for green turtles. In the north, rain-sodden Barra del Colorado attracts anglers from far and wide. To the south, the city of Puerto Limón – famous for its carnival – and the beach towns of Cahuita and Puerto Viejo de Talamanca have strong African-Caribbean identities, where Indigenous Bribri and Cabécar guides can provide a rich insight into their cultures. There are also great places to go surfing and spot wildlife such as howler monkeys and sloths.

Best for
Turtle spotting and Carnaval celebrations

Home to
Parque Nacional Tortuguero, Parque Nacional Cahuita

Experience
Sampling the culinary scene, then patrolling turtle nesting beaches at midnight

PAGE 226

SOUTHERN ZONE

Stretching toward Panama, the Southern Zone bears some of the least-explored, least-developed land in the country. To the north, the peaks of Chirripó invite hikers to power up to the summit. All along the steamy jungled shore, epic breaks attract surfers to chilled-out Dominical and Pavones. Down south, the rainforest-swathed Osa Peninsula hugs Golfo Dolce – a calm bay luring sportfishmen eager to hook the big one. Crossing the waters takes you to Isla del Coco to discover pre-Columbian burial sites and hammerhead sharks.

Best for
Untrammeled rainforest, Indigenous cultures, whale-watching

Home to
Parque Nacional Isla del Coco, Península de Osa, Parque Nacional Chirripó

Experience
Scuba diving with sharks off Isla del Coco

←

1 Crowds going about their day in downtown San José.

2 An adrenaline junkie ziplining through the canopy.

3 Drinking coffee in a tree house in Santa Elena

4 La Fortuna waterfall cascading into a pool below.

Costa Rica is remarkably varied for its relatively small size, and it's easy to combine visits to its different regions. The entire country is easily navigated, but requires careful planning. These itineraries will inspire you to make the most of your visit.

2 WEEKS
across Costa Rica

Day 1

Begin in San José with a stroll to the ornate Teatro Nacional (p106), all marble and gilt-work. Stop at the Alma de Café to indulge in your first cup of the country's delicious coffee over lunch. Then visit the Museo de Jade (p117) and its marvelous jade collection. For dinner, fill up on a simple-but-filling *casado* (rice, beans, plantain, and salad), then dance, dance, dance at El Cuartel de la Boca del Monte (2221-0327).

Day 2

Set out early for Parque Nacional Volcán Poás (p145), about 90 minutes north, to arrive before the clouds blanket the peaks by mid-morning. On clear days the vista from above the spluttering *caldera* (collapsed crater) stretches to both coasts. Wend through coffee country to mountainside Villa Blanca Cloud Forest Hotel and Nature Reserve (p140), stopping for a pick-me-up at the coffee shop on the Doka Estate (p145). That night sleep easy in one of the eco-friendly *casitas* (chalets).

Day 3

Rise with the howler monkeys for an early birding walk with a certified guide on the lookout for colorful plumage. After, head to La Fortuna (p202), arriving with time for lunch at Don Rufino (p204) and a hike into the rainforest to see La Fortuna waterfall. Later, soak in thermal pools at Tabacón Thermal Resort and Spa before heading for dinner back in town.

Day 4

Fuel up on *gallo pinto* (rice mixed with black beans) and scrambled eggs, then set out on a hike along the old lava flows inside Parque Nacional Volcán Arenal (p202). Have lunch at Arenal Observatory Lodge (p203), with spectacular views. Give your lunch time to settle before stepping straight into the canopy at Sky Walk (p176). After, head west along the scenic northern shore of Laguna de Arenal (p198) to the artsy Lucky Bug (p203).

Day 5

Arrive in Monteverde (p172) in time for zesty crêpes at Orchid Coffee (www.orchid coffeecr.com), then spend the afternoon wandering the walkable town of Santa Elena, starting at Herpetarium Adventures (p175), a fascinating, well-organized reptile and amphibian centre. Later, head to Frog Pond (p175) for an evening serenade. A night overlooking the jungle awaits at the Monteverde Lodge (p172).

Day 6

Catch the proverbial worm with a dawn birding tour in Reserva Biológica Bosque Nuboso Monteverde (p174). Then head over to Bat Jungle (p175) when it opens, to learn about these animals on the wing. As dusk falls, check out the Tree House (www.trehouse.cr), whose wide-ranging menu features Costa Rican classics that include steaks, burgers, and pizzas.

$\rightarrow$

1

2

3

Day 7

Get an early start on a road trip through ever-changing landscapes, over the Río Tempisque, to the dusty town of Guaitíl (*p192*). Visit its extraordinary Chorotega ceramics workshops and bring home artisan pieces. Pick up *chorreadas* (corn tortillas served like pancakes) for lunch; they're a local specialty. Continue west, following the signs for Marbella and Nosara along some of the country's most wild coastline. Come to a stop at clifftop Tree Tops B&B (*p187*) in San Juanillo, where epic ocean views pour into the restful rooms.

Day 8

Time for a day of rest: loll on the beach in the morning drinking *pipa fría* (ice-cold coconut water) straight from the nut; read a book over a leisurely lunch; drift through the afternoon above the coral reef with a snorkel. Come evening, feast on *corvina y ajo* (sea bass and buttered garlic) at Tree Tops's restaurant (book ahead), before enjoying another soothing night on the edge of the ocean.

Day 9

Head to Santa Cruz and catch a flight to the Osa Peninsula (*p232*), via San José. Fly into Puerto Jiménez's (*p234*) small regional airport. From there, a meandering taxi ride takes you around the tip of the peninsula to blissful Luna Lodge (*p235*). The heavenly spa and mountaintop yoga platform are all you need to shake off the journey before a dinner filled with organic produce grown on-site, perhaps *pescado en salsa palmito* (fish in heart-of-palm sauce).

Day 10

Sun salutations greet the day, then it's on to the crown jewel of lowland tropical rainforest: Corcovado National Park (*p234*). Luna Lodge backs onto the park and has trained naturalist guides to point out crocodiles, white-faced and spider monkeys, and osprey as you descend the trails that weave down past swimming holes fed by cascading waterfalls on the way to the Río Madrigal, for a picnic lunch on the banks. In the evening, relax with a cocktail in the eco-lodge's salt-water pool.

1 A beachside stallholder preparing fresh coconuts.

2 Surfing in the big waves off the coast of Nosara.

3 A crocodile lolling on the edge of Río Madrigal.

4 Wildlife watchers crossing a flooded path in Tortuguero.

5 A Chorotega woman working clay into a pot in Guaitíl.

Day 11

Prepare to cross the country, flying via San José to Parque Nacional Tortuguero *(p218)* and the balmy Caribbean Sea. The village is rimmed with the nesting beaches of green turtles. Arrive at Tortuga Lodge *(p218)* in time for a jerked *pargo* (red snapper) and *plátanos maduros* (fried sweet plantain) lunch. Later, climb into a kayak to pull yourself gently through mangrove-lined canals – if you're lucky you might see a manatee. Return to Tortuguero for coconut-curry mackerel and cool beers at Miss Junie's *(p221)*.

Day 12

Awake to the breeze coming off the Caribbean coast. Wander into the village for a smoothie and a hearty breakfast at Mi Niño *(70205 Limon Pococi)*, before a splash in the surf. When hunger strikes, a spicy *patí* (pastry) will do the trick; this delicious local specialty is some of the best street food in the region. Tonight, join a guided walk along the beach in search of nesting turtles.

Day 13

Enjoy a leisurely breakfast and a refreshing *batido* (fruit smoothie) then hop on a taxi-boat through banana plantations and past wild jungle to meet Tortuguero Wildlife Tour's *(www.tortuguero-wildlife. com)* animal-spotting experts, and spend the afternoon spying three-toed sloths hanging out in the rainforest around Moín. Back in Tortuguero, enjoy heaped plates of ackee and saltfish or beef in tamarind sauce (a house specialty) for dinner in the laid-back gardens of Taylor's Place *(p221)*.

Day 14

Tuck into a hearty *gallo pinto (p42)* breakfast then take to the muddy trail behind Cuarto Esquinas ranger station. It's a short yomp through steaming rainforest to see the stilted mangroves from land. Before heading back to the airport, pop into Casa Cecropia *(2709-8196)* for some divine late-morning chocolate immersion: peel and grind cacao pods to whip into your own chocolatey drink. It's a delicious final treat before leaving for home.

←

1 Steamy views over the valley near Volcán Irazú.

2 A bridge crossing over koi in the Chinese garden at Jardín Botánico Lankester.

3 Oxcart parts being brightly painted at a Sarchí workshop.

4 The spectacular cascade of La Paz waterfall tumbling through tropical rainforest.

5 DAYS
in the Central Highlands

Day 1

Morning Arrive early in Costa Rica's former capital Cartago to visit its majestic basilica *(p136)*, then dip into colorful Jardín Botánico Lankester *(p138)*, the University of Costa Rica's lovely botanic garden.

Afternoon Discover the art of shade-grown coffee at Finca Cristina *(www.cafe cristina.com)*, and enjoy a fresh cup brewed from the estate's beans. Then carry on through the splendid Orosí Valley *(p132)*.

Evening Overnight at Casa Turire *(www. hotelcasaturire.com)*, on Lago Angosturo.

Day 2

Morning Start the day exploring Costa Rica's ancient past at mysterious Monumento Nacional Guayabo.

Afternoon Stop for lunch at a *soda* (lunch counter) and fantastic views along the stupendously scenic backcountry roads up to Parque Nacional Volcán Irazú *(p150)*.

Evening Stay in Santa Bárbara de Heredia at Finca Rosa Blanca Coffee Plantation *(p147)*, overlooking lush fields of coffee.

Day 3

Morning Fuel up with the hotel's delicious huevos rancheros and then see how many of the estate's 130 bird species you can spot during a tour.

Afternoon North along the twisty-turny Carretera 126 is La Paz Waterfall Garden *(p144)*, with its well-marked waterfall trails and fascinating education center.

Evening Take one of the relaxing yoga classes offered by your hotel, before falling into blissful sleep.

Day 4

Morning Drive up and over the slopes of still-puffing Volcán Poás *(p145)* for a close-up look at one of the world's largest craters.

Afternoon Stop off for a lunch of *gallitos* (huge filled tortillas) at Chubascos *(712 Provinica de Alajuela)*, a short drive south of the volcano.

Evening Carry on downhill to a night in the charming rooms at Tacacori Ecolodge *(p140)*, surrounded by lush gardens.

Day 5

Morning Pick up some *empanadas* (savory meat-stuffed pastries) from a roadside stall on your way to Fábrica de Carretas Eloy Alfaro *(2454-4411)* in Sarchí *(p142)*, famous for their brightly motifed hand-painted *carretas* (oxcarts).

Afternoon Grab a refreshing *fresco de cas*, a sweet-sour fresh-pressed juice, then travel north, to delve through cloud forest to the Villa Blanca Cloud Forest Hotel *(p140)* and its hot tub overlooking mist-shrouded mountains.

Evening Feast on *costilla de cerdo horneada* (baked ribs), cooked in the hotel's signature chocolate barbecue sauce. Later take a glass of wine onto the patio and listen to the sounds of the jungle.

←

1 Costa Rica's opulent Teatro Nacional.

2 An ivy-covered house in Barrio Amon.

3 Parque Central peeking at the end of Avenida 2.

4 Shopping for bargains at Mercado de Artesanías.

2 DAYS
in San José

Day 1

Morning Start your visit to San José at the impressive Catedral Metropolitana (p112), built in 1871 and known for its colorful frescoes and figure of Christ draped in the colors of the Costa Rican flag. Pick up some mango (sold in plastic bags garnished with lime juice and a dash of salt) from one of the vendors in Parque Central to nibble on as you stroll across to Plaza de la Cultura. This otherwise unremarkable square is highlighted by the magnificent Teatro Nacional (p106), but the real draw is the Museo de Oro Precolumbino (p108), under the plaza, where its stunning collection of priceless pre-Columbian artifacts dazzles.

Afternoon After a lunch of casado (a generous plate of rice, black beans, plantain, salad and a tortilla) at a soda (lunch counter), walk south to Mercado Municipal de Artesanias (p113) and dodge the heat of the day perusing the dozens of stalls selling everything from artisan-made cowboy boots to carefully crafted masks. Later, wander back up to pedestrian-only Avenida Central and head east to shady Parque Nacional (p118).

Evening Feast on vacío (bavette steak) at buzzy La Esquina de Buenos Aires (p115), then join the bright young things at El Cuartel de la Boca del Monte (2221-0327) for cocktails and boisterous bands. When the Sandman calls, a quiet night at Hotel Auténtico (p119) is the answer.

Day 2

Morning Fuel up on gallo pinto (p42), a typical Tico breakfast, before diving into the best of the city's art. Barrio Bird Walking Tours (p114) offers great guided tours, given by artists, activists, and historians, through streets, parks, and arty Barrio Amon, stopping to investigate everything from sculptures to political graffiti. Afterwards, duck into Galería Namú (p113), best known for its wonderful collection of folk art and exquisite Boruca masks. Then savor lunch in nearby Kalú (p115), passing the quaint remnants of the defunct Antigua Estación Ferrocarril al Atlántico, the Atlantic Railroad Station (p118), on your way.

Afternoon People watch as you walk the length of Avineda Central on your way to the wonderfully curated Museo de Arte Costarricense (p120), to take in some of the most important examples of Costa Rican art dating back centuries. When you need a break, Parque Sabana (p119), behind the museum, is ideal for watching the world go by with paper-wrapped patacones (deep-fried plantain) from a nearby stall.

Evening Finish up your stay with a jaunt out to the suburb of Escazú (p120), in the west end of the city, and enjoy a fresh seafood dinner at the always popping Alma de Café (p115) before getting into the groove at the nearby Jazz Café (www.jazz cafecostarica.com).

Rescue and Recovery

Want to help protect your favorite species? Volunteer with Sea Turtle Conservation (*www.conserveturtles.org*) to help tag nesting green turtles and count eggs at Parque Nacional Tortuguero *(p218)*; tagging teams are also a strong deterrent to poachers. On the other side of the country, take part in rehabilitating spider monkeys at Rescate Wildlife Rescue Center *(p140)*, ready for release in Nicoya.

←

A green turtle digging a hole to nest on the beach near Tortuguero village

COSTA RICA FOR
WILDLIFE

From astonishing butterflies to nesting sea-turtles, Costa Rica is a wildlife-lovers' dream. The country's astoundingly diverse ecosystems are crammed with creepers and crawlers, howlers and prowlers. For close encounters, visit centers that rescue animals from trafficking and captivity.

TOP 4 PLACES TO SEE WILDLIFE

San Gerardo de Dota
The best place to see the resplendent quetzal *(p150)*.

Río Tárcoles
Crocodiles loll log-like along the riverbank in Parque Nacional Carrara *(p165)*.

Veragua Rainforest
Colorful poison dart frogs hop along the trails *(p216)*.

Parque Nacional Marino Ballena
Watch humpback whales breaching the water *(p241)*.

Sounds of the Jungle

A walk through the jungle can feel like an assault on the senses, but pause to listen. That reverberating boom as you cross the swamp to Parque Nacional Marino Ballena *(p241)* is the lowing bay of crocodiles. That rustling crack as you stand under an almond tree in Rara Avis *(p211)* are toucans breaking open nut shells. That haunting roar rippling through the canopy in Cahuita *(p220)* is the uncanny call of howler monkeys sharing news of your presence.

↑ A group of shaggy-haired howler monkeys greeting the day

Whale of a Time

Sealife throngs in the waters flanking Costa Rica. Jump in with a scuba-diving class in the turquoise seas around Isla del Coco *(p236)* and swim with hammerhead schools. Non-divers can come face to face with jellynose fish and whale sharks from the safety of a semi-submersible.

💬 INSIDER TIP
Go Local

Hiring a licensed local guide, such as through the Asociación Guías U-Suré *(www.usurecr. org)* is the best way to encounter the local wildlife – and help the local economy too. Book at least one week in advance.

↑ A giant whale shark drifting past a scuba diver in the seas around Isla del Coco

Gravity's Rainbows

Butterflies flit across Costa Rica's hiking trails in an all-too-fleeting technicolor ballet. See their full spectrum at the enclosed butterfly gardens in Selvatura Park *(p176)* or Selva Verde *(p209),* where the pretty papilionids stop at feeders long enough to to let you Instagram their brilliance.

←

Getting up close to a black-and-white zebra butterfly in Monteverde

Nocturnal Critters

Unravel the mysteries of Costa Rica's forests – at night. Join a night walk at Parque Nacional Corcovado *(p234)* to shine a light on the nocturnal antics of leaf-cutter ants and red-eyed tree frogs. On the Caribbean side, let the moon light the way at Tortuguero to watch leatherback turtles lumber up the beach to nest.

→

Leafcutter ants carrying a leaf under the cover of darkness

The White City

Liberia's *(p183)* whitewashed, colonial *bahareque* (clay-built) houses and white dirt roads have loaned it the nickname *La Ciudad Blanca* (White City). The fetching townscape dazzles in the sun, especially in the harsh light of midday. Photographing the scene any time around lunch can be a challenge, so underexpose to boost the blue, blue sky; if photographing people, find shade. Stay long enough to take to the streets to shoot around sunset, when the city is bathed in an inviting warm glow.

← Blue skies providing a dazzling contrast to the whitewashed façade

COSTA RICA FOR
PHOTOGRAPHY

Costa Rica is shutterbug paradise, deliverings memorable images around every bend. Whether you're snapping the magnificent landscapes, sensational wildlife, or iconic traditional oxcarts, here are a few tips to capture sensational shots.

Volcanic Vistas

For the most iconic scenery in Costa Rica, shoot Volcán Arenal *(p202)* from the hilltop Arenal Observatory Lodge *(p203)*. The perfectly conical volcano is poised on the edge of Laguna de Arenal *(p198)*, punctuating rolling plains. For maximum effect, use a wide-angle lens to capture the cone rising from the treeline.

↑ The distinctively conical Volcán Arenal surging up from the rolling plains

Costa Rican Pastoral

With its coffee-workers in dusty straw hats and scarves hand-picking beans, villagers playing dominos in the shade, and cowboys on horseback, Costa Rica is full of bucolic tableaux. Many locals are happy to strike a pose, but be sure to engage with your subject and ask if you can take their photos. Use a zoom lens to get up close to capture their *pura vida* spirit.

←

Striking a pose, a *sabanero* (cowboy) at a rustic hacienda in rural Guanacaste

💬 INSIDER TIP
Get Protected

To protect your camera gear from humidity and rain, place it inside a zip-lock bag containing a silica gel pack at night to absorb any moisture inside your camera and lens. A waterproof cover for your camera bag is also a good idea.

Snapping Wildlife

Jazz up your photo album with colorful jungle snaps. To capture the best shot, drop to eye level to frame your subject in Parque Nacional Tortuguero *(p218)*. When shooting quetzals in San Gerardo de Dota *(p150)*, aim for a shallow depth of field to ensure the bird appears sharp against a blurred forest backdrop.

→

Photo opportunities from colorful fish *(inset)* to black vultures silhouetted at dusk

Surf's Up!

A surfers' paradise, Costa Rica is blessed with epic waves and a host of surf schools to choose from. Board masters can test their moves at "Salsa Brava", over razor-sharp coral reefs off Puerto Viejo *(p223)* or the two-minute perfect break that stretches from Pavones *(p243)*. Novice surfer? Take a lesson from the renowned Witch's Rock Surf Camp *(www. witchsrocksurfcamp.com)* at Tamarindo *(p187)*.

←

Coasting in on a low rippling wave at popular Playa Tamarindo

COSTA RICA FOR
ADVENTURERS

Costa Rica is a nirvana for outdoor adventurers. Local operators are constantly pioneering new activities, so there are always fresh opportunities for thrill-seekers to test their mettle, plus staples from scuba diving to white-water rafting to zipline canopy tours.

Soar Through the Canopy

Pioneered by biologists wanting to study Costa Rica's forests without leaving a footprint in the 1970s, ziplining is now an eco-tourism staple. Adrenaline junkies can go whizzing hundreds of feet above the forest floor across the country. Many national parks have facilities for ziplining, but Parque Nacional Volcán Arenal *(p202)*, in the Northern Zone, combines ziplining with an aerial tram, a rather more sedate way of seeing the canopy from the inside.

→

Flying above the canopy, harness and helmet strapped in place

HIDDEN GEM
Lost River

Take a hike into Río Perdido ("Lost River"), in darkest Guacacaste, and you'll come across three waterfall rappels and multiple climbing routes into a slot canyon. A Tarzan swing gets you over the abyss. Screaming encouraged.

Into the Deep

Although it has few coral reefs, the awesome opportunities for diving with big pelagics makes Costa Rica a major scuba center. Boat out to Isla del Coco *(p236)* with Undersea Hunter *(www.underseahunter.com)* to swim with hammerhead sharks. Alternatively, take the plunge off the Islas Murciélagos, in northern Nicoya, to get nose-to-nose with huge bull sharks.

→

Flipping off the edge and into the crystal-clear turquoise water below

Sportfishing

Costa Rica's oceans teem with game fish, from snook to sailfish. Sportfishing is fantastic year-round, although prime spots depend on the season. Boat operators in Quepos *(p166)* and Parque Nacional Tortuguero *(p218)* will get you out to the right spot at the right time to hook the big one.

←

Seeking big game fish surrounded by miles of empty deep sea

Chasing Big Water

Costa Rica's world-class white-water rivers offer thrills alongside outstanding natural beauty. Head to Río Pacuaré, with its large flows and rolling waves, to snatch up a paddle with top-pick Aguas Bravas *(www.aguasbravascr.com)* for a heart-thumping guided high-water run.

→

Paddling through a stretch of boiling rapids along the Río Pacuaré

Visit a Coffee Estate

Many estates – from small organic farms to large *fincas* – welcome visitors; not only can you buy the beans, but most give tours and many have an education center for visitors. A tour of an independent organic farm, like Finca Cristina *(www.cafecristina. com)*, reveals the close symbiotic relationship between birds, lizards, and orchids and the coffee bushes they live within. On the other side of San José, every stage of cultivating and preparing coffee is explained at Costa Rican coffee mecca, the Doka Estate *(p145)* on the slopes of Volcán Poás.

↑ Leaning in to look at coffee seedlings, during a tour of the Doka Estate

COSTA RICA FOR
COFFEE LOVERS

Across the country wafts the sharp aroma of fresh-roasted coffee beans. Costa Rica's volcanic slopes, corduroyed with dark green coffee bushes, offer ideal conditions for growing the best beans, with fertile soil, high altitudes, and well-defined rainy and dry seasons. If you're buzzed about coffee, this is the place to be.

Shopping for the Best

The best coffee beans are sold on the estates and in specialist roasteries, such as Café Bohío *(p35)* in Jacó. The beans to avoid: *café puro* (unadulterated) or *café traditional* (laced with sugar), sold loose in markets.

←

Roasted A-grade coffee beans for sale in a farm shop on a coffee estate

DRINKS

Caféoteca
The coolest boutique café in San José takes coffee seriously.

AD3 **Ⓜ**San José
C2253-8426

$⑤⑤

KOKi Beach Restaurant & Bar
Come here for espresso martinis after dark.

AG4 **Ⓜ**Puerto Viejo de Talamanca
C2750-0902

$⑤⑤

Café Bohío
Exceptional coffee, roasted on-site.

AC4 **Ⓜ**Jacó
Wcafebohio.com

$⑤⑤

Getting from Bean to Cup

↑ Prepping the harvested coffee cherries to be processed at a mill

Starting in November, coffee beans are hand picked and transported to *beneficios* (processing mills) to be pulped, dried, and sorted. Harvest the ripe red cherries at Finca Rosa Blanca *(p147)*, then reap the rewards with a tasting at Feria del Café de Frailes *(www. feriadelcafe.co.cr)*, an annual coffee fair in the heart of the central valley with a full tasting menu.

Discover the History

Costa Rica offers unparelleled opportunities for uncovering the history of the *grano de oro* (golden bean). At Costa Rica's most famous coffee brand, Café Britt *(p146)*, an estate tour turns into fun-filled educational theater. Nearby, Hacienda Espíritu Santo *(4104-0500)* reveals the history of coffee-growing in Costa Rica, as well as the role of the national symbol, the oxcart, that's as eye-opening as a fresh cappuccino. History addicts can also get a fix at the off-the-beaten-track Coffee Museum *(www.costa rica estatecoffee.com)*, at family-run Hacienda Río Jorco.

→

Actors weaving a tale of the history of coffee cultivation in the Central Highlands

Hands-On Experience

Ancestral narratives are integral to many of Costa Rica's indigenous cultures, and finished products are often infused with mythological symbolism. Create your own necklace using traditional techniques during a sit-down session at the Sarapiquís Rainforest Lodge *(p206)*, while listening to ancestral stories told by Malekú storytellers. Nearby, try your hand at painting the rainbow on intricately carved Malekú *jícaras* (hollowed gourds) at Pueblo Malekú *(www.indigenas malekus.com)*. If northern Sarapiquí is too far to travel, opt for magicking clay into three-legged cow vases at the Oven Store's *(p181)* classes in the town of Guaitíl in Guanacaste.

$\longrightarrow$

Twisted strands of colorful beads ready to be turned into a handmade memory

COSTA RICA FOR
INDIGENOUS CRAFTS

From pots and masks to textiles and jewelry, Costa Rica's millennia-old tradition of handmade crafts is undergoing an artisan renaissance. Whether you're looking to pick up a bargain or learn from the masters, Costa Rica's craft scene offers something for everyone.

Boruca *diablitos*, in hand-carved masks *(inset)*, ready to face their foes $\uparrow$

Learn from the Experts

Costa Rica's artisans possess immense skill and patience, perfecting age-old techniques as they hone their craft. Many are keen to demonstrate their skill to visitors and answer questions about their craft. Meet traditional weavers, historically women, at the Reserva Indígena Boruca *(p242)* and watch as they create intricate patterns using a handmade backstrap loom. Alternatively, head south to the Panamanian border learn how Ngäbe fabric is dyed, using natural dyes, through Pavones Ecotours *(www. pavonesecotours.com)*, then pick between bolts of vividly printed fabric.

A Boruca weaver preparing a backstrap loom with colorful cotton yarns

¡Fiesta Time!

Costa Rica's traditional crafts are celebrated in festivals, some of which go back hundreds of years. The hand-painted *máscaras* (masks) of the Rey and Boruca peoples, hand-carved from locally sourced balsa wood, are central to the Fiesta de los Diablitos (Festival of the Little Devils), held in February and December each year. Immerse yourself in the festivities in tiny Curré, east of Palmar *(p243)*: cheer on the *diablitos* (Boruca people) and boo the *toro* (Spanish troops), as they battle for glory. Then watch a master woodworker make one of the ceremonial "devil" faces at their workshop. Return in October for the Día de las Culturas, which brings together Indigenous groups from around the country to celebrate their artistic heritage.

TOP 5 FAIR-TRADE SHOPS

Galería Namú
San's José's premier gallery of Indigenous Costa Rican crafts *(p113)*.

Dantica Gallery
Indigenous-made items from around Latin America, in Jacó *(p161)*.

Chietón Morén
An early Fair Trade adopter, in San José, representing 25 indigenous groups *(p113)*.

Oven Store
Locally crafted ceramics by Chorotega artisans in Guaitíl *(p181)*.

Boruca Cooperatives
These cooperatives sell hand-carved balsa masks and more *(p243)*.

Birding for Shutterbugs

Photographing birds can be challenging. The best tools to take with you are a telephoto lens, tripod, a synchronized flash, and plenty of patience. Join a birding tour who also specializes in photography, such as Trogon Photo Tours *(www.trogontours.net)*, and they'll set you up in Carara National Park *(p164)* to capture scarlet macaws in the wild, or along one of the birding trails at Los Cusingos Bird Sanctuary *(www.cct.or.cr)* to snap the rarer baird's trogon and spot-crowned euphonia.

→

A dramatic fanning of the scarlet macaw's brilliant plumage caught in mid-flight

COSTA RICA FOR
BIRDERS

A birders' paradise, Costa Rica is home to more than 900 bird species. Migratory flocks of casual twitchers and hard-beaked ornithophiles find opportunities across the country to see everything from tiny scintillant hummingbirds to giant king vultures.

Volunteers of a Feather

Conservation efforts invite birders to help save some of Costa Rica's most endangered species, across the country. Want to pitch in? On the Caribbean side, release green macaws into the wild with Ara Manzanillo *(www.ara manzanillo.org)*. Farther north, at Parque Nacional Palo Verde *(p181)*, help out with their seasonal species count.

←

Black-bellied whistling ducks arriving at Parque Nacional Palo Verde

Sneaky Beaks

A guide in the know can help you spot even the most camouflaged birds. Eco-conscious tour companies, such as Eagle-Eye Tours *(www.eagle-eye.com)* and San Isidro de El General-based Tropical Feathers *(www.costaricabirding tours. com)*, will get you sightings across the country.

→

Bird-spotting from a bridge hanging through the canopy at La Selva Biological Station

Hike or Hide?

Costa Rica is home to 35 bird species on the endangered species list, yet many of these can still be seen in the wild. Take to the trails of Parque Nacional Los Quetzales *(p138)* between February and July to see the resplendent quetzal on full display, as males compete for mating rights. But the best chance to see the country's bucket-list birds is to let them come to you. At Laguna del Lagarto, on the Nicaraguan border, birders can spot king vultures from inside a hide, binoculars at the ready.

→

A young male resplendent quetzal perched in Los Quetzales National Park

Volcanic Peaks

From ash-spewing peaks to silent giants, a series of volcanoes trace a spine down Costa Rica's core. Ringed by bubbling hot springs, passive Volcán Arenal (p202) is the most famous, but not the only one worth visiting. Climb its active cousin Volcán Poás (p145) to the summit to peek into its simmering crater. Alternatively, sink into the hot springs near Rincón de la Viejo (p182) for a bit of thermal therapy after a hike.

←

Looking across the tranquil valley toward majestic Volcán Arenal

COSTA RICA FOR
INSPIRING LANDSCAPES

Costa Rica has few rivals when it comes to spectacular scenery. Flanked by two vast bodies of water, its dramatic geography is studded with majestic volcanoes, amazing wetlands, pristine tropical forests, and breathtaking waterfalls plunging into turquoise pools.

TOP 4 NATURAL LANDMARKS

Volcán Arenal
This perfectly conical, dormant volcano is Costa Rica's defining landmark (p202).

Barra Honda Caves
Vast limestone caverns full of eerie stone formations (p193).

Cerro Chirripó
Costa Rica's highest peak is a must for intrepid hikers (p230).

Corcovado Rainforest
A seemingly endless panorama of lush living canopy (p234).

Wonderful Waterfalls

Mountainous terrain and high rainfall combine in stupendous cascades across the country, reached by trails through gorgeous forest. Bring a raincoat to towering La Paz Waterfall Garden (p144): the spray is intense. Take a swimsuit to others, like those tumbling through Parque Nacional Volcán Tenorio (p205), where crystal-clear pools are ideal for a dip. For a different perspective, rappel into Cavernas de Venado (p204) to marvel at cascades deep beneath the earth.

→

Taking the plunge into a natural pool in Parque Nacional Volcán Tenorio

Amazing Rainforests

Thrumming with life, Costa Rica's celebrated rainforests are a major draw for wildlife lovers. Commune with monkeys on a treetop platform at Hacienda Barú *(p242)* one day, then follow a local guide the next through the undergrowth in Parque Nacional Corcovado *(p234)* to spot shy baird's tapirs and still shier spotted cats.

←

A river winding a lazy path through endless miles of verdant rainforest

Parched Forests

Tall grasses and clusters of vibrant flowering trees rustle with wildlife in Guanacaste's savanna-like tropical dry forests. Take to the short Indio Desnudo trail in Parque Nacional Santa Rosa *(p178)* and peer through peeling guanacaste trees and the powder-puff flowers of the rosy trumpet tree to see anteaters, iguanas, and black vultures, as well as petroglyphs carved into the rock.

←

Strolling along the sloping Indio Desnudo trail in Parque Nacional Santa Rosa

Wild Wetlands

Across Costa Rica, wetlands teem with life and there are lots of ways to see it. Join local tour operator Tortuguero Adventures *(www.tortuguero-adventures. com)* to kayak Parque Nacional Tortuguero's *(p218)* languid lagoons and get eye-to-eye with the crocodiles and manatees that live there. On the Pacific side, putt-putt across El Viejo's wetlands *(www.elviejowetlands. com)* past flocks of jabirus.

→

A crocodile seen in Parque Nacional Tortuguero

Get Cooking

Got a taste for *gallo pinto*? Try your hand at traditional home cooking in a cookery class. Often, courses include a visit to a local market or farm with the chef, who will then show you how to use the ingredients to make iconic Costa Rican dishes, such as in a hands-on class at Costa Rica Cooking *(www.costarica cooking.com)* in La Fortuna. Alternatively, take a deep dive into an Indigenous cuisine at the Bribrí reserve near Puerto Viejo. A Foodie Tour *(www.foodietourscr. com)* with a Bribrí chef combines cooking with traditional storytelling.

↑ Learning about local Costa Rican cooking and culture, in a cookery workshop

COSTA RICA FOR
FOODIES

The feel of fresh mango juice dribbling through your fingers; the sizzle of chillies in the pan; the scent of barbequed fish and seafood on the Caribbean coast – Costa Rican food is full of simple pleasures.

Traditional Dishes

Costa Rica's signature *comida típica* (traditional food) dish is *gallo pinto*. It's so beloved that a common Costa Rican saying is "*Más Tico que gallo pinto*" ("More Costa Rican than *gallo pinto*"). The hearty and healthy dish consists of rice and beans, cooked with onions, sweet peppers, and heaps of garlic. It's usually served with scrambled or fried eggs, cheese, avocado and a side of *plátano maduro* (ripe plantain) as part of a *casado*, another traditional dish that literally translates to "married". Eat it at any *soda* (lunch counter), pepped up with spicy Lizano sauce.

←

Fresh-cooked *gallo pinto* with a bottle of spicy Costa Rican favorite, Lizano sauce

Ripe Pickings

A cornucopia of tropical fruits fill markets and roadside stalls nationwide, and it's impossible to pass by without picking some up. Look out for *maracuya* (passion fruit), *carambola* (star fruit), *pejibaye* (peach palm fruit), and *guanabana* (soursop); eat them raw. In the towns and cities, treat yourself to "street mango" Tico-style: a bag of salted fresh-cut mango garnished with a dash of chili powder. Wash it down with a refreshing *pipa fría* – coconut water drunk straight from the just-husked *coco*.

←

Shopping for local produce at San José's Central Mercado

Fisherman's Friend

Flanked on either side by fish-filled seas, it's no surprise that Costa Rica's kitchens send divine seafood dishes to the table. Sourcing sustainable seafood takes priority in hotels and restaurants across the country. Eco-conscious Cayuga Collection group has paired its kitchens around Costa Rica with small-scale fisheries, to ensure their fish dishes use only low-impact wild seafood. Go to Malpaís *(p162)* and know your plate of fresh-as-can-be warm-water oysters and pan-seared tuna were sustainably caught by local fishersmen. Check out websites like Dock to Dish *(www.docktodish.com)* that make tracing the origins of the daily catch easy.

↑ Preparing grilled snapper and fried plantain on the sands

DRINKS TO KEEP COOL

Agua de Sapo
Literally translated as "toad water", this delicious lemonade made with brown sugar and ginger tastes a lot better than it sounds.

Granizados
As much a dessert as a refreshing beverage, this tasty, teeth-zinging sugar rush is made of shaved ice flavoured with condensed milk and sweet fruit syrup.

Naturales
Also known as *batidos*, these fresh fruit juices are heaped with ice and hand-pressed at a standalone kiosk.

Pipa Fría
Refreshing coconut water sipped through a straw straight from the coconut shell. Half the fun is watching the seller cut it open using a machete in front of you.

Thar She Blows!

In the warm, delft-blue waters off Costa Rica's Pacific shores, whales and dolphins gather to breed, offering unparalled chances to see these magnificent creatures in the wild. Head to Parque Nacional Marino Ballena *(p241)* where tour operators, such as Uvita-based Bahía Adventures *(www.bahiaaventuras.com)*, must employ 64 practices for sustainable marine tourism in order to maintain their license, and launch into the ocean to marvel at whales blowing spray into the sky and leaping from the water.

→

A humpback whale breaching in Parque Nacional Marino Ballena

COSTA RICA FOR
ECO-TRAVELERS

An early pioneer of eco-friendly, sustainable travel, Costa Rica continues to be a world leader in environmental conservation and education. An abundance of choice awaits eco-travelers, from innovative, low-impact nature experiences to local sustainability projects. Travel wide, think local!

Chocolate Indulgence

Cacao is integral to Caribbean communities, where artisanal chocolate makers use organic cacao sourced from Indigenous farmers. Join a guided tour of sustainable cacao farm Caribeans Coffee and Chocolate *(www. caribeanschocolate.com)*, then sample the tangy flesh of the cacao fruit - and pieces of delicious artisan-finished chocolates - right at the source.

Mouth-watering chocolate being cooked in a cacao farm ↑

TOP 4 ECO-FRIENDLY CANOPY TOURS

Rainforest Aerial Tram
Get eye-level with the monkeys *(p210)*.

Veragua Rainforest Eco-Adventure
Soar through the trees from the renowned eco-lab *(p216)*.

Mistico Arenal Hanging Bridges Park
Discover the forest from floor to canopy *(p204)*.

Sky Walk/SkyTrek
Walk or whizz through Arenal's treetops *(p176)*.

Give or Take

From hiring local guides to assisting wildlife conservation projects, Costa Rica has countless ways to pitch in. Team up with Dream Volunteers *(www.dreamvolunteers.org)* to turn your vacation into something that gives back, by helping to develop local environmental projects that will last a lifetime.

A volunteer helping to care for an orphaned monkey at a wildlife rehabilitation center ↑

REFORESTATION

By 1985, Guanacaste's tropical dry forest had been devastated by 250 years of cattle farming. That year, a project was initiated in Parque Nacional Santa Rosa to recoup the lost forest and retain farmers within the ecotourism industry. Today, with more than 50 percent regrowth, the restoration of the region's dry forest is Costa Rica's biggest turn-a-leaf eco-success story.

Bird's-eye view of Lapa Ríos eco-lodges snaking through the jungle ↑

Stay at an Ecolodge

Rustic or deluxe, there's eco-sensitive accommodation to suit all tastes. Look for the Certificate for Sustainable Tourism (CST) "leafs", which rate eco-friendliness and sustainability. Stay in Lapa Ríos *(p235)* or Selva Verde Lodge *(p211)*, and sleep well in the knowledge that you're supporting the local environment and the local economy in one.

The Great Escape

If the thought of crowd-happy beaches makes your head spin, Costa Rica has escapes galore. Along both coasts awaits a wealth of pristine, hidden jungle-ringed beaches where your only company will be the occasional seabird. Escape Parque Nacional Manuel Antonio to tranquil Quepos *(p166)* and its under-the-radar idyll Playa Biesanz. Cusped by coral reefs, the seas are ideal for snorkeling and you'll have the whole beach to yourself.

Farther north, hop in a 4WD at Sámara *(p190)* and take the single-track path to the palm-fringed bliss of remote Playa Barrigona, a virginal swath of pink-champagne sands tucked in an unspoiled cove.

↑ A visitor ambling in the distance at the exquisitely remote Playa Barrigona

COSTA RICA FOR
BEAUTIFUL BEACHES

Lapped on either side by the Caribbean Sea and the Pacific Ocean, Costa Rica has enough palm-fringed beaches for everyone. Take your pick – from sugary sands to wild jungle-backed strands, each beach offers something a little different.

Family-Friendly Sands

Shielded by imposing Punta Catedral (Cathedral Point), the calm seas and fabulous beaches to either side of a tombolo teeming with wildlife make Parque Nacional Manuel Antonio *(p158)* a terrific choice for families with children of all ages. For a different day out, check out pelican-patrolled Playas del Coco *(p189)*, a Tico family favorite, with a boardwalk lined with pizzerias, fruit stalls, and family-friendly resorts offering fun activities.

→

Walking towards the sunset in family-friendly Parque Nacional Manuel Antonio

RIPTIDES

Fast-moving riptides are caused by a high volume of incoming surf meeting funnels of retreating water. These create dangerous narrow channels as the water gets sucked back into deep water, which can drag even experienced swimmers out to sea. If caught in a riptide, don't panic or try to swim against the tide. Swim parallel to the beach to exit the narrow rip current, then swim to shore.

↑ An experienced surfer keeping ahead of the crest of the wave as it rolls toward Playa Tamarindo

Surf Meccas

Wildly popular, the beach at Tamarindo *(p187)* has perfect surfing-for-everyone waves, from beginner beach breaks to deep-water pinwheelers ideal for kamikazes. Test your board skills with a surf lesson with Tamarindo-based Witch's Rock Surf Camp *(www.witchsrocksurfcamp.com)*. For less crowded waters, join a class at Costa Rica Surf Camp *(www.crsurfschool. com)* in laid-back Dominical *(p240)*.

Beaches for Wildlife Spotting

Costa Rica's jungle-framed beaches and marine-rich seas are ideal for spotting wildlife in all directions. Gaze out at the ocean at Playa Ostional *(p190)* in search of the regular *arribadas* (mass arrivals) of olive ridley turtles swimming to shore to nest. Above the sugar-white sands at Playa Blanca in Cahuita *(p220)*, on the Caribbean side, you'll see everything from slow-moving sloths to howler monkeys swinging through the trees. Farther south at Manzanillo *(p222)*, get into the water, mask and snorkel in place, to check out the mantas and schools of tropical fish flitting around the coral reefs as you drift along on the surface of the crystal-clear water.

→

Watching the progress of tiny olive ridley turtle hatchlings down the beach

A YEAR IN
COSTA RICA

JANUARY

Copa del Café *(1st week)*. International junior tennis champs battle it out for the "Coffee Cup".

△ **Fiestas de Santa Cruz** *(2nd week)*. Santa Cruz rings in the new year with folk dancing, rodeos, concerts, and fireworks.

FEBRUARY

Bamboo Bass Festival *(late Feb)*. Bass music pounds through Jacó, loud enough to wake the dead.

△ **Envision Festival** *(late Feb)*. Music, yoga, and fire dancers cram onto the beach at Uvita.

Viva el Café Festival *(end Feb)*. Two days of super-caffeinated fun in La Sabana, with tastings and the all-important championship of baristas.

MAY

△ **Día de los Trabajadores** *(1 May)*. Trade unions march across the country on Labor Day.

Día de San Isidro Labrador *(15 May)*. Street parties, processions, and an agricultural fair take over San Isidro de Pérez Zeledón.

Carrera de San Juan *(17 May)*. Crowds cheer on marathon runners, from Cartago to San José.

JUNE

△ **Marcha De Diversidad** *(end Jun)*. A party atmosphere takes over San José as the Pride parade rounds off a month of celebrations.

Compañía de Lírica Nacional *(mid-Jun–mid-Aug)*. The National Lyric Opera Company kicks off a resounding two-month festival of opera.

SEPTEMBER

△ **Día de Independencia** *(14 Sep)*. The entire country stops to sing the national anthem at 6pm as the "Freedom Torch" arrives in Cartago, all the way from Guatemala. School bands lead the nation in festivities the next day.

International Beach Clean-Up Day *(3rd Sat)*. Volunteers across the country pitch in to clean up rivers, beaches, and the ocean.

OCTOBER

Día de la Raza/Carnaval Limón *(mid-Oct)*. Mardi Gras in miniature, Costa Rica's main carnival is a week-long, dance-fueled, costume-filled, float-parading, high-energy party, culminating in the selection of the Carnival Queen.

△ **Upala Fiestas de Maiz** *(mid-Oct)*. Corn-themed parades, the crowning of a Corn Queen, and street parties welcome in the corn harvest.

MARCH

△ **Día del Boyero** *(second Sun)*. Revelers take to the streets of San Antonio de Escazú with music, dance, and colourful *carretas* (oxcarts) to honor the humble *boyero* (oxcart driver).

Jungle Jam *(mid-Mar)*. Beachfront Jacó reverberates during a three-day musical takeover, with tunes ranging from reggae to the psychedelic.

Easter Week *(varies)*. Towns nationwide host religious processions and costumed re-enactments during Semana Santa (Holy Week).

APRIL

△ **Juan Santamaría Day** *(11 Apr)*. Parades and street parties take over Alajuela in celebration of Costa Rica's victory over William Walker's mercenaries at the Battle of Rivas in 1956.

International Festival of the Arts (FIA) *(mid-Apr)*. Arts lovers descend on San José for a week of theatre premiers, dance performances, art exhibitions, and music, with heaps of free events across the city.

JULY

Virgin of the Sea Festival *(Sat closest to 16 Jul)*. A colorful regatta tops this vibrant Puntarenas *fiesta*.

△ **Costa Rica Piano Festival** *(mid-Jul)*. Take in free lessons and recitals across San José.

National Surfing Championship *(from late Jul)*. Amped local enthusiasts and pros alike surf the breaks to win at Playa Hermosa.

AUGUST

△ **La Romería Pilgrimage** *(2 Aug)*. The devout make their pilgrimage to the Virgin of Los Angeles, in Cartago's basilica.

Mes Histórico de la Afrodescendencia *(Aug)*. A month of activities and events to celebrate the influence of Black Costa Ricans on the country's heritage and culture.

NOVEMBER

Día de los Muertos *(2 Nov)*. The entire nation pauses to honor the dead.

La Ruta de los Conquistadores *(mid-Nov)*. A week-long mountain bike championship retraces the route of the Spanish conquistadors across some of Costa Rica's most challenging terrain.

△ **El Desfile de Carretas (Ox-Cart Parade)** *(last week)*. Oxcarts parade through downtown San José.

DECEMBER

Fiesta de los Negritos *(8 Dec)*. The Indigenous Boruca peoples celebrate the Virgin of the Immaculate Conception with music, dancing, and other activities.

Festival de la Luz *(2nd Sat)*. Spectacularly lit floats parade through the center of San José to launch the Christmas season.

Fiestas de Zapote *(last week)*. The San José suburb of Zapote explodes with carnival rides, rodeos, and horse parades.

△ **Fiesta de los Diablitos** *(30 Dec-2 Jan)*. Boruca masked re-enactors battle it out between "little devils" and Spanish colonialists.

A BRIEF
HISTORY

Costa Rica has been shaped by a mysterious ancient past and the early adoption of democracy. The country's declaration of neutrality in 1948, following a brief civil war, continues to forge its identity as a stable democratic nation determined to leave an eco-positive legacy.

Pre-Columbian Costa Rica

Costa Rica was settled by nomadic groups moving between what are now Mexico and Peru, around 8000 BC. These groups spread across Costa Rica, establishing small fishing and farming communities along the coasts and in the central highlands. While no written record has been found, a bounty of gold and jade artifacts suggests they were wealthy, artistic cultures.

Bustling with 10,000 inhabitants at its peak, the city of Guayabo was founded in 1000 BC. Though a center of politics, culture and religion, it was mysteriously abandoned by AD 1400.

1 Early map showing Costa Rica.

2 Plate of Isla Uvita, beyond Puerto Límon.

3 Colorized photograph of 19th-century coffee workers drying beans.

4 Lustrous gold artifacts on display at the Museum of Pre-Columbian Gold.

Timeline of events

8000 BC
First Indigenous peoples settle across the region.

800 BC
Guayabo established on the slopes of Volcán Turrialba.

500 BC– AD 800
Artisans craft fine pendants and figures using jade; by 500 AD gold begins to replace.

AD 400– 1000
Granite spheres are made on Isla del Caño for ceremonial purposes.

1400
Guayabo is mysteriously abandoned.

1502
Columbus lands on Isla Uvita, off the Caribbean coast.

Spanish Conquest

Columbus landed off the Caribbean coast on his fourth trip to the Americas. Spanish conquistadors soon followed, driven by the promise of the "Rich Coast". When that failed, they colonized the land, driving out or enslaving local populations.

Subsistence Era

By the 18th century, farming settlements were concentrated in the central valley. Meanwhile, the Caribbean coast had become a haven for pirates, smugglers, and people escaping slavery on the Caribbean islands. In some respects these settlements were relatively egalitarian, but Indigenous peoples were excluded and repeatedly forced out of their lands. The resulting tensions between far-off Spain and the Central American colonies came to a head in El Salvador in 1811, leading to a demand for independence, which was granted to Central America in 1821. Costa Rica was torn between those in favor of total independence, and those who sought to join the newly formed Mexican empire. The discord erupted into a brief civil war, which led to Costa Rica's formation as an independent nation state.

WHERE TO SEE PRE-COLUMBIAN COSTA RICA

What remains of Costa Rica's pre-Columbian artifacts are best seen in situ, at the Guayabo National Monument. The largest archaeological site in the nation provides great insight into this former city. In San José, Museo de Oro Pre-Columbino, Museo de Jade, and Museo Nacional all host extensive collections of pre-Columbian artifacts.

1506

Diego de Nicuesa is named governor and begins an ill-fated attempt at colonization.

1563

Governor Juan Vásquez de Coronado founds Cartago.

1641

Survivors of a slave-ship establish the free community of Miskitos.

1737

Villanueva de la Boca del Monte is founded; it is later renamed San José.

1747

Talamanca peoples are forcibly resettled in the highlands.

1838

Costa Rica splits from the Federation of Central America to become its own nation state.

Coffee Era

About a decade before Central America was granted its freedom, coffee became the country's dominant crop. A wealthy merchant class of *cafeteleros* (coffee barons) grew, and income from *grano de oro* (grain of gold) exports funded free public education, public buildings, and national defense – including the defeat of William Walker in 1856 – plus street lighting in San José. Costa Rican farmers struggled when the Depression hit the market in 1930. In response, the government laid the foundations of the production structures that still exist today.

The 1948 Civil War

Costa Rica was beset by social unrest between the World Wars, which culminated in a violent civil war in 1948. On 11 March, José Figueres Ferrer declared the War of National Liberation, following the annulment of election results. After 44 days of fighting, the undemocratic government was toppled. Figueres became provisional president, initiated a new constitution, disbanded the army, declared Costa Rica neutral, and enacted far-reaching social reforms.

1 Coffee workers in the fields in the 1890s.

2 Costa Rican soldiers during the 1948 civil war.

3 Presidents Ronald Reagan and Luis Alberto.

4 Visitors marveling at Cabo Blanco's wildlife.

97.8%

Costa Rica's literacy rate, thanks to 150 years of free, compulsory education.

Timeline of events

1849
Cafeteleros elevate fellow coffee baron Juan Rafael Mora to power.

1856
William Walker's mercenary invasion of Costa Rica is defeated.

1897
Teatro Nacional is completed, built using taxes on coffee exports.

1871
General Tomás Guardia establishes compulsory, free education for all.

1934
Plantation workers win the right to unionize.

1948
José Figueres Ferrer launches the War of National Liberation.

Years of Dangerous Instability

Following three decades of increasing prosperity, Costa Rica's stability was shaken by the 1979 Sandinista Revolution in Nicaragua that toppled Anastasio Somoza's dictatorship. The Contras, Somoza's right-wing supporters, set up clandestine bases in Costa Rica, aided by the CIA, turning the northern lowlands into a war zone, compromising Costa Rican neutrality. In 1986, Figueres's protegé Óscar Arias Sánchez beat Luis Alberto Monge for the presidency. The youthful leader ejected the Contras and, in defiance of American President Ronald Reagan, negotiated a peaceful resolution to Central America's regional conflicts, earning the 1987 Nobel Peace Prize.

Costa Rica Today

The 1990s saw the beginning of a huge tourism boom, fueled by Costa Rica's stewardship of its natural resources. Two decades of economic and political scandals, demonstrations, and natural disasters bedeviled successive administrations. But none of this slowed the development of ecotourism, and Costa Rica continues to be an active voice in support of tackling climate change.

NICOLAS WESSBERG

Swedish national Nicolas Wessberg, with foreign aid, created Cabo Blanco, Costa Rica's first wildlife reserve, from a sliver of primary forest on the Nicoya Peninsula. In 1963, the park was granted the status of *reserva absoluta*, allowing only rangers inside. Assassinated in 1975, Wessberg's legacy lives on in Costa Rica's national park system.

1949
Figueres is made provisional president, instituting a new constitution and abolishing the army; he gives up his power 18 months later.

1955
Nicaraguan invaders are repulsed at Santa Rosa.

1963
Cabo Blanco becomes the country's first nature reserve.

1987
Óscar Arias Sánchez wins the Nobel Peace Prize.

2010
Laura Chinchilla is elected, becoming Costa Rica's first female president.

2020
More than 99 per cent of electricity comes from renewable sources.

FIELD GUIDE

An iguana eyeing up the dense undergrowth of the rainforest

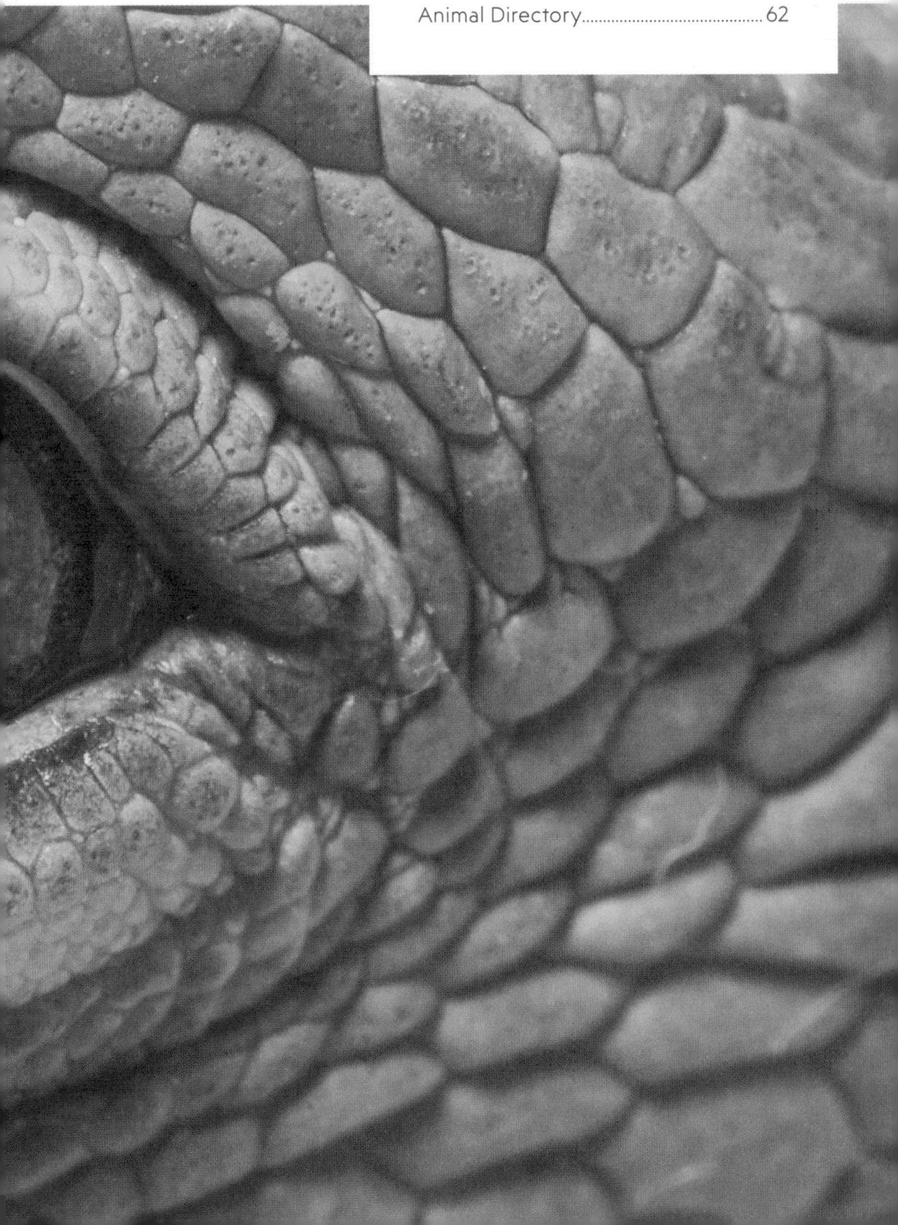

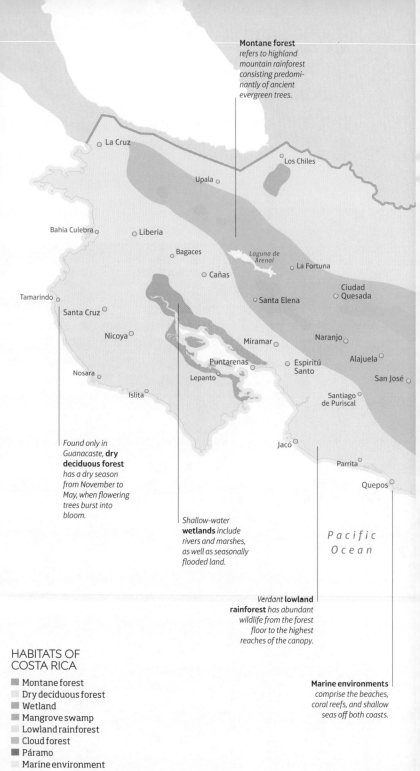

Montane forest *refers to highland mountain rainforest consisting predominantly of ancient evergreen trees.*

La Cruz

Los Chiles

Upala

Bahía Culebra

Liberia

Bagaces

Laguna de Arenal

La Fortuna

Cañas

Ciudad Quesada

Tamarindo

Santa Cruz

Santa Elena

Nicoya

Miramar

Naranjo

Alajuela

Puntarenas

Espíritú Santo

San José

Nosara

Lepanto

Islita

Santiago de Puriscal

Found only in Guanacaste, **dry deciduous forest** *has a dry season from November to May, when flowering trees burst into bloom.*

Jacó

Parrita

Quepos

Shallow-water **wetlands** *include rivers and marshes, as well as seasonally flooded land.*

P a c i f i c   O c e a n

Verdant **lowland rainforest** *has abundant wildlife from the forest floor to the highest reaches of the canopy.*

HABITATS OF COSTA RICA

- Montane forest
- Dry deciduous forest
- Wetland
- Mangrove swamp
- Lowland rainforest
- Cloud forest
- Páramo
- Marine environment

Marine environments *comprise the beaches, coral reefs, and shallow seas off both coasts.*

COSTA RICA'S
HABITATS

Until about three million years ago, North and South America were not connected. As the Central American isthmus rose from the sea, Costa Rica became a hotspot of biological intermingling, leading to the evolution of new, distinctly tropical flora and fauna. The country's diversity of climates, terrains, and habitats has fostered an astonishingly rich animal and plant life.

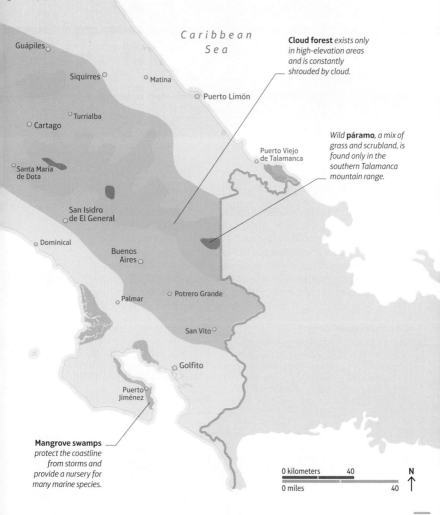

Barra del Colorado

Tortuguero

Puerto Viejo de Sarapiquí

Caribbean Sea

Guápiles

Siquirres

Matina

Puerto Limón

Turrialba

Cartago

Santa María de Dota

Puerto Viejo de Talamanca

San Isidro de El General

Dominical

Buenos Aires

Potrero Grande

Palmar

San Vito

Golfito

Puerto Jiménez

Cloud forest *exists only in high-elevation areas and is constantly shrouded by cloud.*

Wild **páramo**, *a mix of grass and scrubland, is found only in the southern Talamanca mountain range.*

Mangrove swamps *protect the coastline from storms and provide a nursery for many marine species.*

0 kilometers   40

0 miles   40

N ↑

TERRAIN AND FLORA

Few countries on earth can rival Costa Rica for biodiversity. Despite its tiny size, the nation is home to almost 5 percent of the world's identified living species, including an estimated 1,200 types of butterflies. This astonishing wealth of wildlife is due to the country's great variety in relief and climate, from lowland wetlands to cloud-draped mountains. As a result, Costa Rica has several distinct "life zones," each with a unique combination of climate, terrain, flora, and fauna.

Lowland Rainforest

Tropical rainforests cloak many of the plains and lower mountain slopes of the Caribbean lowlands and Pacific southwest, their canopies forming an uninterrupted sea of greenery. These complex ecosystems harbor much of the country's wildlife. Hardwood trees, such as mahogany and kapok, may tower 200 ft (61 m) or more, and rely on widespreading roots to support their weight. These forests comprise distinct layers, from ground to treetop canopy. Each layer has its own distinct microclimate as well as flora and fauna, with the vast majority of species concentrated at higher levels. Tapirs and jaguars inhabit the ground level, while birds and monkeys cavort in the treetops. Animals such as kinkajous, sloths, and arboreal snakes are also adapted for life in the branches, which are weighed down by vines, epiphytes, and other vascular plants.

Montane and Cloud Forests

Named for the ephemeral mists that envelop them, Costa Rica's cloud forests are typically found at elevations of 3,300 ft (1,000 m) above sea level, which accounts for more than half of Costa Rica's terrain. These areas show extreme local variations in flora. On wind-swept exposed ridges, trees and shrubs grow closer to the ground, forming forests with a primeval quality.

① Verdant lowland rainforest.
② Shrouded montane cloud forest.
③ Tangled mangrove swamps.
④ Dry deciduous forest.
⑤ Rocky marine environments at low tide.

Protected areas have taller vegetation with several levels, although the lush canopies rarely reach 100 ft (30 m). Epiphytic plants such as orchids and bromeliads cling to branches, which also drip with lichen, fungi, mosses, and liverworts. The interplay of sunshine, clouds, and rainfall produces flora of astounding diversity. Fauna is correspondingly abundant, although the mists and thick foliage hamper sightings.

Páramo

Páramo ecosystems, a mix of grassland and scrubland, are found in small regions above the forest line. These arid treeless uplands are a populated by tenacious species of rodents, lizards, and snakes, and are valuable hotspots for observing the processes of evolution.

Dry Deciduous Forest

Once covering most of Guanacaste and Nicoya, dry forests today cover only about 200 sq miles (520 sq km) of Costa Rica. The mostly deciduous flora sheds its leaves during seasonal droughts, making wildlife easier to spot. Conservationists are trying to revive dry forest ecosystems.

Wetlands and Mangroves

Wetlands range from coastal mangroves, such as the Terraba-Sierpe delta in the Pacific southwest, to inland lagoons, such as Caño Negro in the north. Many habitats are seasonal, flooding in the wet season from May to November; wildlife gathers in the December–April dry season. Mangroves thrive in alluvial silts deposited by rivers, forming a vital coastal nursery for marine creatures, such as the olive ridley turtle, and avian fauna, such as the frigate bird.

Marine Environments

Costa Rica's coastline stretches over 800 miles (1,290 km). Promontories and scalloped bays are common on the Pacific side, while the Caribbean coast is almost ruler straight. Small patches of coral reef fringe the coast off the central Pacific and southern Caribbean shores. Many beaches, notably Tortuguero on the northern Caribbean coast, provide nesting grounds for turtles. Bahía Ballena ("Whale Bay") on the southern Pacific side is a famous birthing ground for colossal humpback whales (and coincidentally features a sandbar shaped exactly like a whale's tail).

CONSERVATION

Costa Rica suffered severe deforestation and a rapid decline in the populations of many animal species in the 20th century. The rise of ecotourism and Costa Rica's efforts to protect its flora and fauna have led to the creation of a network of protected areas. Occupying about one-third of the country, this network includes 29 national parks, 25 wildlife refuges, 10 wetlands, and 8 biological reserves.

Habitat Loss

The main environmental threat to Costa Rica comes from deforestation fueled by agricultural and real-estate development. More than 60 species of trees are now protected. Other threats include pollution from fruit plantations, trawl nets, and uninsulated electricity cables.

Hunting and Poaching

Hunting is legal in Costa Rica except in national parks and reserves. Nonetheless, illegal hunting continues even within protected zones. Some farmers treat wild cats as pests, shooting them on sight. The illegal pet trade has contributed to the severe decline of parrots and monkeys; and turtle nests are often poached for eggs.

Endangered Species

Costa Rican law protects 166 animal species from hunting, capture, or sale. One of the most endangered is the leatherback turtle, which faces threats from fishing, egg poaching, pollution, and rampant development. Efforts to save these populations are finally bearing fruit.

Ecotourism

The popularity of ecotourism has done wonders for conservation efforts in Costa Rica. Economic incentives to protect, rather than cull, local wild- and plantlife are becoming increasingly evident. Greater ecological sensitivity has also seen Costa Ricans successfully lobby against proposed gold-mining and offshore oil-drilling projects.

1 Cleared lowland rainforest.
2 Protected turtle nesting grounds.
3 A turtle laying eggs on the beach.
4 A near-threatened jaguar.
5 A rescued baby sloth.

Macaw-Breeding Programs

The scarlet macaw is considered a species of least concern. However, it has disappeared from many parts of Costa Rica, and its cousin, the great green macaw is now listed as endangered. Several private initiatives have been set up to reverse the dramatic decline in population, by breeding macaws for release into the wild as sustainable-size flocks, including in areas from which they have disappeared.

CITES

The Convention on International Trade in Endangered Species of Wild Fauna and Flora (CITES) is an agreement that aims to regulate the trade in plant and animal products and ensure that such trade does not threaten the species' survival. Signed in 1963, CITES protects more than 33,000 species. Costa Rican species listed as threatened or endangered include 16 bird, 13 mammal, 8 reptile, and 2 amphibian species, plus several dozen plants. CITES requests that any listed products be traded only with a permit. Unfortunately, many species are trafficked illegally.

IUCN RED LIST

The International Union for Conservation of Nature (IUCN) Red List of Threatened Species assesses the extinction risk of a plant or animal. The categories are:

Extinct (EX) - No individuals known to survive.
Extinct in the Wild (EW) - Survives only in captivity or as an introduced population outside its natural range.
Critically Endangered (CE) - Extremely high risk of extinction.
Endangered (EN) - Very high risk of extinction within the foreseeable future.
Vulnerable (VU) - Significant medium-term risk of extinction.
Near Threatened (NT) - Close to qualifying for Threatened status.
Least Concern (LC) - No significant risk of extinction at present.

CATS

Elusive, solitary, and mainly nocturnal, cats belong to the *Felidae* family. Among the most difficult mammals to spot in the wild, these agile killers feed on living creatures, from fish, rodents, and small birds to deer and tapirs. Each species varies in size and coloration, yet all cats are shaped like their domestic cousins, with round heads, keen eyes, and prominent canines; large paws with long, retractable claws; and sinuous bodies, plus long tails that aid balance. Most are well adapted to hunt both on the ground and in trees.

TAXONOMY

Costa Rica is home to six felid (wild cat) species. These are ocelot, margay, oncilla, cougar (variously known as mountain lion, puma, catamount, and panther), jaguarundi, and jaguar. They are divided into three genera. Leopardus, small to medium-sized spotted cats, are often similar to typical domestic cats in their size and stature. Two species of Puma, representing larger cats, which have uniform coloration; both live in Costa Rica. Panthera, so-called "big cats", such as lions, tigers, and leopards, have larynx modification permits them to roar, growl, and shriek. The jaguar is Costa Rica's only Panthera.

Ocelot (LC)

Species *Leopardus pardalis* **Seen** *Cahuita National Park, Santa Rosa National Park*

The largest of Costa Rica's small felids, this graceful yet secretive cat is widely distributed throughout lowland and mid-elevation habitats, from the dry savannas of Guanacaste to the rain forests of Corcovado. Called *manigordo* by the locals, the ocelot has a stocky body; it can grow to 39 in (100 cm) in length and weigh up to 22 lb (10 kg). Its short, sleek, and golden or cream-colored fur is spotted with orange rosettes ringed by black and arranged in irregular chains along its back. Like its cousins, the margay and the oncilla, the ocelot has a black stripe on each cheek and twin black stripes running up its forehead, plus a black-banded tail. Adults are solitary and will often defend their territories – which they mark with pungent urine and feces – to the death. Like all cats, the ocelot has superb night vision, which it puts to good use when prowling dense forests in search of prey. A more diverse feeder than most cats, the ocelot will even feed on amphibians, fish, and small reptiles, although its main diet consists of small mammals, such as rabbits and rodents. Females typically give birth to a single cub – but, occasionally, two or even three kittens – every two years. Once hunted extensively for its fur and for the illegal pet trade, the ocelot is now considered of least concern on the IUCN list of endangered species and can be found in a wide area ranging from northern Mexico to the Tropic of Capricorn.

Margay (NT)
Species *Leopardus wiedii* **Seen** *Corcovado, Tapantí-Macizo la Muerte*

Less frequently seen than its larger cousin the ocelot, the margay prefers dense forest, in which it is supremely adapted for life in the trees. This medium-sized cat also has a longer tail and legs, and a smaller head with larger eyes. An agile climber, it spends much of its time hunting birds and other treetop creatures, and it has evolved a special ankle structure that permits it to turn its feet 180 degrees. Capable of prodigious leaps, the margay can run headfirst down tree trunks and even hang from branches.

Oncilla (VU)
Species *Leopardus tigrinus* **Seen** *Braulio Carrillo, Monteverde*

Almost entirely nocturnal, this ground-loving forest dweller prefers higher elevations than its cousins the ocelot and the margay. While it bears a close resemblence to the margay, the oncilla – or *tigrillo*, as the locals call it – is much smaller, growing to only 23 in (59 cm) in length. It also has a short, narrow jaw, and unmistakable huge, round eyes. Heavily hunted for its fur, the oncilla is currenty listed as vulnerable by the IUCN.

Cougar (LC)
Species *Puma concolor* **Seen** *Chirripó, Santa Rosa*

Known locally as *león*, the cougar is the most adaptable of the American felids – in Costa Rica it is found in every habitat. This master of the ambush stalks large prey such as deer but also eats rodents, reptiles, and even insects. The cougar has the longest hind legs relative to body size of any American felid, good for big leaps and short sprints of up to 35 mph (56 km/h). The cougar's unicolored coat can range from silvery to chestnut, depending on its habitat.

Jaguarundi (LC)
Species *Puma yagouaroundi* **Seen** *Barra Honda, Rincón de la Vieja*

This smaller relative of the puma is found in grassland, lowland scrub, and mid-elevation forest. Its coat ranges from chestnut to dark chocolate, and its long body and short legs have earned it the nickname "otter cat." Its ears are short and rounded, and its small face features piercing blue-green eyes. As well as chirping and whistling, it purrs and hisses like a domestic cat. The jaguarundi is mainly diurnal, which makes it the most readily seen of Costa Rica's felids.

JAGUAR

The largest land predator and the only Panthera species in Central America, the elusive jaguar resembles the African leopard, but it is stockier and more powerful. Although this cat can climb trees, it mostly prowls the dense forest floor. Adult jaguars require a vast range for hunting. Habitat fragmentation and illegal hunting have caused a decline in numbers, and today the jaguar is confined to a few protected areas, notably Corcovado, where fewer than 50 individuals remain.

KEY FACTS

Species
Panthera onca. Local name: Tigre.

Size
Height: 26–30 in (65–75 cm); Weight: up to 350 lb (160 kg).

Population in Costa Rica
Unknown.

Conservation Status
NT.

Reproduction
Females reach sexual maturity at two years; litters of one to four cubs every 18–24 months.

Habitat
From dry deciduous forest to seasonally flooded wetlands and lowland rainforest.

Seen
Corcovado, Santa Rosa, Talamancas, Tortuguero.

Family and Breeding

Like all American cats, the jaguar is a loner. Each adult carves out a large territory for itself, marking it with scent trails. Females' home ranges may overlap, but individuals avoid each other and chance meetings trigger an aggressive reaction. Males, whose territories cover 2–3 times the area of females, defend their turf against intrusions by other males, although actual fights between rivals are rare. Male and female adults generally meet only to mate, an ill-tempered affair that can occur at any time of year. Females then provide all the parenting. Cubs can stay with their mother for up to two years before leaving to establish their own territory. Females are fiercely protective of their cubs, against external predators, but also against male jaguars, which often kill existing cubs when taking over a rival's territory.

Feeding

Jaguars are solitary nocturnal hunters who rely on stealth rather than speed to ambush prey. They eat a wide variety of animals, from agoutis to caimans, but prefer large ungulates such as tapirs and brocket deer. Jaguars that inhabit coastal terrain are also known to hunt marine turtles. Uniquely, they kill their prey with a bite to the skull using their huge canines. The jaguar's bite is by far the strongest of all felids – twice as powerful as that of a lion.

Communication and Voice

Fearsome and furtive, adult jaguars rely on silence and guile to catch their prey and are thus not given to extensive articulation. When females come into estrus (heat), they communicate their fertility by marking territory with urinary scents and by vocalizations, ranging from purrs, mews, and grunts to the jaguar's characteristic hoarse, cough-like roar. Males emit a series of deeper roars, repeated several times, to advertise their presence to females and to warn off rivals. Clashes between males elicit much snarling and hissing.

Did You Know?

Jaguars' canine teeth are strong enough to pierce even the shells of a mature turtle.

OTHER MAMMALS

Costa Rica supports over 200 mammal species. This figure includes about two dozen species of non-felid carnivorous mammals, although most are omnivorous to various degrees. A few are easily observed, while others are highly elusive or rare – the olingo, for example, is a creature of the night and not likely to be readily seen. On the other hand, the raccoon and the coati are diurnal and often become quite bold in approaching lodges and tourists in the hope of being fed. Mammals that are active by day include rodents, ungulates, and the three-toed sloth. There are also approximately 100 species of bats, the only mammals in the world that have evolved for powered flight – their wings are really webbed forelimbs. Exclusively nocturnal, they navigate by emitting ultrasonic squeaks and track the echoes with special receptors. This is known as echolocation.

TAXONOMY

Costa Rica's mammals, of which there are 260 species, are grouped into 11 orders including carnivores across three suborders: felids, canids, and procyonids (raccoons). Anteaters, tamanduas, and sloths belong to the diverse order Pilosa. Bats, which make up the majority of mammalian species on Costa Rica, belong to the Chiroptera order. Peccaries and deer are among the even-toed ungulates – hoofed animals.

Brown-Throated Three-Toed Sloth (LC)

Species *Bradypus variegatus* **Seen** *Braulio Carrillo, Cahuita, Manuel Antonio, Tortuguero*

The three-toed sloth – more accurately called "three-fingered", since the two-toed sloth, confusingly, also has three "toes" on its hind limbs – can be seen in every kind of forest in Costa Rica. It has a round face with a blunt nose, a black eye mask, and a prominent forehead, and it can rotate its neck by 360 degrees. Sloths spend virtually their entire lives suspended by their hook-like claws, or otherwise curled up asleep in the forks of branches. Active by day, they feed exclusively on the leaves of several tree species, notably the cecropia. The three-toed sloth's thick, long gray fur runs from its belly to its back in order to facilitate the drainage of rain while it hangs upside down. Green algae grow on its fur, providing natural camouflage and food for a species of moth.

Hoffmann's Two-Toed Sloth (LC)
Species *Choloepus hoffmanni* **Seen** *Cahuita, Corcovado, Tapantí-Macizo*

This nocturnal animal has many similarities to its smaller three-toed cousin, but it has only two claws on its forelimbs. It also has a much more extensive diet that includes insects, fruit, and birds' eggs, as well as plant material. It has a cream-colored face and bulbous brown eyes. Although it is clumsy on the ground, it is a good swimmer. Females give birth to a single baby once a year and carry it clinging on their chests; if a baby falls, its calls are ignored and it is doomed – a meal for snakes, cats, or hawks.

Northern Tamandua (LC)
Species *Tamandua mexicana* **Seen** *Caño Negro, La Cruz, Santa Rosa*

This semi-arboreal mammal, a dedicated eater of ants and termites, supplements its diet with tiny beetles and other insects. The tamandua has a coarse cream coat with a shoulder band and black flanks. It uses its strong forearms and huge claws to tear open ant nests. Its elongated snout tapers to a tiny mouth, through which an extremely long, narrow tongue darts to lick up insects. A long prehensile tail helps to climb trees in its preferred lowland-forest habitats.

Giant Anteater (VU)
Species *Myrmecophaga tridactyla*
Seen *Corcovado*

The largest of the three anteater species can exceed 7 ft (2.1 m) in length, half being its bushy tail and another 20 in (50 cm) its slender snout. This gray, black, and white mammal shuffles along on its knuckles like a chimpanzee. Its large front claws are perfect for ripping apart termite mounds, but also for defense – the anteater rears up on its hind legs to slash at attackers. This extremely rare animal is now thought to be restricted to Corcovado.

Silky Anteater (LC)
Species *Cyclopes didactylus* **Seen** *Braulio Carrillo, Corcovado, Monteverde*

Also called the pygmy anteater for its relatively small size, this nocturnal animal is arboreal by nature. During the day, it sleeps curled up into a ball high up a tree, and by night, it hunts for ants, termites, and beetles. Resembling a teddy bear, it has soft, honey-colored fur, a short pink snout, and a long prehensile tail. The silky anteater forages in a variety of forest types and nests in tree hollows, where it gives birth to a single pup each year.

BAIRD'S TAPIR

The largest neotropical land mammal, Baird's tapir resembles the offspring of a horse and a pig. It has good hearing and a long, prehensile snout, and its keen sense of smell makes up for its poor vision. The tapir's thick hide and huge bulk help protect it against jaguars and crocodiles. Sadly, this shy, reclusive creature fares less well against illegal hunters. The Cordillera Talamanca is a rare sanctuary with a stable population, but elsewhere numbers are dropping: it is estimated that fewer than 3,000 individuals remain in the wild.

KEY FACTS

Species
Tapirus Bairdii. Local name: Danta.

Size
Shoulder height: 3.9–5 ft (1–1.5 m); weight: up to 880 lb (350 kg).

Population in Costa Rica
Less than 1,000.

Conservation Status
EN.

Reproduction
Females typically conceive after two years and give birth every two years.

Habitat
Humid habitats from sea level to 11,400 ft (3,500 m).

Seen
Corcovado, La Amistad, La Selva, Rincón de la Vieja.

Family and Breeding

Adult tapirs mostly keep to themselves, although the bond between mother and calf is strong. Rival males fight to mate with a female. The excited winner initiates an elaborate courtship by spraying urine. The couple dances a quickening duet, sniffing each other's genitals, before violent copulation begins. Females give birth to a single calf, weighing about 15 lb (7 kg). The calf is weaned for a year, then spends another year or two with the mother. Males do not contribute to raising their offspring.

Adult tapirs have a thick, tough skin, especially on their hind legs, which are covered with bristly, tightly packed hairs. Individuals that live at higher elevations, such as the páramo of Parque Nacional Chirripó, grow thicker coats as protection from the cold.

Feeding

This tapir is a grazer-browser that feeds primarily at twilight and by night, using its long prehensile snout to forage for and pluck leaves and fruit. Its diet consists largely of fruit and berries, plus tender shoots and young leaves supplemented by aquatic vegetation. Weighing up to 880 lb (350 kg) in the wild, this rapacious eater can devour one-tenth of its own body weight in vegetation daily. The tapir's tendency to follow well-worn paths that meander through the thick forest undergrowth makes it relatively easy to find – for both hunters and wildlife fans.

Communication and Voice

Solitary, unsociable, and territorial, tapirs mark their home ranges with urine and dung. Except for in breeding season, tapirs that come into contact react aggressively by baring their teeth. If neither retreats, a fight can occur, with each trying to bite the other's hind legs – their sharp incisors can inflict serious wounds. Tapirs vocalize with shrills, snorts, squeaks, and whistles. These vary in pitch depending on meaning and are especially loud when the animal is sexually excited.

Did You Know?

Baird's tapir is named for American naturalist Spencer Fullerton Baird, who studied them in the 1840s.

Red Brocket Deer (Data Deficient)
Species *Mazama americana* **Seen** *Arenal, Cahuita, Rincón de la Vieja*

Endemic to Central America, this small deer inhabits thick forests, where its rust-brown fur is camouflaged by dark shade. The red brocket deer's lower legs are edged with black, while its throat and inner legs are whitish. Juveniles have two rows of white spots running along each flank, and adult males grow small, spike-like antlers. The red brocket deer dines mostly on fruits, but it also browses on leaves. A shy creature, it is less commonly seen than the white-tailed deer.

White-Tailed Deer (LC)
Species *Odocoileus virginianus* **Seen** *Barra Honda, Caño Negro, Santa Rosa*

The white-tailed deer tends to prefer grassland, wetland, and dry deciduous forest over dense evergreen forests, and it is particularly active around dawn and dusk. It is gray-brown to rust in coloration and displays the white underside of its tail when alarmed. Capable of huge leaps, it relies on speed and agility to outwit cougars, coyotes, jaguars, and human hunters. Males spar for dominance in breeding season, when they lose weight due to a singular focus on mating.

Paca (LC)
Species *Cuniculus paca* **Seen** *Braulio Carrillo, Corcovado, Tortuguero*

A cousin of the agouti, the paca (called *tepezcuintle* in Costa Rica) is distinguished by its shiny dark-brown fur spotted with several parallel lines of white dots along its sides. A nocturnal animal, this herbivore enjoys a diet of seeds, roots, fruits, and flowers. A good climber and swimmer, where possible it flees to water to escape danger. It is illegally hunted for its meat, and many *campesinos* (subsistence farmers) raise pacas commercially.

Agouti (LC)
Species *Dasyprocta punctata* **Seen** *La Selva, Corcovado, Manuel Antonio*

Known as *guatusa*, this large ground-dwelling rodent has grown so accustomed to humans that in many national parks it can be seen at close range, grooming or feeding on palm nuts, which it stores in the ground. Its chestnut-brown coat is glossy, and the male's rump hairs form a fan-shaped crest that is displayed during territorial disputes. Monogamous for life, the agouti breeds year-round. During courtship, the male sprays the female with urine.

Nine-Banded Armadillo (LC)
Species *Dasypus novemcinctus* **Seen**
Arenal, Caño Negro, Santa Rosa

Of South American origin, the armadillo is
protected by a bony shell of interlinked scales.
Armed with powerful claws for burrowing, it
thrives only in soft-soil environments, where it
digs for termites, grubs, and tubers at dusk.
Although it typically ambles, it can flee quickly
from danger and – being capable of holding its
breath for several minutes – it can easily run
along riverbeds or even swim across. The nine-
banded armadillo can reach 42 in (110 cm) in
length, nose to tail.

Collared Peccary (LC)
Species *Pecari tajacu* **Seen** *Braulio Carrillo,*
Corcovado, Santa Rosa

One of two peccary species in Costa Rica, this
large cousin of the pig stands up to 24 in (60 cm)
tall. It is covered in thick gray bristles, and has
short legs and a massive head tapering to a tiny
snout for sniffing out fruits, nuts, and tubers. It
roams lowland environments, from savanna to
rainforest. The collared peccary typically lives
in groups of up to 20 individuals. Herds of the
more aggressive white-lipped peccary can
contain more than 100 animals.

Kinkajou (LC)
Species *Potos flavus* **Seen** *Corcovado, La*
Selva, Monteverde

An arboreal mammal related to the cacomistle,
raccoon, and olingo, the kinkajou is distinguished
by its prehensile tail. It uses its dexterous fore-
paws to hold and eat figs and other fruits and
insects, and its long, extrudable tongue to
scoop up honey and nectar. Kinkajous are social
animals and sometimes forage in groups. They
are hunted for their short golden fur, as well as
for the illegal pet trade. Your best chance of
seeing this nocturnal mammal is on a night tour.

Cacomistle (LC)
Species *Bassariscus sumichrasti* **Seen**
Braulio Carrillo, Carara, Corcovado

Much smaller in size than its cousin the raccoon,
the cacomistle is also far rarer. Living in the
upper levels of moist forests, it has been heavily
impacted by deforestation – in Costa Rica it is
listed as an endangered species. It has huge
black eyes for vision while prowling at night for
insects, small vertebrates, and fruit. With a
narrow nose and extremely long, pointed ears,
its face is catlike – indeed, cacomistle means
"half-cat" in the Nahuatl language.

White-Nosed Coati (LC)

Species *Nasua narica* **Seen** *Arenal, Cahuita, Manuel Antonio*

The white-nosed coati (*pizote* to the locals) is a cousin of the raccoon and commonly seen in Costa Rica from sea level to an altitude of about 11,500 ft (3,500 m). Females and juveniles forage in bands of up to 30 individuals; males are solitary, only coming into contact with females to mate. The coati's chestnut body contrasts with its silvery chest and white nose, which is long and pointed. Ringed with black and white, the long tail is held aloft while walking, and it aids balance when climbing trees.

Northern Olingo (LC)

Species *Bassaricyon gabbii* **Seen** *Carara, Corcovado, La Selva, Selva Verde*

This bushy-tailed arboreal mammal, with short legs and small rounded ears, is almost always nocturnal. Lively and furtive, it lives in the upper forest canopy, where it feeds on insects, fruit, and small vertebrates. Its soft, dense fur is pale cream on the belly and dark brown around the midriff, and its tail makes up more than half of its 35-in (90-cm) length. The olingo is a popular (but illegal) pet, which causes it to be poached from the wild.

Northern Raccoon (LC)

Species *Procyon lotor* **Seen** *Cahuita, Santa Rosa, Tortuguero*

Familiar to North Americans almost everywhere, the northern raccoon (*mapache*) is found in most parts of Costa Rica. Although mostly nocturnal, this unfussy omnivore also forages by day, using its impressive front paws, second only to monkeys in terms of dexterity, to manipulate objects. It can also rotate its paws backward to descend trees headfirst. It stands up to 12 in (30 cm) tall and has gray fur and a white face with trademark black mask.

Crab-Eating Raccoon (LC)

Species *Procyon cancrivorus* **Seen** *Manuel Antonio, P. Verde, Terraba-Sierpe*

Native to Central and South America, the crab-eating raccoon shares the coloration of the northern raccoon, but its shorter fur gives it a smaller, leaner look. This coastal dweller favors shoreline forests, especially mangrove swamps. Although it scavenges for birds' eggs, lizards, and fruits, its diet consists mainly of crabs and other crustaceans. Crab-eating raccoons are often seen begging or trying to steal tidbits from visitors at Manuel Antonio National Park.

Gray Fox (LC)
Species *Urocyon cinereoargenteus*
Seen *Guanacaste, Rincón de la Vieja*

The gray fox is easily recognized by its silvery coat, with white bib and rust-red underparts and neck; its large, alert ears; and its bushy, black-tipped tail. A stealthy, nocturnal predator, it hunts for small mammals and birds both on the ground and in trees, which it is able to climb thanks to the strong, curved claws on its hind paws. The best time to see one is around dawn or dusk, and the best location is the lowlands of Guanacaste, especially during the dry season when foliage is more sparse.

Coyote (LC)
Species *Canis latrans* **Seen** *Palo Verde, Rincón de la Vieja, Santa Rosa*

These opportunistic hunters often pair up to kill rodents and ground-nesting birds. Their diet also includes snakes and large invertebrates. Closely resembling the gray fox, coyotes tend to be more robust, standing up to 26 in (65 cm) tall at the shoulder, which is crossed by black-tipped guard hairs. A coyote's howl is often heard around dusk in many areas of Costa Rica; it is renowned for its adaptability to different environments, from cities to scrublands.

Tayra (LC)
Species *Eira barbara* **Seen** *Arenal, Braulio Carrillo, La Amistad*

A forest-dwelling weasel, the tayra *(tolomuco)* averages 24–28 in (60–70 cm), plus tail. It is black except for a white throat, though its neck and head silver with age. Armed with large claws and powerful legs, this diurnal hunter is an expert climber capable of leaping between branches in pursuit of small monkeys, birds, and other prey. It also eats fruit, eggs, and honey. Although it prefers rainforest environments, it can sometimes be found in dry forests.

Neotropical Otter (NT)
Species *Lontra longicaudis* **Seen** *Cahuita, G'ca-Manzanillo, Tortuguero*

Known in Costa Rica as *nutria*, this sleek, robust aquatic mammal inhabits lowland riverine and swamps, where it feeds on fish, amphibians, and crustaceans. It requires unpolluted waters and healthy riparian vegetation. It has short legs, a long body, a thick neck, and a flat head with tiny ears and a broad, thickly whiskered muzzle. Its pelt is dense and sleek, and its webbed feet and powerful tail provide propulsion in the water, They are frequently spotted playing in groups.

Honduran White Bat (NT)
Species *Ectophylla alba* **Seen** *Cahuita, Hitoy-Cerere, Tortuguero*

This tiny bat averages less than 2 in (5 cm) in length. It has snow-white fur and an orange nose, ears, legs, and wings. Mostly a fruit eater, it lives only in the Caribbean lowland rainforest, where it roosts communally, shoulder to shoulder, inside "tents" made by chewing the veins of heliconia leaves until they fold. Usually the group comprises a single male with his harem. Sunlight filtering through the leaf makes the Honduran white bat's fur appear green, providing camouflage.

Jamaican Fruit Bat (LC)
Species *Artibeus jamaicensis* **Seen** *Arenal, Cahuita, Rincón de la Vieja*

One of the most important pollinators in the neotropics, this large bat has a short, broad snout topped by a nose leaf. Its gray-brown fur has a distinctive soapy smell. It snatches wild figs and other small fruits in flight and returns to its roost to eat the pulp. Like the Honduran white bat, it is one of 15 species that form a tent from large leaves; the Jamaican fruit bat prefers broad-leaf palms, but it also lives in hollow trees.

Common Vampire Bat (LC)
Species *Desmodus rotundus* **Seen** *Barra Honda, Caño Negro, Santa Rosa*

Costa Rica has three vampire bat species that feed on the blood of cattle and other mammals and birds, usually while they sleep. A vampire bat typically crawls toward its victim, whose fur it trims with clipper-like teeth, then pierces the skin with two sharp fangs. Its saliva contains an anticoagulant substance called draculin, which permits it to suck up free-flowing blood. After feeding, the bat uses its powerful pectoral muscles to leap into the air and take flight.

Greater Bulldog Bat (LC)
Species *Noctilio leporinus* **Seen** *Drake Bay, Gandoca-Manzanillo, Tortuguero*

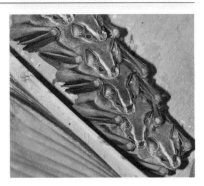

Visitors to Tortuguero are virtually guaranteed a sighting of the greater bulldog bat, also known as the "fishing" bat, swooping low over the lagoons to snatch fish with its long claws. Its reddish fur is water repellent, and its narrow wings act as oars to gain speed and take off if it falls in the water. The greater bulldog bat can be seen wherever there are large bodies of water, including sheltered coves on both the Caribbean and Pacific shores.

Mexican Tree Porcupine (LC)
Species *Sphiggurus mexicanus* **Seen** *Rincón de la Vieja, Santa Rosa*

As its name suggests, this porcupine is arboreal. It is mostly nocturnal, with a prehensile tail that aids in maneuvering around the treetops. It inhabits most forest types but prefers drier habitats and is rare in rainforest. Covered almost entirely in thick quills mixed with white-tipped black fur, this porcupine has a small round head and a fleshy snout. It eats leaves, fruits, and seeds. Normally silent, it wails during breeding season, when it can also emit a foul-smelling garlicky odor.

Striped Hog-Nosed Skunk (LC)
Species *Conepatus semistriatus* **Seen** *Poás, Cahuita, Santa Rosa*

A solitary creature that lives in habitats from lowland grassland and scrub to moist mid-elevation forest, the *zorrillo* (as it is known locally) emerges at night to hunt for fruit and small invertebrates. Including its long bushy tail, this black-and-white striped animal grows up to 20 in (50 cm) in length. Infamously, the skunk wards off potential predators by spraying a foul-smelling sulfurous chemical from its anal scent gland.

Variegated Squirrel (LC)
Species *Sciurus variegatoides* **Seen** *Carara, Monteverde, San Gerardo de Dota*

Related to North American and European squirrels, the variegated squirrel is endemic to Central America. This squirrel, the most frequently seen of five local species, has a copper-colored body with a black back and gray bushy tail, which typically curls along its back. It nests inside trees, and – unlike other squirrels – it feeds mostly on fruit, although it often scampers onto restaurant tables to steal food.

Common Opossum (LC)
Species *Didelphis marsupialis* **Seen** *Cahuita, Carara, La Selva*

The opossum is the only marsupial in Costa Rica. A primitive yet adaptable creature, it inhabits a wide range of habitats below 6,600 ft (2,200 m), including urban environments. Often active at night, it spends most of its time on the ground but can also climb trees in search of fruit and birds' eggs. Females give birth several times a year to tiny babies that emerge after only two weeks' gestation and climb into their mother's pouch to suckle.

PRIMATES

Costa Rica has four of the 156 species of American primates, which are limited to a spectrum of tropical forest. They differ from their Old World counterparts in having flat noses with side-facing nostrils, plus (in many species) strong prehensile tails that can grasp branches and aid maneuvering through the treetops. The Costa Rican species are small to mid-sized, arboreal, and mostly herbivorous – only capuchin monkeys are adept at foraging on the forest floor. Intelligent and entertaining, primates also have a complex social structure.

TAXONOMY

Costa Rica's four diurnal primate species are all classified as American monkeys, or platyrrhines ("flat-nosed") – that is, monkeys that chiefly populate tropical Central and South American habitats. White-faced capuchins and Central American squirrel monkeys are in the Cebidae family; mantled howler and Geoffroy's spider monkeys (among the largest monkeys in Central America) belong to the Atelidae family.

White-Faced Capuchin (LC)

Species *Cebus capucinus* **Seen** *Cabo Blanco, Cahuita, Manuel Antonio*

This long-lived monkey is named for its black cloak and cap and white chest, neck, and shoulders, which hint at the dress of the namesake Franciscan friars. Mischievous or malicious, depending on your point of view, this hyperactive and agile animal spends much of the day searching for food from ground to treetop, and it will snatch human belongings (such as bags left unattended on the beach) in its search for tidbits. An omnivore weighing 5.5–7.7 lb (2.5–3.5 kg), it eats everything from buds, fruits, and nuts to birds' eggs, insects, and small vertebrates. The white-faced capuchin is the most intelligent of the American monkeys: it uses twigs to forage for insects and stones to crack open crab shells; it even rubs itself with crushed millipedes to repel mosquitoes. Highly gregarious, this monkey lives in groups of ten to 35 members dominated by an alpha male and female. Territories tend to overlap, leading to hostile encounters that often result in infanticide by males that take over a group. The white-faced capuchin is widely distributed throughout Costa Rica, where it lives in almost every kind of forest below 6,500 ft (2,000 m).

Central American Squirrel Monkey (VU)
Species *Saimiri oerstedii* **Seen** *Corcovado, Golfito, Manuel Antonio*

Handsome and tiny, the endearing squirrel monkey *(mono titi)* is restricted to the Central and Southern Pacific coasts. Unlike other local primates, its tail is not prehensile – it is used purely for balance. These monkeys live in groups of up to 100 members, and adult males share females. Rather than fighting, males engorge themselves to attract female attention. They have short-cropped fur with an olive or orange body, white chest and face, and black mouth, hands, cap, and tail tip. When predators are detected, male sentinels issue alarm calls, and the monkeys dive for cover. The species' population is recovering after a steep decline caused by deforestation.

Mantled Howler Monkey (LC)
Species *Alouatta palliata* **Seen** *Manuel Antonio, Santa Rosa, Tortuguero*

Weighing up to 23 lb (9 kg), the mantled howler monkey *(mono congo)* is the largest Costa Rican primate and the most widespread, found in most national parks and reserves. It is named for the male's loud, throaty roar, emitted at dawn and dusk and to intimidate interlopers. The mantled howler is black, with a chestnut-colored coat on its flanks and back. Its long, prehensile tail acts as an extra arm for gripping branches. The mantled howler eats mostly leaves, fruit, and flowers, and it spends much of the day snoozing to digest its low-energy food source. It lives in troops of up to 20 animals and is the most resilient of the monkey species to forest disturbance due to its small home range and low-energy lifestyle.

Geoffroy's Spider Monkey (EN)
Species *Ateles geoffroyi* **Seen** *Arenal, Braulio Carrillo, Corcovado, Palo Verde, Santa Elena*

A gangly acrobat, this rust-colored monkey is named for its disproportionately long limbs, supremely adapted to life in the canopy. This monkey brachiates, or swings, beneath branches aided by its long prehensile tail, which is tipped by a palm-like pad and can support its entire weight. Its hands have long, hook-like fingers but only a vestigial thumb, and it has pale flesh-coloured "spectacles" around the eyes. It lives in bands of up to 35 individuals, but by day it forages in smaller groups. The spider monkey inhabits several forest habitats, from dry deciduous to cloud forest. It is one of the first mammals to disappear due to habitat disturbance.

SEALIFE

Costa Rica's large pelagic animals include rays, sharks, dolphins, humpback whales, and other cetaceans. Whales and dolphins are frequently seen in Golfo Dulce, Golfo de Nicoya, and in the warm waters surrounding Isla del Caño and Isla del Coco. Scuba divers and snorkelers can enjoy closeup encounters with groupers, hammerhead sharks, whale sharks, and other marine creatures, including more than 120 species of fish that swim among the 35 different types of coral. Five of the world's seven marine turtle species nest on Costa Rican beaches, especially around Tortuguero and Nicoya.

TAXONOMY

Dolphins and whales are in the Cetacean order of air-breathing mammals that evolved for aquatic life. Fish, on the other hand, belong to several dozen groups of loosely related marine vertebrates. Sharks and rays that belong to the Elasmobranchii order swim in the waters on both sides of the country. Each of Costa Rica's five marine turtle species is the only species in its genus, except the ridley, which is one of two species in the Lepidochelys genus. All belong to the Cheloniidae family, except the leatherback, which belongs to the Dermochelyidae family.

Leatherback Turtle (VU)

Species *Dermochelys coriacea* **Seen** *Gandoca-Manzanillo, Playa Grande*

The largest of the sea turtles, the leatherback can measure 6.5 ft (2 m) and weigh up to 1,200 lb (550 kg). It roams the world's oceans powered by massive front flippers. Its body is pewter-colored, pink underneath, covered with white blotches, and lined with seven ridges for hydrodynamic efficiency. Instead of a hard carapace, it has thick cartilaginous skin overlaying a matrix of small, polygonal bones and fatty flesh that permits it to resist the extreme cold of Arctic waters and the pressure of deep ocean dives. Backward spines in its throat aid in eating slippery jellyfish, its main food source. Female leatherbacks nest at night on both the Caribbean (February to July) and Pacific (October to March) shores of Costa Rica and prefer soft-sand beaches facing deep water, such as Pacuaré and Playa Grande. The female lays 50–100 eggs in a deep nest dug with her rear flippers, before filling in the pit by flinging sand with her front flippers. The leatherback matures at about 10 years and can live to 40 years or more. Up until recently, these turtles were listed as critically endangered due to ocean pollution, incidental capture by long lines and drift nets, and the poaching of eggs by animals and humans, but thanks to earnest conservation efforts, the ICUN have upgraded them to "vulnerable" status.

Loggerhead Turtle (VU)
Species *Caretta caretta* **Seen** *Gandoca-Manzanillo, Tortuguero*

With the exception of its copper-colored /'shell, the loggerhead turtle is similar in size and appearance to the green turtle. Females mate with several partners and can store sperm until ovulation. Like all turtles, the female loggerhead lays as many as 50–100 eggs, principally nesting on the Caribbean shores, and more infrequently on the Pacific side. The loggerhead turtle has a varied diet, but it mostly feeds on bottom-dwelling invertebrates, which it crushes with its powerful jaws.

Green Turtle (EN)
Species *Chelonia mydas* **Seen** *Gandoca-Manzanillo, Pacuaré, Tortuguero*

The green turtle is the largest of the shelled species and can grow up to 5 ft (1.5 m) in length. Named for the green layer of fat under its shell, it has a small round head and a broad, heart-shaped carapace resembling that of the smaller hawksbill turtle. Uniquely, this turtle is a herbivore and grazes on shallow-water sea grasses. It has separate Atlantic and Pacific populations; in Costa Rica it is primarily found at Parque Nacional Tortuguero.

Hawksbill Turtle (CR)
Species *Eretmochelys imbricata* **Seen** *Gandoca-Manzanillo*

This delicate-looking turtle is in fact extremely aggressive – it is named for its sharp beak-like mouth, which it uses to defend itself. It prefers shallow coastal waters and is frequently seen swimming around coral reefs. A solitary nester, the hawksbill turtle comes ashore in Costa Rica along both coasts. Adults eat all manner of sealife, including jellyfish. This turtle is targeted by hunters for its uniquely patterned, reddish-brown, and slightly iridescent carapace.

Olive Ridley (VU)
Species *Lepidochelys olivacea* **Seen** *Camaronal, Ostional, Santa Rosa*

The smallest of Costa Rica's five turtle species, the olive ridley is remarkable for nesting en masse at a few select locations worldwide. In Costa Rica, these include five or six beaches along the shores of Nicoya and Guanacaste. Each female nests up to three times per season. Arrivals take place as often as twice-monthly from July to December, peaking in September and October, when tens of thousands of female turtles arrive to lay eggs.

MANATEE

A large, lumbering marine mammal, the manatee is a placid aquatic herbivore. This distant relative of the elephant lives in warm brackish tropical and sub-tropical waters. Sometimes reaching lengths of more than 10 ft (3 m), manatees can remain underwater for long periods, surfacing for air at regular intervals. Spotting one is an exciting feather in the cap for nature lovers, who can encounter them in the back-waters of Tortuguero and Gandoca-Manzanillo.

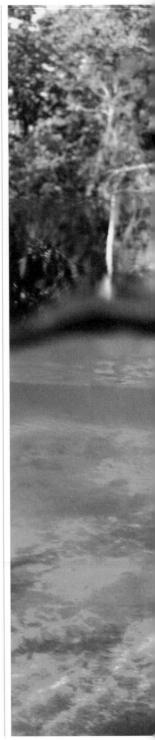

KEY FACTS

Species
Trichechus manatus. Local Name: Sea cow, manatí

Size
Length: up to 12 ft (3.9 m); Weight: up to 3,910 lb (1,620 kg).

Population in Costa Rica
200+.

Conservation Status
VU.

Reproduction
Females first conceive at about five years of age, then every 2–5 years.

Habitat
Shallow coastal lagoons and rivers of the Caribbean.

Seen
Barra del Colorado, Gandoca-Manzanillo, Tortuguero.

Family and Breeding

Although generally solitary, manatees are sometimes spotted in groups. Females can come into estrus through-out the year, and about two years after giving birth. Like their cousin the elephant, males form ephemeral mating herds around estrus females and compete for their turn at copulation. Male–female bonds do not form. Females give birth to a single baby – or, rarely, twins – after about 13 months. The calf nurses from nipples just behind the mother's flippers. Mother and calf form a strong bond, and will remain together for two years during weaning. Gentle and slow-moving, manatees face the greatest danger from fast-moving vessels. Every year, many sustain nasty injuries from boat propellers and hull collisions. Boat traffic along the canals and lagoons of Tortuguero National Park scares them into the back-waters. Other threats include pesticides washing down from banana plantations.

Feeding

Manatees are opportunistic browsers, with a varied diet consisting of over 60 different aquatic plant species, including seagrasses, water hyacinths, and mangrove leaves. They spend the greater part of the day grazing and can eat up to 10 percent of their body weight daily. Lacking incisors and canine teeth, manatees rely on large back molars that, uniquely among mammals, are constantly replaced as they become worn down and fall out.

Communication

Manatees use a repertoire of chirps, squeaks, and grunts to communicate. Variations in pitch and tone have specific meanings – for example, short, harsh squeaks indicate anger or annoyance, while squeals reveal alarm or fear. Hungry calves squeak until allowed to nurse, while calves separated from their mum will cry until she answers – from as far away as 197 ft (60 m). Smell, taste, and touch are also used for communication: during mating season, males caress females and utter excited squeals.

Did You Know?

The manatee's taxonomic order, Sirenia, is named for the sirens of Greek mythology.

Humpback Whale (LC)

Species *Megaptera novaeangliae*
Seen *Whale Marine National Park, Isla del Caño, Drake Bay*

Twice a year (December–March and July–October), schools of humpback whales arrive in the waters off southwest Costa Rica to breed and give birth. These giants have long pectoral fins and a black-and-white tail fin; despite weighing up to 40 tons (36,000 kg), they like to perform spectacular leaps, or breaches, into the air above the surface. Males compose complex communal songs that females respond to during courtship.

Pilot Whale (LC)

Species *Globicephala melas* **Seen** *Whale Marine Nat. Park, Isla del Caño*

An ocean nomad, this whale actually belongs to the dolphin family. It prefers deep waters, especially those at the edge of the continental shelf, where it feeds primarily on squid. Dark gray in color, the pilot whale is recognizable by its high, blunt forehead; sweeping dorsal fin set forward toward the rear of its head; and tiny tail flukes. It typically lives in groups of 10–30 individuals. Adult males can measure 16–20 ft (5–6 m) and females 11–17 ft (3–5 m).

Bottlenose Dolphin (LC)

Species *Tursiops truncatus* **Seen** *Gulf of Papagayo, Whale Marine National Park, Golfo Dulce*

This playful and extremely intelligent creature with a gray body and pale-pink belly can grow to 12 ft (4 m) long and weigh up to 1,400 lb (635 kg), although those found in Costa Rican waters tend to be smaller. It mostly eats fish and squid, which it tracks using echolocation and chases at speeds of up to 20 mph (30 km/h). Highly social, it typically lives in groups of several hundred individuals.

Spinner Dolphin (LC)

Species *Stenella longirostris* **Seen** *Drake Bay, Gulf of Nicoya, Isla Caño*

This long, dark-gray mammal is named for its acrobatic displays, performed either singly or alongside a pod of fellow dolphins. Unusually long fins help power the spinner dolphin, which can leap high enough in the air to spin many times before splashing down in belly or back flops. It can even execute spectacular somersaults. Spinner dolphins communicate by slapping the water and by trailing bubbles from their blowhole.

Whale Shark (EN)
Species *Rhincodon typus* **Seen** *Gulf of Papagayo, Isla del Caño, Isla del Coco*

This gentle giant – the world's largest fish – can grow to 40 ft (12 m), yet it is so docile that it will let swimmers touch it. It scoops up plankton and tiny sea creatures as it swims slowly, with its vast mouth open. Its gray upper body is marked with striped hoops interspersed with rings of pale spots; three ridges run along each flank. Whale sharks exist in large numbers around the Bat Islands, in the Gulf of Papagayo, and in the nutrient-rich waters around Isla del Coco.

Hammerhead Shark (EN)
Species *Sphyrna lewini* **Seen** *Gulf of Papagayo, Isla del Caño, Isla del Coco*

The scalloped hammerhead, one of nine shark species named for a flattened cephalofoil head, inhabits the Pacific coastal waters and throngs around Isla del Coco. Its hammer-shaped head, lined with super-sensitive receptors, offers 360-degree binocular vision. Unlike other sharks, hammerheads swim in huge schools that can number in the hundreds. At night individuals break off to hunt for small fish. The scalloped hammerhead is not dangerous to humans.

Sailfish (LC)
Species *Istiophorus platypterus* **Seen** *Gulf of Papagayo, Central Pacific*

Unlike its cousins the marlin and the swordfish, the sailfish has a huge dorsal fin that forms a retractable sail. Taller than the fish itself, this fin is laced with blood vessels and thought to aid in cooling and heating. It is also useful when herding prey, though it is folded down for swimming. Like a chameleon, the sailfish can change body color and even flash iridescent hues across its skin. Capable of incredible leaps, the sailfish swims even faster than marlin.

Black Marlin (Data Deficient)
Species *Makaira indica* **Seen** *Gulf of Papagayo, Central Pacific waters*

One of three marlin species in Costa Rican waters (along with the blue and striped marlins), the black marlin has a long, sharp upper jaw, or bill, which it uses to slash at small tuna and other prey. Its streamlined body is dark blue above and silvery-white below, with faint blue stripes. Capable of speeds of up to 65 mph (100 km/h), it is the most highly prized game fish. However, local sportfishers practice catch-and-release, except for trophy-size specimens.

AMPHIBIANS AND REPTILES

Despite the fearsome reputation of toxic poison-dart frogs, venomous snakes with potentially lethal bites, and man-eating crocodiles, most of Costa Rica's amphibians and reptiles are perfectly harmless to humans. These cold-blooded creatures have variable body temperatures and depend on their surroundings for warmth, so they can frequently be spotted basking in the sun. Most amphibians lay their eggs in fresh water, which they also need to stay moist. Prolific in warmer lowlands, they are relatively scarce at higher elevations.

TAXONOMY

Reptiles are arranged in four orders: Crocodilia, Squamata (snakes and lizards), Testudines (turtles and tortoises), and Sphenodontia. They share several character-istics with amphibians. Although they were once classified as reptiles, today amphibians are classified separately as Amphibia, and include Caudata (newts and salamanders) and Anura (frogs and toads).

American Crocodile (VU)

Species *Crocodylus acutus* **Seen** *Barra del Colorado, Corcovado, Río Tárcoles, Tortuguero*

One of the largest of the family (up to 23 ft or 7 m) – this crocodile inhabits the lagoons of Tortuguero, on the Caribbean; the Tempisque and Tárcoles rivers; and Corcovado National Park, on the Pacific. Its broad, olive-green body tapers to a narrow, elongated head. The American crocodile can remain submerged for more than an hour and is capable of rapid bursts of speed on land, where it spends long hours in the sun to heat its body. It primarily feeds on fish, but occasionally seizes unwary mammals that come to the rivers to drink. Crocodiles are felicitous parents, and both male and female will guard the nest and their hatchlings to protect them from predators. American crocodiles use the ocean to migrate between rivers, but rarely attack surfers and swimmers. Since at least 2007, they have even been spotted in Lake Arenal. How they got there is a mystery.

Green Iguana (VU)
Species *Iguana Iguana* **Seen** *Corcovado, Manuel Antonio, Palo Verde, Santa Rosa*

The green iguana is a scaly, dragon-like lizard that can grow up to 6.5 ft (2 m). Mature iguanas can range in color from gray-olive to dark brown, although all juveniles are lime green. During the mating season (November to December), males turn bright orange and advertise their prowess from the treetops. The green iguana inhabits various low- and mid-elevation ecosystems, and it roams at ground level on cold days. An agile climber, it eats flowers, fruits, and leaves. A spiny crest extends along its back; its regenerative tail can be discarded to escape predators, which it detects with the aid of a primitive third eye atop its head. Females lay 20–70 eggs in the ground, but newborns must fend for themselves.

Spectacled Caiman (LC)
Species *Caiman crocodilus* **Seen** *Caño Negro, Tortuguero, Gandoca-Manzanillo*

Abundant throughout Costa Rica's Caribbean and Pacific lowland rivers and wetlands, this small olive-brown crocodilian is commonly seen basking in the sun along riverbanks. It grows up to 8 ft (2.5 m) in length and is easily identified by dark crossbands on its body and tail, and by a bony ridge resembling the bridge of a pair of spectacles between its eyes – hence its name. A nocturnal hunter, it eats mainly fish and amphibians. Caimans breed primarily in the wet season. Females lay up to 40 eggs in nests scraped together from leaves, twigs, and sand; males will stay close by and help to guard them. Raccoons prey on the nests, and baby caimans can be seized by herons and other birds of prey.

Slider Turtle (LC)
Species *Trachemys scripta* **Seen** *Caño Negro, Palo Verde, Tortuguero, Gandoca-Manzanillo*

The slider, the most common freshwater turtle in Costa Rica, has two subspecies: the ornate and the Mesoamerican (or Nicaraguan) slider, limited to the extreme north. This mid-size turtle has dark-olive skin striped with yellow markings, yellow eyes, and a yellow underside to its carapace. They are usually seen in or close to large ponds and rivers, or sunning on rocks or logs, often piled up one atop the other. Sliders are omnivores and eat anything from insects to fish to aquatic vegetation. They mate in spring and fall, when they sink to the bottom of the river or lake to copulate. The population is at risk from illegal poaching for the pet trade.

Poison-Dart Frogs (LC)
Family *Dendrobatidae* **Seen** *Barbilla, Braulio Carrillo, Corcovado, La Selva*

Small (0.6–2.4 in/1.5–6 cm) and brightly colored, these ground-dwelling frogs are named for their toxic skin secretions, which derive from their diet of ants and tiny beetles. The poison varies in potency, and only three species found in Panama and Colombia are strong enough to kill humans. Costa Rica has several species, including the red-and-blue *Oophaga pumilio* and the green-and-black *Dendrobates auratus*. By day, they hop about the moist forest floor, safe from predators thanks to their gaudy coloration, which serves to advertise their toxicity. Females lay their eggs in moist places. Newly hatched tadpoles typically hitch a ride on their mother's back to be carried to water, where they can feed.

Red-Eyed Tree Frog (LC)
Species *Agalychnis callidryas*
Seen *Cahuita, Corcovado, La Selva*

This arboreal frog has a lime-green body, blue sides streaked with yellow, orange toes, and red eyes with narrow black pupils. It measures 1.5–2.75 in (4–7 cm), but more than twice that with its limbs extended. An excellent climber, it moves slowly and stealthily, feeding on moths and other flying insects, which it snares with its long, sticky tongue. When in danger, it flashes its bright body parts to startle the predator and facilitate escape. The red-eyed tree frog is a nocturnal hunter, and by day it sleeps folded on the underside of large leaves, using suction cups on its feet to hang upside down. During breeding season (October to March), the forests at night resound with the croaking of males calling for mates.

Glass Frogs (LC)
Family *Centrolenidae* **Seen** *La Selva, Monteverde*

Named for their transparent bodies, glass frogs are nocturnal, mostly arboreal, difficult to spot in the wild, and generally small, rarely exceeding 3 in (7.5 cm). Although the upper body is green and often spotted, the abdominal skin is translucent, exposing the frog's internal organs, such as its heart, intestines, and liver. Some species are entirely transparent. Denizens of the humid forests of Costa Rica at most elevations, glass frogs are particularly common and diverse in montane cloud forests. Living mostly near rivers and streams during the breeding season (and occupying the canopy the rest of the year), the females lay their eggs on leaves that hang over water and catch the tadpoles once they hatch.

Common House Gecko (LC)
Species *Hemidactylus frenatus*
Seen *Barra Honda, Cahuita, Santa Rosa*

Costa Rica has nine species of this adorable creature. The common house gecko is ubiquitous by night, its presence given away by its loud chirp, which is used by both sexes to attract mates and warn off competitors. Found across the country, this particular lizard species seems to find its way into every dwelling in Costa Rica. Measuring up to 6 in (15 cm), most geckos have velvety pinkish-gray skin with specks or stripes. They can scurry upside down across branches or ceilings thanks to their toe pads, which are covered with bristles, or setae, so fine they tap into electrical attraction at a molecular level. A devourer of mosquitoes, the gecko has such keen eyesight that it can detect color at night.

Anoles (LC)
Family *Polychrotidae* **Seen** *Manuel Antonio, Rincón de la Vieja, Selva Verde*

Costa Rica has more than two-dozen species of anoles, a common and diverse neotropical lizard family that includes more than 400 species. These creatures typically measure 3–8 in (8–20 cm) and have pointed snouts and long slender tails that they can break off to escape predators. Normally green or brown, anoles can change color depending on mood and temperature. Semi-arboreal and active by day, they stake out a territory around low-lying foliage. When an intruder is near, the male performs "push-ups" and displays the orange or red dewlap beneath its throat. If this does not scare away the intruder, a fight might ensue, in which the competitors bite at each other's necks.

Basilisk Lizard (LC)
Species *Basiliscus plumifrons* **Seen** *Corcovado, Gandoca-Manzanillo, Tortuguero*

Ranging from bright green to olive, the basilisk lizard is known by several names, including the plumed or double-crested lizard, but it is most famously known as the Jesus Christ lizard thanks to its unique ability to dart across water, aided by its long, slender webbed toes, which create air pockets above the surface and prevent it from sinking. Suitably, it is generally found in lowland rainforests close to streams – it is also an excellent swimmer. The basilisk can grow to about 2 ft (60 cm) in length. Males have crests atop their heads and backs, which they use to court females. Hatchlings are born ready for the wild, having most of the survival capabilities of adults.

Coral Snakes
Family *Elapidae; Genus: Micrurus*
Seen *Cahuita, Carara, Gandoca-Manzanillo, Tortuguero*

Distinctive for their black, red, and yellow-white banding, coral snakes possess the most potent venom of all New World snakes. Small and with tiny heads, they spend most of their time underground or in leaf litter, emerging to breed or hunt for frogs, lizards, and rodents. Coral snakes have non-retractable teeth and hold on to a victim when biting. The rhyme "red on yellow, kill a fellow; red on black, friend of Jack," used to identify coral snakes in North America, does not apply in Costa Rica, where the order of the bands cannot be used as a gauge. Several species of coral snakes inhabit Costa Rica's lowland and mid-elevation habitats. Allen's coral snake is found only in the Caribbean.

Neotropical Rattlesnake (LC)
Species *Crotalus durissus* **Seen** *Barra Honda, Palo Verde, Rincón de la Vieja, Santa Rosa*

The only rattlesnake in Costa Rica, the *cascabel*, as it is known, is found solely on the Northern Pacific slopes. It prefers low-elevation dry forest, savanna, and scrub, for which it is well camouflaged, with a blotchy beige-and-brown skin patterned with dark triangles and diamonds. Twin stripes run along the top of its neck. Rattlesnakes are born without the ability to rattle; they gain this after shedding their skin three or four times (which takes around a year). Adults will typically have around ten segments in their rattle. When threatened, it vibrates its rattle and lifts the front third of its body off the ground in preparation to strike. Its venom is one of the most toxic of all rattlesnake species.

Boas
Family *Boidae* **Seen** *Braulio Carrillo, Cahuita, Manuel Antonio, Santa Rosa*

The thick-bodied boa constrictor is the largest snake in Costa Rica, growing to a length of 10 ft (3 m). Two smaller rainbow boa species also strangle their prey, and live only in moist areas. These wide-ranging snakes are semi-arboreal, though they are also quite adept in the water All are patterned cream, gray, and brown, with darker saddles; they shine with a blue radiance when exposed to direct light. Boas are often illegally killed for their skins and their generally docile nature has made them valuable as pets. The biggest threat, however, is from deforestation, which destroys their prime habitat and has the knock-on effect of allowing rodent populations to increase.

Fer-De-Lance
Species *Bothrops asper* **Seen** *Cahuita, Corcovado, La Selva, Tortuguero*

This large, highly venomous pit viper, called *terciopelo* (meaning "velvet") locally, is the most feared snake in Costa Rica, accounting for half of all bites and most fatalities. Growing to 8 ft (2.5 m) and about as thick as a man's arm, the fer-de-lance inhabits a wide range of lowland habitats and is common along riverbanks. It is easily identified by its skin pattern of diamonds and diagonal stripes in various shades of brown and by its large, sharply triangular head (*fer-de-lance* means "spearhead" in French). Mostly nocturnal, it rests in leaf litter by day. Unpredictable when disturbed, it is aggressive and fast-moving in defense. Females give birth to 20–100 young, which are fully envenomed and can be as deadly as their parents.

Yellow-Bellied Sea Snake (LC)
Species *Pelamis platurus* **Seen** *Golfo de Papagayo, Isla del Caño*

Sometimes seen washed up on Pacific beaches, the yellow-bellied sea snake lacks the flat belly that gives land snakes traction on land, and so otherwise spends its entire life at sea, feeding on fish and eels, and propelling itself with its spatulate tail or taking advantage of ocean currents to cover longer distances. It can stay underwater for up to an hour and a half, and mates and breeds entirely at sea. These abilities have helped it to become the most widespread species of snake on the planet. Averaging 18–25 in (45–65 cm) in length, its yellow belly is contrasted by its dark, black back, possibly acting as a warning to potential predators. Although extremely venomous, this sea snake is docile and reluctant to strike.

Eyelash Viper
Species *Bothriechis schlegelii* **Seen** *Braulio Carrillo, Cahuita, Corcovado, Tortuguero*

The sinister beauty and small size (22–32 in/ 55–80 cm) of this forest-dwelling pit viper belie its potentially lethal bite. Named for the large scales fanning out above its eyes, this nocturnal arboreal snake has varying markings, ranging from bright yellow to olive green, brown, and even sometimes pink. Even vipers from the same litter can vary in their coloration and patterning. The eyelash viper lives in moist forests up to 4,900 ft (1,500 m) and spends its days coiled up on branches; hikers should watch where they put their hands. Males compete for females by facing off with heads erect and attempting to push the other to the ground.

BIRDS

With over 850 species grouped into 75 different families, Costa Rica's avifauna is exceptionally varied, exceeding that of the United States and Canada combined. More than 630 are resident species, although only eight are endemic. Any part of the country is suited to successful birding, with many places offering the chance to see more than 100 species a day – take a guided tour or just follow your beak. Avian diversity peaks between October and April, when migrants flock in, filling the skies and trees with a carnival of color and sound.

TAXONOMY

A growing body of genetic and fossil evidence has demonstrated that birds (more properly referred to as the class Aves) are, along with their closest relatives the crocodiles (the order Crocodilia), in fact the only living members of the Archosauria family, a group that also includes the extinct dinosaurs. The widespread opinion is that birds survived a massive extinction event some 66 million years ago and migrated around the planet. All birds have in common feathers, toothless beaked jaws, and a lightweight skeleton, and the fact they lay hard-shelled eggs.

Great Green Macaw (EN)
Species *Ara ambiguus* **Relatives** *Scarlet macaw*

The third largest of the world's 18 macaw species (after the hyacinth and red-and-green macaws), the great green, or Buffon's, macaw is known locally as *lapa verde* or *guacamayo*. It sports a bright-red fuzzy forehead, lime-green plumage that merges into teal-blue wings, and a blue-and-scarlet tail. Its massive hooked beak is designed to break open the nut of the almendro tree, its main source of food. In fact, research has found that the great green macaw is so particular about its diet that it favors individual trees whose nuts are the most nutritious. These macaws are also especially noisy, and there is a great deal of variation in their vocalization, depending on the locality and even from one bird to another. By the time they are adults, they will have amassed a comprehensive vocabulary of shrills, shrieks, and squawks with distinct meanings. As a result of deforestation and poaching for the illegal pet trade, only an estimated 300 great green macaws remain in the wild, including about 50 breeding pairs, who lay one or two eggs at a time. Great green macaws typically live to around 30 years of age.

Scarlet Macaw (LC)
Species *Ara macao* **Relatives** *Green macaw*

The smaller of Costa Rica's two macaw species, the scarlet macaw grows up to 36 in (90 cm) in length. It has a scarlet body and tail, turquoise rump, bright-yellow upper wings, and blue wing feathers. Today it occupies only a fraction of its former range, being almost entirely restricted to Carara National Park and the Peninsula de Osa. Seasonally monogamous, the scarlet macaw emits loud, throaty squawks, especially when flying in pairs or flocking at clay licks. It nests in cavities in tall trees, where females lay one or two eggs (Dec–Apr).

Keel-Billed Toucan (LC)
Species *Ramphastos sulfuratus*
Relatives *Chestnut-mandibled toucan, collared aracari, emerald toucanet, fiery-billed aracari, yellow-eared toucanet*

Costa Rica has six of the 50 toucan species. The most recognizable is the keel-billed toucan, with a black body, yellow bib, red abdomen, and rainbow-hued bill. Toucans – whose main food is fleshy fruit, supplemented by small reptiles, hatchlings stolen from nests, and eggs – eat by throwing their head back and dropping the food into their throat.

Montezuma Oropendola (LC)
Species *Psarocolius montezuma*
Relatives *Chestnut-headed oropendola*

A common resident of humid forests up to 3,300 ft (1,000 m), the oropendola is a deep-chestnut color, with a black head, turquoise cheeks, a pink wattle, an orange-tipped bill, and a bright-yellow tail. Living in huge colonies in tall, free-standing trees, females weave vines and twigs into pendulous nests. When courting (Jan–May), the male makes rapid cooing calls and performs a somersault around a branch, then ruffles her feathers prior to mating.

King Vulture (LC)
Species *Sarcoramphus papa*
Relatives *Black vulture, turkey vulture, yellow-headed vulture*

A relative of the Andean condor, with a 6.5-ft (2-m) wingspan, the king vulture is a large lowland forest dweller. It has a white body and black wing and tail feathers; its bare neck, face, and beak are brightly colored in red, yellow, black, and purple. Mature birds also have a wrinkled fleshy swelling atop their beaks. The king vulture soars high in the sky; a sighting would be a feather in the cap for any birder.

RESPLENDENT QUETZAL

Catching a glimpse of the quetzal, one of the most striking and beautiful tropical birds, is the reason many people visit Costa Rica. The male, with its iridescent metallic-green feathers and arrestingly intense blood-red chest, bedazzles everyone who sees it in its cloud forest habitat. It also features 24-in- (60-cm-) long tail feathers that it uses to impress females during mating displays. The female is less flamboyant.

KEY FACTS

Species
Pharomachrus mocinno

Size
Body length: 14–16 in (36–40 cm); tail (male): 24 in (60 cm); weight: 7–8 oz (200–225 g).

Population
2,800–4,800.

Conservation Status
NT.

Reproduction
Females begin to reproduce in their second year and lay one or two eggs each season.

Habitat
Subtropical forests; clearings above 3,300 ft (1,000 m).

Seen
Chirripó, La Amistad, Monteverde, San Gerardo de Dota.

Feeding

Although the quetzal's mixed diet includes caterpillars, insects, and even small frogs and lizards, it is primarily a frugivore that relies on wild avocados *(aguacatillos)* and other fruits of the laurel family. The quetzal is an altitudinal migrant, and its seasonal movements – between 3,300 ft and 9,800 ft (1,000 m and 3,000 m) – are dictated by the fruiting of various laurel species at different times of year. The pit of the wild avocado fruit, which the quetzel eats whole, is too big to pass through the bird's digestive tract, so it vomits it up after digesting the pulp – in the process becoming an important propagator of the laurel tree. The quetzal is threatened by deforestation at lower altitudes, to which it descends during the non-breeding season.

Family and Breeding

A solitary bird when not breeding, the quetzal is mono-gamous and territorial in the breeding season (Febuary to April). Couples use their beaks to hollow out nests in soft, dead, or rotten trees. The cock and the hen take turns incubating the pale-blue eggs – the male by day and the female by night. Hatchlings typically emerge after 18 days, to be fed insects, larvae, and worms by both parents. Eventually, the female abandons the nest, leaving her young in the care of the male. Fledg-lings leave the nest after about one month. Young quetzals are fed larvae, insects, and worms.

Communication

The male quetzal is a true showman that attempts to impress a potential mate by flaunting its extraordinary tail feathers In spectacular mid-flight displays. Loose and slender, the feathers ripple gracefully behind it like the long ribbons of a rhythmic gymnast as the quetzal flies upward then swoops down in a graceful arc. Male quetzals also vocalize with at least six distinct calls, including a repetitive and slightly slurred "kwuee, kwuee, kwuee," shrill calls that resemble a cat's meow, and the striking of a high-pitched tuning fork.

Did You Know?
——
Notoriously fragile, there is only one known case of the quetzal being successfully bred in captivity.

Black Vulture (LC)

Species *Coragyps atratus* **Relatives**
King vulture, turkey vulture, yellow-headed vulture

Known by Costa Ricans as *zopilote*, this black-feathered scavenger is present nationwide below 6,600 ft (2,000 m). It stands 25.5 in (65 cm) tall and has a 5-ft (1.5-m) wingspan. The black vulture has a bald dark-gray head and a short hooked beak. It is frequently seen sunning itself, with its impressive wings outstretched, or hovering in the sky with its eye out for roadkill and other carrion, its main source of food.

Bare-Throated Tiger Heron (LC)

Species *Tigrisoma mexicanum*
Relatives *Great blue heron*

This elegant upright wader can grow up to 3 ft (90 cm) tall, and is distinguished by its long, thick neck and gray-brown feathers striped with black streaks. Juveniles tend to have more pronounced "tiger stripes" against their orange plumage. The most widespread of the several beautiful heron species in Costa Rica, it is often seen standing motionless beside watercourses and ponds, ready to skewer fish and frogs with its long yellow bill.

Slaty-Tailed Trogon (LC)

Species *Trogon massena* **Relatives**
Collared trogon, emerald trogon, violaceous trogon

Like all of Costa Rica's 11 trogon species, this cousin of the resplendent quetzal *(p92)* has an iridescent-green body, a short bill, and a long tail. Its abdomen is blood red. The slaty-tailed trogon likes humid lowland forest and can spend hours motionless on a perch. It flies short distances on sallies to snatch insects and fruits on the wing, and it makes its home in rotten trees or termite nests.

Anhinga (LC)

Species *Anhinga anhinga* **Relatives**
Neotropic cormorant

Commonly seen swimming with only its neck above the surface, this large freshwater bird has evolved for diving in search of fish and amphibians. It dries out its feathers by perching on branches and spreading its wings. Mostly black, with a brownish neck and a yellow beak, the anhinga has wings streaked with silver feathers. It has a long bill and an even longer S-shaped neck that explains its more common name: "snakebird."

Fiery-Throated Hummingbird (LC)
Species *Panterpe insign* **Relatives** *Green-crowned brilliant, rufous-tailed hummingbird*

One of the most colorful of Costa Rica's 50-odd hummingbird species, this handsome bird is found only in the highlands. It grows to 4.5 in (11 cm) in length and has scintillating green and blue plumage, an orange throat, and a blue chest. It uses its straight, black bill to feed on tiny insects and the nectar of the flowers of epiphytes, Ericaceae and bromeliads. Males aggressively defend their territories against intruding competitors.

Three-Wattled Bellbird (VU)
Species *Procnias tricarunculata*
Relatives *Bare-necked umbrella-bird, snowy cotinga*

This elusive denizen of the cloud forest is famous for the male's distinctive three-part vocalization, which resembles the clang of a bell. Growing up to 12 in (30 cm) long, it has a copper-colored body, a white head, and three worm-like wattles dangling from atop its bill (hence its name). Unfortunately, its population is in rapid decline, but lucky birders might see one in Monteverde.

Sunbittern (LC)
Species *Eurypyga helias* **Relatives** *Sungrebe*

The sole member of the Eurypygidae family, this bird is similar to a heron but with a more horizontal posture and shorter legs. It stalks small vertebrates and fish along streams and in ponds in lowland forest. Its plumage – in multiple shades of gray, black, and brown – is broken up with linear patterns for camouflage in dappled sunlight. During courtship, or when threatened, it spreads its wings to display vivid red, yellow, and black eyespots.

Great Curassow (VU)
Species *Crax rubra* **Relatives** *Black guan*

The great curassow is a large, turkey-sized ground bird, conspicuous by the prominent forward-curling crest on its head and its long tail. Males are usually a lustrous blue or black with a bulbous yellow beak, while females are striped with brown or black and white. Restricted to national parks as a result of hunting and deforestation, it lives in humid lowland forests, such as that at La Selva Biological Station. The curassow runs rather than flies, and forages in the undergrowth for fruits, seeds, and insects.

Northern Caracara (LC)
Species *Caracara cheriway*
Relatives *Red-throated caracara, yellow-head caracara*

One of the most common birds of prey in Costa Rica, the northern caracara is a lazy hunter that prefers to scavenge carrion than hunt its own prey, if it can. It is often seen stalking crabs and eels washed up on beaches, or perched road-side awaiting a chance kill. Standing up to 23 in (58 cm), it is brown except for a cream chest and head capped in black, plus yellow legs and a red cere at the base of its sharply hooked gray beak.

Jabiru Stork (LC)
Species *Jabiru mycteria* **Relatives** *Wood stork*

The huge Jabiru stork is unmistakable thanks to its massive, intimidating black bill, which is upturned at the tip. Standing up to 5 ft (1.5 m) tall, it is a common sight along rivers and wetlands such as Palo Verde National Park, where it lives in large groups that forage for fish and amphibians. It is conspicuous for its snow-white body and wings, which contrast with the red band around its neck and its soot-black head and legs.

Blue Dacnis (LC)
Species *Dacnis cayana* **Relatives** *Scarlet-thighed dacnis, yellow-throated euphonia*

A characteristic passerine, this brightly colored member of the tanager family stands out for its azure plumage and turquoise cap, which contrast against its black wings and eye mask. The female is bright green, with blue head and shoulders. Common in the Pacific lowlands, it likes to hawk its insect prey at the forest edge, but it is also seen feasting at the banana feeders that are often placed in hotel gardens to draw butterflies.

Boat-Billed Heron (LC)
Species *Cochlearius cochlearius*
Relatives *Bare-throated tiger heron, tri-colored heron*

One of the oddest-looking members of the heron family, the boat-billed heron has a large beak that is far broader than it is deep, looking not unlike an upturned boat. Its huge black eyes hint at its nocturnal nature. Gray, fawn, and white, this handsome bird lives in mangroves and at the edge of freshwater habitats, where it hunts frogs, crabs, and fish. It will crouch for hours, awaiting prey.

White Ibis (LC)
Species *Eudocimus albus* **Relatives** *Glossy ibis, roseate spoonbill*

The sight of a white ibis soaring through the sky with its neck outstretched is a genuine thrill for birders. Colonial by instinct, the white ibis nests communally, often with hundreds of other individuals. Its preferred habitats are mangroves and brackish marshes, where it feeds on crayfish and crabs. Its long, down-curved bill and gray-pink face mask turn flush during mating season. The black tips of its wings can be seen only in flight – the bird is all white when at rest.

Blue-Footed Booby (LC)
Species *Sula nebouxii* **Relatives** *Brown booby, masked booby*

A delight to watch, either in flight or performing its trademark courtship dance, the blue-footed booby nests on rocky offshore islands from Nicoya to Isla del Coco. This long-winged seabird has fawn and white plumage and unmistakable bright-blue feet, which the male displays – first one foot, then the other – to impress females while pointing its long, pointed beak and tail skyward. It feeds on fish and has nostrils that are sealed for diving.

Roseate Spoonbill (LC)
Species *Platalea ajaja* **Relatives** *Green ibis, white-face ibis*

Inhabiting shallow freshwater and brackish lagoons, this bird is named for its spatulate bill, which it sweeps from side to side in the water to sift aquatic beetles and vertebrates. This long-necked wader stands up to 31 in (80 cm) tall atop long legs. Its back, neck, and head are typically white, while its pink wing plumage derives from the shrimp in its diet. Like other members of the Threskiornithidae family, it lays eggs in a treetop stick nest.

Frigate Bird (LC)
Species *Fregata magnificens* **Relatives** *Great frigatebird*

An agile aerial pirate that feeds primarily by harassing other birds until they release or regurgitate fish, this huge iridescent-black seabird has a wingspan up to 85 in (215 cm) and the lightest weight-to-size ratio of any bird in the world. The frigate bird never lands on water, for which it is ill-suited. It has a forked tail, crooked wings, and a long, sinister beak. During courtship, roosting males inflate a red sac on their throat while females fly overhead.

INSECTS AND ARACHNIDS

Costa Rica hosts hundreds of thousands of insect species, including more than 1,250 species of butterflies. No one knows the exact number of beetle species or ants, which are in their thousands. Bees, wasps, and myriad other flying creatures buzz about, while an astounding profusion of other types of insects creep, crawl, or leap. Many advertise their toxicity with gaudy coloration. Others have adopted clever techniques of disguise to prey or avoid being preyed upon. Scorpions and other arachnids – from tiny jumping spiders to giant tarantulas – are ubiquitous too. Costa Rica celebrates its arachnid and insect diversity in butterfly gardens and insect museums around the country. The insects and arachnids highlighted here are not on the IUCN list.

TAXONOMY

Costa Rica's ubiquitous insect population (of the class Insecta) are the most diverse group of organisms in the country: as more are discovered every year, estimates range from anywhere from 5,000 up to 300,000 species. Arachnid (Arachnida) species are fewer in number, but are still thought to be in the thousands.

Rhinoceros Beetle

Subfamily *Dynastinae* **Seen** *Palo Verde, Corcovado, Tortuguero, Caño Negro*

Rhinoceros beetles are named for the male's characteristic long curved horn. Sometimes growing up to 6 inches (15 cm) in length, they primarily eat fruits and leaves and are entirely harmless to humans. They're mostly nocturnal and can be found by day hiding under leaf litter or rotting logs. Two of the most recognizable species in this subfamily are the Hercules beetle *(Dynastes hercules)* and the elephant beetle *(Megasoma elephas)*. Hercules beetles are distinguishable by their gigantic, shiny, downward-curving horns, and are so named for their prodigious strength; they have been observed lifting objects up to a hundred times their own weight. The elephant beetle is somewhat unusual among rhinoceros beetles in that most of its body is covered with a dense coat of microscopic hairs (commonly known as a "carpet"). Male rhinoceros beetles use their giant horns to do battle during mating season. The victor will then mate with the (hornless) female, who will produce up to 50 eggs and die shortly thereafter.

Leaf-Cutter Ants
Genera *Atta and Acromyrmex*
Seen *Anywhere and everywhere*

Present in most lowland and mid-elevation environments, leaf-cutter ants scythe fresh leaves and other plant parts and transport them long distances to vast underground nests. They compost the vegetation to farm a fungus whose spores feed the colony, which can number millions of individuals. Communities are divided into different-size castes, each with its own specialized task. Large "major" ants with powerful jaws defend the "median" sherpas and the colony from invaders.

Praying Mantis
Family *Mantidae*
Seen *Golfo Dulce, Monteverde*

With elongated body parts resembling twigs and foliage, leaf-green mantis' are superbly camouflaged for their prime purpose: ambush. These exquisite insects adopt an upright posture with forearms folded in prayer-like stance, belying their rapacious behavior. Their enlarged forelegs are spiked for grasping as they devours their prey. A sexual cannibal, a female will often devour her mate during the process of mating.

Tarantulas
Family *Theraphosidae* **Seen** *Palo Verde, Carara, Santa Rosa*

Tarantulas are large, hairy spiders that live in underground burrows. Costa Rica has several species, including the Zebra tarantula, named for its black-and-white striped legs. They are mostly nocturnal, emerging at night to hunt insects and small vertebrates. Unlike their fearsome reputation, they are relatively shy and non-aggressive towards humans. Females can live 20 years. Costa Ricans nickname them *pica caballos* from a false belief that they bite horses.

Morpho Butterflies
Genus *Morpho* **Seen** *Cahuita, Corcovado, Monteverde, Santa Elena*

Morphos are dazzling, neon-bright butterflies whose iridescent upper wings flash with a fiery electric-blue sheen in flight. The wings are actually brown, not blue. The illusion is caused by the tiny, layered, glass-like scales on the upper wing, which absorb the entire light spectrum except blue. There are more than 50 species of this neotropical butterfly, commonly seen flitting along forest pathways in a wave-like motion. They can grow up to 8 inches (20 cm).

EXPERIENCE

Neck-craning rainforest at La Selva Biological Station

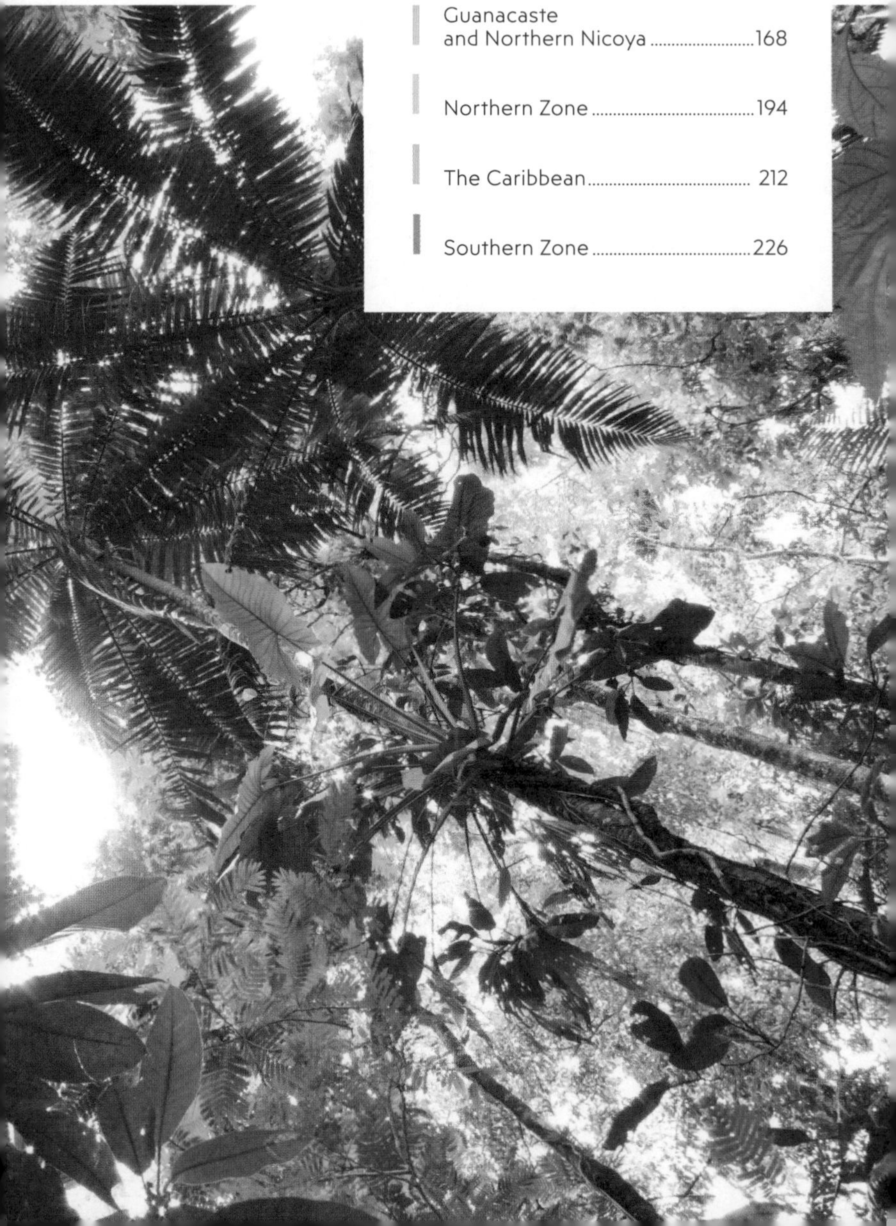

SAN JOSÉ

Nestled amid craggy peaks, Costa Rica's capital city enjoys a splendid setting with the Poás, Barva, and Irazú volcanoes rising over the city to the north, and the rugged Talamanca Mountains to the south. Founded in 1737, San José grew slowly through its first 100 years. Its creation on the eve of the coffee boom in the heart of coffee country, however, was advantageous. By the early 1800s, the town had grown to challenge Cartago – then capital – for supremacy. Following a brief civil war in 1823, San José replaced Cartago as capital and soon eclipsed other cities as prominent *cafetaleros* (coffee barons) hired skilled artisans to beautify the city with fine structures. Among them is the opulent Teatro Nacional (National Theater). Paid for in 1897 by money raised through the controversial coffee tax, it remains a symbol of the golden age of Costa Rican coffee.

SAN JOSÉ

Must Sees

1. Teatro Nacional
2. Museo del Oro Precolumbino
3. Centro Costarricense de Ciencias y Cultura

Experience More

4. Catedral Metropolitana
5. Mercado Central
6. Teatro Mélico Salazar
7. Parque Morazán
8. Edificio Metálico
9. Parque España
10. Edificio Correos
11. Barrio Amón
12. Museo Nacional
13. Museo de Jade Fidel Tristán Castro
14. Centro Nacional de la Cultura
15. Asamblea Legislativa
16. Parque Nacional
17. Antigua Estación Ferrocarril al Atlántico
18. Universidad de Costa Rica
19. Parque Sabana
20. Museo de Arte Costarricense
21. Parque Diversiones (Pueblo Antiguo)
22. Escazú
23. Museo de Ciencias Naturales La Salle

Eat

1. Kalú
2. La Esquina de Buenos Aires
3. Sapore Trattoria
4. Alma de Café

Drink

5. Tintos y Blancos
6. Stiefel
7. Bebedero

Stay

8. Hotel Grano de Oro
9. Hotel Auténtico
10. Casa de las Tías

Shop

11. Chietón Morén
12. Galería Namú
13. Mercado Municipal de Artesanías

1 ⬡ ⬡ ⬡

TEATRO NACIONAL

⊙ C4 ⌂ Calles 3/5, Ave 2 🚌 Cemeterio-Estadio ⊙ Building: 9am–4pm Mon–Sat; shows: Mar–Dec: 8pm Thu and Fri, 10:30am Sun 🌐 teatronacional.go.cr

Opened in 1897 with a performance of *El Fausto de Gournod* by the Paris Opera, the National Theater is a lavish confection of marble and gilt, flanked by statues of 19th-century luminaries of the arts. Its cultural significance was recognized in 1965 when it was declared a national monument.

The ruling coffee barons levied a tax on coffee exports to fund the building of this grand theater, following a snub by Spanish-born prima donna Adelina Patti, who refused to perform in Costa Rica during a Central American tour due to the lack of a suitable venue. The theater has a lavish Neo-Baroque interior, replete with statues, paintings, marble staircases, and parquet floors made of 10 species of hardwood. A double staircase with gold-gilt banisters leads to the magnificent foyer, which features pink marble and a surfeit of crystals, gilt mirrors, and gold-leaf embellishments. Splendid murals show scenes of Costa Rican life. Depicting a coffee harvest, the huge mural on the ceiling of the intermezzo, between the lobby and the auditorium, was painted in 1897 by Milanese artist Aleardo Villa. The scene is full of errors, the most notable being coffee shown as a coastal crop instead of a highland one.

The Palco Presidencial, or presidential balcony, has a ceiling mural, Alegoría a la Patria y la Justicia, painted in 1897 by Roberto Fontana.

The black-and-white tile Alma de Café, which adjoins the lobby, has marble-topped tables and a ceiling painted with a striking triptych.

Allegorical statues of the Muses of Music, Dance, and Fame top the Neo-Classical facade.

Statue of 17th-century dramatist Calderón de la Barca

The small formal garden

The pink marble floor and bronze-tipped Corinthian marble columns of the lobby hint at the splendors to come.

A 19th-century statue of Ludwig van Beethoven, by Adriático Froli, stands in an alcove.

The marble-and-gilt foyer

1 The design of the building is based on the architecture of the Paris Opera House.

2 The theater's foyer is a marble, gilt-encrusted marvel of ornamentation.

3 Taking tea beneath the exquisite hand-painted ceiling of the Parisian-style Alma de Café

← Illustration of the historically important National Theater

A frescoed rotunda ceiling dominates the red-and-gold auditorium.

The sandstone exterior is given structural support from a steel frame.

Did You Know?

Collectors seek out the old five colón banknote, which featured the Teatro Nacional's coffee mural.

→ Adriático Froli's 1890s statue of pre-eminent German composer Ludwig van Beethoven

BEETHOVEN

2

MUSEO DEL ORO PRECOLOMBINO

📍 C4 🏛 Plaza de la Cultura, Calle 5 and Aves Central/2 🚇 🕐 9:15am–5pm daily
🌐 museosdelbancocentral.org

Occupying the starkly modern subterranean space beneath the Plaza de la Cultura, the Museum of Pre-Columbian Gold has a dazzling display of ethnographic objects dating back to AD 500.

The mainstay of the museum's collection consists of more than 1,600 pieces of pre-Columbian gold. Archaeological evidence indicates that these objects first appeared in Costa Rica sometime between 300 and 500 AD, and became most prevalent from around 700 AD until Spanish contact in the 1500s. The majority of the items recovered in Costa Rica come from the South Pacific, where there is a wealth of natural gold and copper deposits in the region, but many were also found in the Central Caribbean. Most of the amulets, earrings, shamanic animal figures, and erotic statuettes exhibited here originated in southwest Costa Rica and attest to the sophisticated art of the Diquís culture. The uses and crafting of these items are demonstrated with the help of models and other displays, which also depict the social and cultural evolution of pre-Columbian cultures.

A spiral staircase descends to the second level of the building where visitors are given an introduction to pre-Columbian culture and metallurgy. Temporary exhibitions that are changed every four months are also held here. The third level features an auditorium as well as the main gallery, which displays a permanent exhibition of ancient gold items.

Did You Know?

The museum's gold collection weighs 22,000 troy ounces – more than a ton.

↑ All that glitters: visitors admiring the stunning pieces of pre-Columbian gold artifacts

LOST WAX TECHNIQUE

Pre-Columbian groups, notably the Chibchas and Diquís of the Pacific southwest, were masterful goldsmiths, skilled in the use of the "lost wax" technique. In this technique, artists carve the desired form in wax, which is then molded with clay and baked. The wax melts, leaving a negative into which molten metal is poured to attain the required result. Most pre-Columbian pieces were alloys of gold and copper, with the alloy *tumbaga* being the most commonly used.

← Dioramas and maps showing pre-Columbian cultures and settlements, and where to find them

→ The utilitarian entrance of the subterranean museum, belying the exquisite collections within

③ 🖋 🎨 🖥 🏛

CENTRO COSTARRICENSE DE CIENCIAS Y CULTURA

📍 B2 🚇 Calle 4 and 110 yd (100 m) N of Ave 9 🚌 Sabana-Cemetario 🕐 8am–4:30pm Tue-Fri, 9:30am–5pm Sat & Sun 🌐 museocr.org

Housed in the fortress-like former *penitenciario central* (central penitentiary) built in 1910, the Costa Rican Science and Cultural Center was inaugurated in 1994 to promote science, technicological innovation, and the arts in education. The complex contains a number of important cultural institutions.

The center is the brainchild of former First Lady Gloria Bejarano Almada, who wanted to rehabilitate the abandoned hub-and-spoke-shaped prison into a positive space. Today each of the "spokes" of the building is dedicated to a different exhibition space. In one, the airy Galería Nacional features paintings, sculptures, and other art forms by Costa Rica's leading exponents of avant-garde art. In another wing, the playful Museo de los Niños is a capitvating space with dozens of thematic hands-on exhibits that provide children with an understanding of nature, science, technology, and culture. For an insight into the prison's history, visit the Museo Penitenciario. The center hosts lectures, as well as national and international performances of music and dance in the Teatro Auditorio Nacional.

Sala Kaopakome is named for the Bribri word meaning "Hall of Meetings".

The stained-glass ceiling was designed by Italian artist Claudio Dueñas.

Contemporary artists painted the eastern wall.

The old Jail cells are preserved in their original condition at the Museo Penitenciario.

1917

The year a gunpowder explosion destroyed a large part of the building.

The Galería Nacional occupies 14 large rooms upstairs.

↑ San José's star-shaped cultural center, a former prison

The dramatic ocher façade of the former prison, topped by crenellations

Must See

Museum Spaces

Museo de los Niños

▶ Vibrant and full of wonder, there is nothing about the Children's Museum to suggest the space was once a notorious prison. In repurposed former jail cells, hands-on exhibits forge links between art, culture, science, and technology, and invite young visitors to discover how ancient cultures practiced recycling. Special events are hosted year round.

Teatro Auditorio Nacional

◀ The versatile National Theater Auditorium hosts all kinds of special events, from audiences with renowned authors to international dance competitions and theatrical performances. The theater also has an educational season with the National Symphony Orchestra, to introduce children to classical music from around the world.

Galería Nacional

▶ A celebration of contemporary art, the National Gallery showcases rotating exhibits of visual artworks by nationally and internationally renowned artists in spotlit rooms converted from former jail cells. The gallery hosts five exhibitions every month.

Museo Penitenciario

▼ In 1979, historic San José Central Penitentiary was closed after 70 years of human rights violations of prisoners. Today, many of the old jail cells are preserved. Restored graffiti left on the walls is a potent reminder of the human tragedy that once played out here.

🔍 HIDDEN GEM
Jailhouse Rocks

Past the mock-medieval entrance, keep an eye out for a multifaceted sculpture by Jorge Jiménez Deredia. Called *Genesis* (1998), it depicts a woman evolving from an egg.

Imagen Cósmica (1998) by Jorge Jiménez Deredia, is in bronze and marble.

The entrance is in the form of a medieval castle, with twin turrets.

Museo de los Niños is spread across 39 rooms.

Escuela "El Grano de Oro" has exhibits on Costa Rican coffee culture.

An electric train and carriages date from 1928–30.

111

EXPERIENCE MORE

❹ Catedral Metropolitana

📍 C4 🏛 Calle Central and Aves 2/4 📞 2221-3820 🕐 7am-7pm Mon-Sat, 6:30am-8pm Sun

San José's pre-eminent church, the Metropolitan Cathedral was built in 1871 to replace the original cathedral, which had been destroyed by an earthquake in 1820. Designed by Eusebio Rodríguez, the austere-looking structure combines Greek Orthodox, Neo-Classical, and Baroque styles. Its linear façade is supported by an arcade of Doric columns and topped by a Neo-Classical pediment with steeples on each side. Inside, a vaulted ceiling runs the length of the nave, supported by two rows of fluted columns. In a glass case to the left of the entrance is a life-size statue of Christ.

Although entirely lacking the ornate Baroque gilt of many other Latin American churches, the cathedral has many fine features, notably an exquisite 19th-century tiled floor and beautiful stained-glass windows depicting biblical scenes. The main altar, beneath a cupola, comprises a simple wooden base atop a marble plinth and supports a wooden figure of Christ and cherubs.

To the left of the main altar is the Capilla del Santísimo (Chapel of the Holy Sacrament), with flower-painted wooden quadrants decorating the walls and ceilings. The short gallery that leads to the chapel contains a glass-and-gilt coffin with a naked statue of Christ draped with a sash in the red, white, and blue of the Costa Rican flag.

To the south of the cathedral is La Curía (The Palace of the Archbishop), built in 1887. This two-story structure, which has been remodeled, is closed to the public. A small garden in front features a life-size bronze statue of Monseñor Bernardo Augusto Thiel Hoffman (1850–1901), the German-born second archbishop of Costa Rica. Hoffman lies buried in the crypt of the cathedral, alongside former president Tomás Guardia.

On the cathedral's north side is a contemporary marble statue of Pope John Paul II by Jiménez Deredia.

> ## Did You Know?
>
> Locals colloquially refer to San José as "Chepe" – the nickname for anyone named José.

❺ Mercado Central

📍 B4 🏛 Calles 6/8 and Aves Central/1 🕐 6:30am-6pm Mon-Sat (daily in Dec)

An intriguing curiosity, San José's Central Market was built in 1881. The building, which takes up an entire block northwest of the Catedral Metropolitana, is itself rather

← The simple columns and decoration of the Metropolitan Cathedral

↑ The Teatro Mélico Salazar, a "Specialist Cultural Institution" of the Costa Rican state

uninspiring, but its warren of narrow alleyways, hemmed in by more than 200 stalls, immerses visitors in a slice of Costa Rican life. This quintessential Latin American market thrives as a chaotic emporium. Every conceivable item is for sale here, from herbal remedies and fresh-cut flowers to snakeskin boots and saddles for *sabaneros* (cowboys). Toward the center, *sodas* (food counters) offer inexpensive cooked meals sold at the counter. The market extends one block north to Mercado Borbón, which has stalls of butchers, fruit sellers, fishmongers, with buyers crowded into the aisles looking for a bargain. Next to the market's entrance on the southeast corner, the wall is lined with plaques that honor the country's important political figures.

Pickpockets are known to operate within the tightly packed alleys of the market, so it is best to leave your valuables in your hotel safe when visiting, and to keep phones and cameras out of sight when not in use.

Teatro Mélico Salazar

⊠ C4 ⌂ Calle Central and Ave 2 🕐 8am–4pm Mon-Fri ⓦ teatromelico.go.cr

One of the city's landmarks, this theater was built in 1928 as the Teatro Raventós, and was a venue for *zarzuelas* – light, often comic Spanish operettas. After a spell as a movie theater in the 1960s it was damaged by fire but was restored and reopened in 1986, and renamed in honor of Manuel "Mélico" Salazar Zúñiga (1887–1950), a celebrated Costa Rican tenor. Designed by architect José Fabio Garnier, it has a Neo-Classical façade adorned with fluted Corinthian pilasters. To the left of the entrance is a larger-than-life bronze bust of Zúñiga. To the right is a bas-relief plaque honoring José Raventós Gual, who had the theater built.

The handsome lobby, in checkered green-and-black tile, leads into a triple-tiered, horseshoe-shaped auditorium, where theatrical and musical events, as well as folk dance shows are staged. The auditorium has a striking parquet wooden floor and a soaring wood-paneled ceiling, decorated with a simple mural and a wrought-iron chandelier.

SHOP

Chietón Morén
Specializing in quality arts and crafts, this "fair deal" store represents Costa Rica's Indigenous communities.

⊠ E4 ⌂ Calle 17 and Aves 2/6 ⓦ chietonmoren.org

Galería Namú
Known for its Boruca masks, Galería Namú also sells locally made baskets, hammocks, jewelry, and folk art by contemporary artists.

⊠ D3 ⌂ Calles 5/7 and Ave 7 ⓦ galeria namu.com

Mercado Municipal de Artesanías
This is the principal market in San José for all manner of artisanal crafts, and it has dozens of stalls selling a miscellany of goods, from carvings to cowboy boots.

⊠ D4 ⌂ Plaza Artigas, Calle 11 and Aves 4/6

> **Mercado Central's warren of narrow alleyways, hemmed in by more than 200 stalls, immerses visitors in a slice of Costa Rican life.**

↑ The bandstand in Parque Morazán, popular with office workers, schoolchildren, and lovers

❼ Parque Morazán

📍 D3 🏛 Calles 5/9 and Aves 3/5 🚌

Laid out in 1881, this small park was later renamed after Francisco Morazán, the Honduran-born Central American federalist who served briefly as president of Costa Rica before being executed in 1842. Shaded by tabebuia trees that bloom in the dry season, the park is popular with locals, and hosts a cultural fair every Saturday,

💬 INSIDER TIP
Walk This Way

Barrio Bird Walking Tours (toursanjosecosta rica.com) offers themed tours through different neighborhoods, led by local artists, entrepreneurs, and others dedicated to downtown revitalization. The "Bird's Nest Tour" offers an overview, but other specialty themes include art, cuisine, and coffee; a "Saturday Favorites" tour combines all three.

as well as occasional concerts. The park's four ornate iron gateways are topped by Roman urns. At its center is the domed Neo-Classical Templo de Música, built in 1920. Busts honor Morazán and other luminaries such as South American liberator Simón Bolívar (1783–1830).

❽ Edificio Metálico

📍 D3 🏛 Calle 9 and Aves 5/7 🚌

Constructed entirely using prefabricated pieces of metal, this intriguing structure, which stands between the Parque Morazán and Parque España, was designed by French architect Charles Thirio. The metal pieces were cast in Belgium in 1892 and shipped to Costa Rica to be assembled, jigsaw-like, in situ. Since then, it has functioned as a local elementary school. A small bust of Minerva, the Roman goddess of wisdom, sits on top of its imposing Neo-Classical façade. An elaborate fountain in the small plaza in front of the school provides an appealing photo opportunity.

❾ ⓜ Parque España

📍 D3 🏛 Calles 9/11 and Aves 3/7 🚌

Shaded by densely packed trees and bamboo groves, this leafy plaza is pleasantly full of birdsong. It was here, in 1903, that the Costa Rican national anthem, written by José María Zeledón Brenes (1877–1949) and Manuel María Guttierez (1829–87), was first performed.

On the northeast corner, a quaint *pabellón* (pavilion), erected in 1947, is inlaid with sepia-toned ceramic murals of the apparition of the Lady of Los Angeles, the church of Orosí, and the cathedral of Heredia. A patinated life-size statue of conquistador Juan Vásquez de Coronado stands at the southwest corner of the park. Brick pathways wind past busts of figures, including Isabel II of Spain (1830–1904) and philanthropist Andrew Carnegie (1835–1919).

❿ Edificio Correos

📍 B3 🏛 Calle 2 and Aves 1/3 📞 2223-9766 🚌 🕐 7am–6pm Mon-Fri, 8am–noon Sat 🚫 Public hols

The building housing the main post office, or Correo Central, was completed in 1917. It was designed by Luis Llach in eclectic style, with Corinthian pilasters embellishing its concrete façade. The arched centerpiece is topped by a shield and supported by angels bearing the national coat of arms. The post office buzzes with the comings and goings of locals picking up their mail at the *apartados* (post office boxes) that fill the ground floor of the atrium.

→

Los Presentes, created in 1979 by well-known sculptor Fernando Calvo

Philatelists can view rare stamps in the small **Museo Filatélico de Costa Rica** (Philatelic Museum of Costa Rica), which occupies six airy rooms on the upper floor. In the first, a range of Costa Rican stamps are offered for sale, and the second has a fine collection of old telephones and telegraphic equipment that goes back more than 100 years. The collection of stamps occupies the other four rooms, which also have exhibits on the history of philately in Costa Rica. The nation's first stamp, from 1863, is displayed here. There are also important and rare stamps from abroad, including the British Penny Black. The entrance fee entitles you to one stamped postcard to send anywhere in the world.

The Edificio Correos is fronted by a pedestrian plaza dominated by a statue of the first president of Costa Rica, Juan Mora Fernández, who was in power from 1824 to 1833. Southwest of the Edificio Correos is another square, Plaza Los Presentes, which forms the setting for sculptor Fernando Calvo's *Los Presentes*, a contemporary monument in bronze to Costa Rican *campesinos* (peasant farmers). The square is the place to go if you want to look your best: shoeshines still ply their trade in the leafy plaza.

Museo Filatélico de Costa Rica

⊛ ☎ 2223-6918 ◷ 8:15–11:30am & 1:15–4:30pm Mon-Fri; 8–11:30am last Sat of month ▣ Public hols

---

⑪ Barrio Amón

▣ C3 ▣ Calles Central/9 and Aves 7/13 ▣

The richest collection of San José's historic homes populate this residential *barrio* (neighborhood), which was founded in the 1890s. The most interesting are along Avenida 9; the stretch between Calles 3 and 7 is lined with beautiful ceramic murals showing traditional Costa Rican scenes, created by Fernando Matamoros.

At Calle 11, No 980 is an elegant two-story mansion; gazing over its railings is a life-size *campesino*. At Calle 9, the Hotel Don Carlos was once the residence of President Tomás Guardia. One block west, at the corner of Calle 7, is Casa Verde, a clapboard building of New Orleans pine dating to 1910. The most audacious building is the Bishop's Castle at Avenida 11 and Calle 3. Built in 1930 in ornate Moorish style, it features keyhole windows, a central dome, and glazed tiles showing scenes from the novel *Don Quixote*.

EAT

Kalú
Fresh seasonal dishes served in an airy and modish restaurant.

▣ B5 ▣ Calle 31 and Ave 5 ⍉ kalu.co.cr

⑤⑤⑤

La Esquina de Buenos Aires
Arty vibes and gourmet cuisine.

▣ D4 ▣ Calle 11 and Ave 6 ⍉ laesquinade buenosaires.net

⑤⑤⑤

Sapore Trattoria
Authentic pizzas, pastas, and risottos.

▣ D4 ▣ Ave 2 and Calle 13 ⍉ sapore trattoria.com

⑤⑤⑤

Alma de Café
Wonderful cakes and a prime location.

▣ C4 ▣ Ave 2 and Calle 3 ☎ 2010-1119

⑤⑤⑤

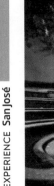

The large, elegant amphitheater outside the Museo Nacional ↑

Museo Nacional

📍E4 🏠Calle 17 & Aves Central/2 🚌 🕐8:30am–4:30pm Tue–Sat, 9am–4:30pm Sun 🚫Public hols 🌐museocostarica.go.cr

Dramatic and imposing, the crenellated, ocher-colored Bellavista Fortress – opposite the Legislative Assembly – was built in 1917 and served as an army barracks. Its exterior walls, with towers at each corner, are pocked with bullet holes from the 1948 civil war. Following his victory, José "Don Pepe" Figueres (p52) disbanded the army, and the fortress became the venue for the National Museum, which had been founded in 1887. The entrance, on the west side, opens to a large netted butterfly garden with a snaking walkway that leads up to a landscaped courtyard displaying pre-Columbian carretas (oxcarts), stone bolas (spheres), and colonial-era cannons. The museum is arranged thematically in a counterclockwise direction around the plaza. Rooms are dedicated to geological, colonial, archaeological, contemporary, and religious history, from the first arrival of humans in Costa Rica to the formation of the nation and recent events. The museum has a particularly impressive pre-Columbian collection, notably of metates (grinding stones) and ceramics, as well as spectacular gold ornaments displayed in the Sala de Oro, in the northeast tower. The Sala Colonial, laid out with rustic colonial furniture, is presented as a typical room would have looked in the 18th century.

The museum is approached via steps from the Plaza de la Democracia, laid out in 1989 to commemorate 100 years of Costa Rican democracy. The stepped plaza hosts a 1994 bronze statue of José Figueres; the Cubist Museo de Jade Fidel Tristán Castro rises on the northwest side.

Did You Know?

Instead of street addresses, locals often use distances from landmarks – many defunct – as locators.

JADE CARVING

Jade carving was introduced to the region by cultures from the north around 500 BC and died out around AD 800, when gold replaced the stone as the material of choice. Saws made of fiber string, as well as drills and crude quartz-tipped chisels were used to carve the stone into necklaces, pendants, and religious figurines bearing replicas of animal motifs.

FROG PENDANT

> **The Sala de Jade displays pendants in kaleidoscopic hues of green and blue, exquisitely backlit to demonstrate their translucent quality.**

to AD 800. The collection also includes *metates* made of volcanic stone, ceramics, and gold ornaments. The Sala de Jade displays pendants in kaleidoscopic hues of green and blue, exquisitely backlit to demonstrate their translucent quality. The jade pieces in this collection did not come from archaeological sites – they were purchased from private collectors who, somewhat controversially, had bought them from looters. The collection is displayed in six themed rooms and includes cultural events, workshops, film screenings, audio guides, and a cafeteria.

Centro Nacional de la Cultura

♀E3 **♙**Calles 11/15 and Aves 3/7 **☎**2255-3190 (ext 210) ▦ **◷**Tours: Tue-Fri, by appointment only

Immediately east of Parque España, the rambling structure of the National Center of Culture (CENAC) takes up a block on the site of the former Fábrica National de Licores (State Liquor Factory); traces of the old distillery can still be seen. The Ministry of Culture is located here, as are venues hosting the National Theater Company and the National Dance Company. Most of the extant buildings date to 1856, as does the perimeter wall, whose stone west gate is topped by a triangular pediment. Note the *reloj de sol* (sun clock), carved into the perimeter wall to the right of the southeast *portalón* (gate) by architect Teodorico Quirós. The **Museo de Arte y Diseño**

Contemporáneo (Museum of Contemporary Art and Design) occupies the southeast part of the complex and features exhibitions of art, architecture, and ceramics. *Evelia con Baton*, a sculpture by Costa-Rican-born Francisco Zúñiga, stands in the west courtyard.

Museo de Arte y Diseño Contemporáneo
◷9:30am-5pm Tue-Sat **🗓**Public hols **ⓦ**madc.cr

15

Asamblea Legislativa

♀E4 **♙**Calles 15/17 & Ave Central ▦ **◷**Entry by guided tour only (2243-2547) **ⓦ**asamblea.go.cr

Costa Rica's seat of government is in an enclave of five buildings, covering two blocks. The main structure, a modern 18-story tower, was inaugurated as the new legislative assembly in October 2020. It replaced the nearby Edificio del Plenario, which was built in 1958 and has a bronze statue of drummer Juan Santamaría (recognized for his actions in the Second Battle of Rivas), torch in hand, in the north courtyard. The pink Casa Rosada, to the northeast, houses the offices of various political parties. The pretty blue Castillo Azul to the southeast was built in 1911 for Máximo Fernández, then a presidential aspirant.

The buildings can only be visited by guided tour. Visitors are also admitted into the legislative assembly to witness debates on weekdays. When in the building, sandals are not permitted for men, nor are bare legs for anyone.

↑ Pre-Columbian ceramics from the Guanacaste region at Museo Nacional

Museo de Jade Fidel Tristán Castro

♀D4 **♙**Ave Central and Calle 13 ▦ **◷**9am-5pm daily **🗓**Public hols **ⓦ**museodeljade.ins-cr.com

Located in a stunning black Cubist monolith on the western side of Plaza de la Democracia, this magnificent museum contains the largest collection of pre-Columbian jade pieces in the Americas. It was founded by Fidel Tristán Castro, the first president of the INS, in 1977. The collection consists of *adzes* (cutting tools), ceremonial heads, and decorative items dating from 500 BC

16

Parque Nacional

♀E4 🚏 **Calles 15/19 and Aves 1/3** 🚌

Laid out in 1895, the largest of San José's inner-city parks is also its most appealing. The peaceful park sprawls across a gentle hill that rises eastward. Stone benches fringe the irregular paths that snake beneath flowering trees, swaying palms, and breezy bamboo groves. The massive Monumento Nacional is at the center, cast in the Rodin studios in Paris. Unveiled on September 15, 1892, it is dedicated to the notable deeds of

the War of 1856. Upon its granite pedestal are five bronze Amazons representing the Central American nations as they repelled mercenary William Walker. Costa Rica stands in the middle, holding a flag in one hand and supporting a wounded Nicaragua with the other; El Salvador holds a sword, Guatemala an axe, and Honduras an arch and shield. Bronze bas-reliefs to each side depict scenes from the different battles. Busts dotted around the park honor famous Latin American figures including the Mexican revolutionary and priest Miguel Hidalgo (1753–1811), the Venezuelan poet and intellectual Don Andrés Bello (1781–1865), and the Cuban patriot and poet José Martí (1853–95).

The park is surrounded by important buildings. The Biblioteca Nacional (National Library) is to the north, and to the south, the Bulevar Ricardo Jiménez, named for the three-time president, runs down three blocks to the building of the Tribunal of Justice.

17

Antigua Estación Ferrocarril al Atlántico

♀F4 **Calles 21/23 and Ave 3** 🚌

To the northeast of the Parque Nacional is the former Estación Ferrocarril al Atlántico (Atlantic Railway Station). Built in 1908, this ornate French Beaux-Arts-style building, which resembles a pagoda, later became the terminus for the famous "Jungle Train," discontinued in 1991 following a devastating earthquake that destroyed much of the rail line. The

---

> **Stone benches fringe the irregular paths that snake beneath flowering trees, swaying palms, and breezy bamboo groves.**

building served as a museum for many years before being resurrected as a functioning station for the Tren Inter-urbano. Rail history buffs can appreciate the vintage rolling stock to the rear and east of the building. This includes Locomotora 59, a 1939 steam locomotive imported from Philadelphia for the Northern Railway Company.

A bust of General Tomás Guardia, under whom the railroad was established between 1871 and 1890, stands in front of the building, next to an obelisk commemorating the abolition of capital punishment in 1877.

18

Universidad de Costa Rica

♀B5 🚏 **Calle Central, San Pedro** 📞 **2511-4000** 🚌

The University of Costa Rica imbues the suburb of San Pedro with an intellectual, arty vibe. The campus entrance is on Calle Central (off Avenida Central), which throbs with student bars and cafés. The campus itself is not particularly appealing, although many busts and statues are sprinkled about the tree-shaded grounds, and a botanical garden is in the southwest corner.

The **Museo de Insectos**, which opened in 1962, is located in the basement of the Music Department in the northeast corner of the campus. It boasts large displays of butterflies, beetles, and other insects numbering almost a million. Visitors can call ahead

←

The Monumento Nacional, topped by a group of Amazons

↑ Abstract figures towering above the lake in La Sabana Park

to book edible-insect-tasting sessions. Finally, **Planetario**, a planetarium in the campus's Ciudad de la Investigación, explores the rich biodiversity of Costa Rica.

Museo de Insectos
☎ 2511-5318 ⏱ 8am-12pm & 1-4:45pm Mon-Fri

Planetario
⏱ 9-11:10am & 1-7pm Mon-Fri, 5-7pm Sat
🌐 planetario.ucr.ac.cr

⑲

Parque Sabana
📍 B5 🏠 Calle 42/Sabana Oeste and Ave las Américas/Sabana Sur 🚌

Officially named Parque Metropolitano La Sabana

> ### Did You Know?
>
> Locals consider Parque Sabana to be the "lungs of San José", akin to New York's Central Park.

Padre Antonio Chapui, after the first priest of San José (1710–83), this park was the city's main airfield until 1955, when it was converted into a bucolic retreat and sports venue. The former airport buildings now house the Museo de Arte Costarricense *(p120)*. Looming over the park are the curving ICE (Costa Rican Institute of Electricity) tower to the north, and the strangely sloping Controlaría de la República, the government's administrative headquarters, to the south.

The park, accessed from downtown via the wide Paseo Colón, is popular with Costa Rican families, who picnic on weekends beneath the pine and eucalyptus groves. The park's facilities include jogging and cycling tracks; basketball, volleyball, and tennis courts; riding trails; a swimming pool; a gymnasium; soccer fields; and the National Stadium, completed in 2011. There is also a rollerskating track at the east end of the park. On the south side, a man-made lake is surrounded by modern sculptures. To the west of the park, a cross honors Pope John Paul II's visit to Costa Rica in 1983.

STAY

Hotel Grano de Oro
This elegant hotel is the city's finest lodging and has a superb restaurant.

📍 B5 🏠 Calle 30 and Aves 2/4 🌐 hotel grano deoro.com

⑤⑤⑤

Hotel Auténtico
Chic décor characterizes this low-rise close to Parque Sabana.

📍 B5 🏠 Calle 40 and Aves 5/7 🌐 autentico hotel.com

⑤⑤⑤

Casa de las Tías
Set in the heart of Escazú, this family-run B&B has a luxuriant garden. Gourmet breakfasts.

📍 A5 🏠 San Rafael de Escazú 🌐 casa delastias.com

⑤⑤⑤

20 Ⓜ

Museo de Arte Costarricense

◆ B5 ⌂ Calle 42 and Paseo Colón 🚌 🕐 9am–4pm Tue–Sun 🚫 Public hols 🖥 mac. go.cr

Costa Rica's leading museum of fine art, on the east side of Parque Sabana *(p119)*, is situated in the colonial-style former airport terminal that closed in the 1950s. The Costa Rican Art Museum displays more than 3,200 important 20th-century works of art by Costa Rican sculptors and painters, as well as a smattering of foreign artists, including Mexican Diego Rivera (1886–1957). Many of the works celebrate a romanticized, pastoral way of life, exemplified by *El Portón Rojo* (1945) by Teodorico Quirós Alvarado.

A highlight of the collection, and not to be missed, are Francisco Amighetti's wooden sculptures and woodcuts. On the second floor, the Salón Dorado has a bas-relief mural in bronze and stucco by French sculptor Louis Ferrón. Sweeping around all four walls, the panorama depicts an idealized version of Costa Rican history from pre-Columbian times to the 1940s.

The Jardín de Esculturas (Sculpture Garden) at the rear exhibits works by prominent sculptors, and also displays pre-Columbian stone *esferas* (spheres) and petroglyphs. Most intriguing are the *Tres Mujeres Caminando*, Francisco Zúñiga's sculpture of three women, and the granite *Danaide*, a female curled up in the fetal position, by Max Jiménez Huete.

---

21 ⊗ 🍴 🛍

Parque Diversiones (Pueblo Antiguo)

◆ A4 ◈ 1 mile (1.6 km) W of Hospital México, La Uruca 🚌 🕐 9am–7pm Fri–Sun (daily Dec–Jan) 🖥 parque diversiones.com

This splendid park, in Barrio La Uruca, 2 miles (3 km) west of downtown, draws local families not only for the roller coasters, water slides, and other pay-as-you-go rides, but also for the marvelously done re-creations of scenes from early 20th-century Costa Rican life in the adjoining Pueblo Antiguo (Old Town).

Pueblo Antiguo is divided into three sections: the capital city, the countryside and the coast. Buildings in traditional architectural style include a church, a market, a bank, a fire station, and a railroad station. There are several original adobe structures, such as a coffee mill, a sugar mill, and a milking barn, which have been moved here from remote rural quarters and rebuilt in their entirety. A farmstead is stocked with live animals.

Kids will enjoy a ride around the village on the electric train, as well as the antics of actors in period costume who can be found all over the village dramatizing scenes from the past. Folkloric shows with music and dance bring the place to life on Friday and Saturday evenings. The park also has a number of craft shops as well as a restaurant that serves Costa Rican fare.

↑ Examining the art in a gallery room at the Museo de Arte Costarricense

DRINK

ChepeCletas
This cultural group leads a nightly tour of San José cantinas.

🌐 chepecletas.com

Tintos y Blancos
Classy wine and tapas bar with live music.

📍 A5 🏠 Centro Comercial Multiplaza
🌐 tintosyblancos.com

Stiefel
A convivial pub in a historic building.

📍 D3 🏠 Calles 13/15 and Ave 7 📞 8850-2119

Bebedero
Retro-styled cocktail bar in a cultural center.

📍 C4 🏠 Calle 1 and Ave 1 📞 8529-4250

Formal displays and eccentric dioramas *(inset)* at Museo de Ciencias Naturales ↑

㉒
Escazú

📍 A5 🏠 2 miles (3 km) W of Parque Sabana 🚌

This upscale district lies west of the Parque Sabana and is accessed by the Carretera Prospero Fernández. Its appeal is partly down to its blend of antiquity and modernity, and partly to its position at the foot of Cerro Escazú mountain. The suburb, which derives its name from the Indigenous word *itzkatzu* (resting place), sprawls uphill for several miles. It is divided into three main *barrios* – San Rafael de Escazú, San Miguel de Escazú, and San Antonio de Escazú.

Everyday life bustles in congested San Rafael de Escazú, where an exquisite colonial-style church, Iglesia

Jiménez y Tandi, designed in the 1930s by Costa Rican-born architect Teodorico Quirós Alvarado, is encircled by high-rise condominiums and US-style malls. Half a mile (1 km) uphill, in San Miguel de Escazú, colonial-era adobe houses are painted with a strip of blue. It is believed that this was done to ward off witches.

San Antonio de Escazú, farther uphill, is a farming community. Time your visit here for the second Sunday of March, when flower-bedecked *carretas* (oxcarts) parade during Día del Boyero (Oxcart Drivers' Day), a festival held in honor of the men who drive the oxcarts. **Barry Biesanz Woodworks** is in the barrio of Bello Horizonte, in east Escazú. This is the workshop of Costa Rica's leading woodcarver and craftsman, who creates elegantly beautiful furniture, bowls, and boxes from Costa Rica's hardwoods. His works are available at the studio and at upscale San José stores.

Barry Biesanz Woodworks
🕒 ♿ 🏠 Barrio Bello Horizonte 🕐 May-Nov: 8am-5pm Mon-Fri; Dec-Apr: 8am-5pm Mon-Fri, 9am-3pm Sat
🌐 biesanz.com

㉓
Museo de Ciencias Naturales La Salle

📍 B5 🏠 Sabana Sur 🚌 🕐 8am-4pm Mon-Sat, 9am-5pm Sun
🌐 museolasalle.ed.cr

Located in the former Colegio La Salle school, La Salle Museum of Natural Sciences houses one of the most comprehensive collections of native and exotic flora and fauna in the world: more than 70,000 items, from molluscs to moths to manatees. The fossil, shell, and butterfly displays are particularly fine. Most exhibits are arranged in dioramas: snakes are poised to strike their prey, and fish swim suspended by invisible wire. The mounted specimens are a bit moth-eaten, and their contrived contortions often comic. Despite this, the museum provides an interesting introduction to Costa Rica's natural world.

A SHORT WALK
SAN JOSÉ CENTER

Distance 1 mile (1.6 km) **Nearest bus stop** Calle 2 and Ave 1
Time 20 minutes

Laid out in a grid of narrow, heavily trafficked one-way streets, San José's tightly packed core contains the city's most significant sights. The main artery, broad Avenida 2, throngs with honking taxis and buses threading past tree-shaded Parque Central. Running parallel to it and to the north is the Avenida Central, a pedestrian precinct lined with department stores, specialist shops, and places to eat. At the heart of this stroll-and-shop area lies the small concrete Plaza de la Cultura. Humming with activity all day, it's a popular meeting place for young people and is packed with hawkers as well as musicians and other street entertainers.

The **Teatro Mélico Salazar** (p113), dating from the 1920s, has a Neo-Classical façade and a simple interior.

START

FINISH

Bustling **Avenida 2** is lined with the city's important buildings. Traffic flows eastward on this four lane-wide avenue, which slopes downhill east of Calle 3.

Bronze statue of a street cleaner

Laid out in 1885 and shaded by palms and guanacaste trees, compact **Parque Central** has an unusual bandstand, which is supported by arches.

CALLE 2

CALLE CENTRAL

AVENIDA 2

CALLE CENTRAL

CALLE 1

AVENIDA 4

0 meters   100
0 yards   100

N

A marble statue of Pope John Paul II by Jiménez Deredia

Blue-domed **Catedral Metropolitana** (p112), built in 1871 in a simple Greek Orthodox style, features an elaborate altar.

La Curia (The Archbishop's Palace)

← Sitting in the shade of the unusual bandstand in Parque Central

↑ The opulent marble lobby of the 19th-century Teatro Nacional

Locator Map
For more detail see p104

SAN JOSÉ

San José Center

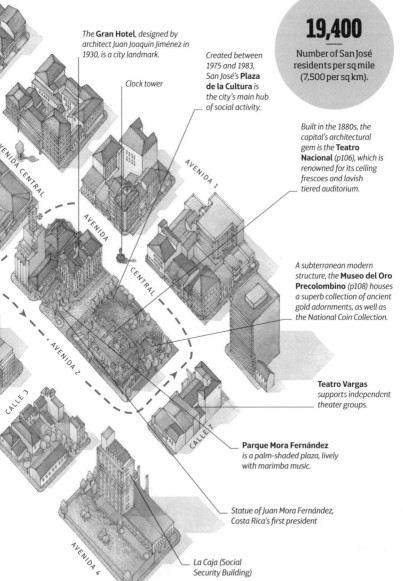

The **Gran Hotel**, designed by architect Juan Joaquín Jiménez in 1930, is a city landmark.

Clock tower

Created between 1975 and 1983, San José's **Plaza de la Cultura** *is the city's main hub of social activity.*

AVENIDA CENTRAL

AVENIDA

AVENIDA 1

AVENIDA CENTRAL

AVENIDA 2

CALLE 3

CALLE 1

19,400

Number of San José residents per sq mile (7,500 per sq km).

Built in the 1880s, the capital's architectural gem is the **Teatro Nacional** *(p106), which is renowned for its ceiling frescoes and lavish tiered auditorium.*

A subterranean modern structure, the **Museo del Oro Precolombino** *(p108) houses a superb collection of ancient gold adornments, as well as the National Coin Collection.*

Teatro Vargas *supports independent theater groups.*

Parque Mora Fernández *is a palm-shaded plaza, lively with marimba music.*

Statue of Juan Mora Fernández, Costa Rica's first president

AVENIDA 4

La Caja (Social Security Building)

A SHORT WALK

AROUND PARQUE NACIONAL

Distance 1 mile (1.6 km) **Nearest bus stop** Parada Parque España **Time** 20 minutes

Commanding a bluff on the east side of downtown, Parque Nacional is a bucolic tree-shaded retreat in the heart of San José. Bordering the park is one of Costa Rica's most important government centers, the Legislative Assembly complex. Nearby cultural sights include the National Museum and National Center for Culture. The area makes for pleasant strolling, especially along the pedestrianized area sloping south from Parque Nacional, a lovely place to sit and relax.

Biblioteca Nacional, erected in 1969–71, houses the national library.

CALLE 17

AVENIDA 3

Occupying the former State Liquor Factory, the **Centro Nacional de la Cultura**'s (p117) attractions include the state-of-the-art Museum of Contemporary Art and Design.

START

FINISH

CALLE 15

AVENIDA 3

A **fish pond**, stocked with koi, swells along the western side of the park.

Epítome del Vuelo statue

AVENIDA 1

The **Tribunal Supremo de Elecciones** building houses the government body that ensures the integrity of elections.

CALLE 11

The small, semi-circular **Plaza de la Libertad Electoral** honors the nation's democracy. Neo-Classical columns enclose a pink granite statue, Epítome del Vuelo *(1996), sculpted by José Sancho Benito.*

←

Passing José Sancho Benito's *Epítome del Vuelo* (1996), which honors freedom

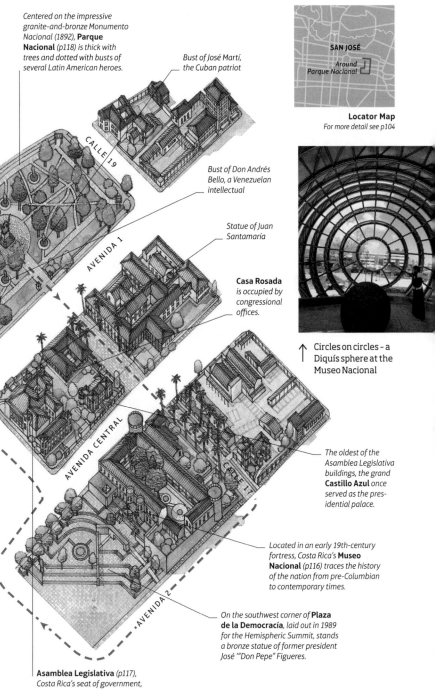

Centered on the impressive granite-and-bronze Monumento Nacional (1892), **Parque Nacional** (p118) is thick with trees and dotted with busts of several Latin American heroes.

Bust of José Martí, the Cuban patriot

CALLE 19

Bust of Don Andrés Bello, a Venezuelan intellectual

AVENIDA 1

Statue of Juan Santamaría

Casa Rosada is occupied by congressional offices.

SAN JOSÉ

Around Parque Nacional

Locator Map
For more detail see p104

↑ Circles on circles – a Diquís sphere at the Museo Nacional

The oldest of the Asamblea Legislativa buildings, the grand **Castillo Azul** once served as the presidential palace.

AVENIDA CENTRAL

Located in an early 19th-century fortress, Costa Rica's **Museo Nacional** (p116) traces the history of the nation from pre-Columbian to contemporary times.

On the southwest corner of **Plaza de la Democracía**, laid out in 1989 for the Hemispheric Summit, stands a bronze statue of former president José '"Don Pepe" Figueres.

AVENIDA 2

Asamblea Legislativa (p117), Costa Rica's seat of government, is housed in three historic buildings dating back to 1914 and built in different styles.

0 meters		100	N ↙
0 yards		100	

125

CENTRAL HIGHLANDS

Simmering volcanoes dominate the landscape of the Central Highlands – a broad valley at an altitude of around 3,300 ft (1,000 m). The mild climate and fertile soils of the *meseta central* (central plateau) attracted pre-Columbian peoples around 7000 BC. One of the most intriguing ancient settlements – Guayabo – was mysteriously abandoned before the arrival of the Spanish in the mid-1500s. In 1563, Juan Vázquez de Coronado founded Cartago, which remained the colonial capital until 1823. Over the next two centuries, the region remained a colonial backwater centered around farming communities near Heredia and Orosí. The region's fortunes changed in 1779 with the introduction of coffee from Jamaica, and following independence in 1830, the *grano de oro* (golden bean) became the region's foremost export, leading to the rise of a merchant class of coffee barons by the end of the century.

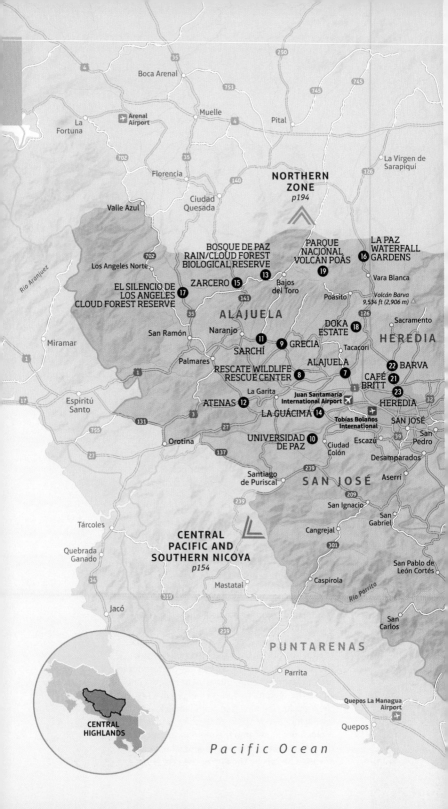

CENTRAL HIGHLANDS

Must Sees

1. Monumento Nacional Guayabo
2. The Orosí Valley
3. Basílica de Nuestra Senora de Los Angeles

Experience More

4. Parque Nacional Los Quetzales
5. Jardín Botánico Lankester
6. San Isidro de Coronado
7. Alajuela
8. Rescate Wildlife Rescue Center
9. Grecia
10. Universidad de Paz
11. Sarchí
12. Atenas
13. Bosque de Paz Rain/Cloud Forest Biological Reserve
14. La Guácima
15. Zarcero
16. La Paz Waterfall Gardens
17. El Silencio de Los Angeles Cloud Forest Reserve
18. Doka Estate
19. Parque Nacional Volcán Poás
20. Parque Nacional Braulio Carrillo
21. Café Britt
22. Barva
23. Heredia
24. Parque Nacional Tapantí-Macizo la Muerte
25. Turrialba
26. Parque Nacional Volcán Irazú
27. San Gerardo de Dota
28. Parque Nacional Volcán Turrialba

EXPERIENCE Central Highlands

MONUMENTO NACIONAL GUAYABO

🅐 E3 🏠 12 miles (19 km) N of Turrialba 🚌 From Turrialba 🕐 8am-3:30pm daily
🌐 sinac.go.cr

On the southern slope of Volcán Turrialba, Guayabo is the nation's most important pre-Columbian site, comprising the remains of a city that is thought to have had a population of 20,000 at its peak. It became a designated national monument in 1973.

Although minor in scale compared to the Mayan remains of Mexico or Machu Picchu in Peru, the site is shrouded in just as much mystery. Most of the site is yet to be thoroughly excavated, but there is much to convince archaeologists that the site is of great cultural and religious significance. Believed to have been inhabited between 1500 BC and AD 1400, Guayabo is said to have supported a population as high as 20,000, before being abandoned for reasons unknown. The jungle quickly reclaimed the town, which was discovered in the late 18th century by naturalist Don Anastasio Alfaro. The peaceful site features residential mounds, the remains of petroglyphs, and a system of paved roads. Most impressive are walled aqueducts and still-funcitonal cisterns. Pottery, flint tools, gold ornaments, and other finds unearthed at the site are displayed in San José's Museo Nacional (p116).

↑ Getting to know the site with a guide

> **INSIDER TIP**
> **Mystic Nights**
>
> Join a local guide for a magical Mystic Night Tour and discover the site after dark. Atmospherically lit tours are given by certified guides (www.usurecr.org), who unravel - at least some - of the site's secrets.

↑ Surveying the sweep of the Guayabo's mysterious causeway from a viewing point

↑ Fit for a king: the "chief's" mound, measuring 98 ft (30 m) across and 15 ft (4.5 m) in height

PETROGLYPHS

Excavations around Guayabo have revealed a wealth of petroglyphs, the prehistoric artform achieved by incising, picking, carving, or abrading a rock surface. The most noteworthy of the petroglyphs scattered around the site are along the Sendero de los Montículos. The Monolito Jaguar y Lagarto has a lizard lounging on one side and, on the other, a spindly bodied jaguar with a round head.

↑ A causeway of circular and rectangular mounds believed to be the foundations of wooden structures

2

THE OROSÍ VALLEY

🅰E4 **📍10 miles (17 km) S of Cartago** **🚍** **ℹ437 yd (400 m) S of church, Orosí; 2533-3640**

Lined with coffee and sugar cane plantations, the Orosí Valley is as rich in scenery as it is in history. Archaeological excavations date human inhabitation back to 1000 BC, and while it was one of the first places to be colonized by the Spanish in Costa Rica, it remains relatively untouched by tourism.

Hemmed to the south by the Talamanca Mountains, the Orosí Valley falls steeply away south of Cartago. The Río Reventazón runs through the valley and drains into Lago de Cachí, which is also fed by other streams and raging rivers that tumble down hills enveloped by cloud forest. The Orosí Valley has been an important center for millennia. It was inhabited by the Huetare, Viceita, and Cabecar peoples, who farmed and hunted the land, until the arrival of the Spanish in the 1500s. The Spanish quickly founded their capital here, in 1563, as well as what are now two of Costa Rica's oldest Christian sites, one of which is the ruins of the 17th-century church in the village of Ujarrás, set at the edge of Lago de Cachí. Looping around the Orosí Valley, Route 224 passes the main points of interest, including hamlet of Orosí, the valley's social hub.

🔍 HIDDEN GEM
Finca Cristina

This small, organic shade-grown coffee farm (cafecristina.com) in the north of the valley doubles as a nature reserve atwitter with bird calls. The coffee bushes are integrated into a diverse tropical ecosystem that draws more than 250 butterfly species, 315 bird species, and a Noah's Ark of mammals and reptiles.

↑ Coffee plants growing under almond trees on the hillsides of the valley

Did You Know?

In the 16th century the valley was a major producer of snuff.

↑ The winding Orosí river, bisecting the valley on its way to Lago de Cachí and *(inset)* the Cachí Dam

EXPLORING THE OROSÍ VALLEY

① Lago de Cachí

⌂ 1.5 miles (2 km) E of Ujarrás

This massive lake was created between 1959 and 1963, when the ICE (Costa Rican Institute of Electricity) dammed the Río Reventazón. The Presa de Cachí (Cachí Dam) funnels water down spillways to feed massive hydroelectricity turbines. Visitors can enjoy kayaking, canoeing, and boating on the lake, arranged by local tour operators. The national tourist board operates Paradero Lacustre Charrarra, a recreational complex that offers swimming, horseriding, and boating from the north shore. On the southern shore is **Casa el Soñador**, the bamboo-and-wood studio of renowned sculptor Macedonio Quesada Valerín (1932–94). Carved figures representing the town gossips lean out of the upper-story windows and a bas-relief of Leonardo da Vinci's *The Last Supper* adorns the exterior. Macedonio's sons carry on their father's tradition of carving ornaments, walking sticks, and religious figures from coffee plant roots. The studio also serves as an art gallery for other local artists.

Casa el Soñador

⌂ 5 miles (8 km) E of Orosí
☎ 8955-7779 ⊙ 9am–6pm daily

---

② Ujarrás

⌂ 8 miles (13 km) SE of Cartago

Located at the edge of Lake Cachí and surrounded by coffee bushes, the hamlet of Ujarrás is home to the ruins of the Iglesia de Nuestra Señora de la Límpia Concepción, completed in 1693. The ruins stand in a charming garden awash with tropical flowers.

The site previously housed the shrine La Parroquia de Ujarrás. According to legend, an indigenous *converso* (Catholic convert) found a statue of the Virgin Mary. He carried it to Ujarrás, where it suddenly became too heavy for even a team of men to lift. The local priest saw this as a sign from God that a shrine should be built here. When pirates led by Henry Morgan attacked the region in 1666, local inhabitants prayed at the shrine for salvation. A defensive force led by Spanish governor Juan Lopez de la Flor routed the pirates and in gratitude built a church, Virgen del Rescate de Ujarrás (Virgin of Rescue), which was later abandoned after a flood in 1833. Every April, pilgrims walk 4 miles (6 km) to the shrine from Paraíso, in honor of the Virgin.

↑ Peaceful gardens surrounding the atmospheric ruins of Ujarrás's 17th-century stone church

↑ The well-preserved Iglesia de San José de Orosí under a delft blue sky

③
Orosí

🏠 6 miles (10 km) S of Paraíso

Nestled neatly on the banks of the Río Grande de Orosí, this small, peaceful village, in a lush forest with tall pine trees, is a coffee-growing center. Mineral-rich hot springs gush from the hillsides and can be enjoyed in well-maintained pools at **Balnearios Termales Orosí**. Orosí's pride is the beautifully preserved Iglesia de San José de Orosí, the oldest church in Costa Rica. Built by Franciscan monks in 1743–66 and dominated by a solid bell tower, the whitewashed church has withstood several earthquakes, despite its plain adobe construction. The interior features a beamed ceiling, terracotta floor, and simple gilt-adorned wooden altar. The Franciscan monastery adjoining the church is now the **Museo de Arte Religioso**, displaying artifacts dating back three centuries.

Balnearios Termales Orosí
🕐 7:30am–4pm Wed–Mon
📞 2533-2156

Museo de Arte Religioso
♿🅿 📞 2533-3051 🕐 1–5pm Tue–Fri, 9am–5pm Sat & Sun

EAT

Orosí Lodge
Enjoy filling alfresco breakfasts and steaming coffee on the deck, then come back later for tempting cakes, ice creams, and shakes.

🏠 Orosí
🌐 orosilodge.com

$$$

La Casona del Cafetal
On the banks of Lake Cachí, this coffee farm restaurant has a superb Sunday brunch buffet and excellent coffee.

🏠 Lago de Cachí
🌐 lacasonadel cafetal.com

$$$

Backerei Café y Panadería Suiza
Delicious handmade pastries and superb breakfasts are on offer from the break of dawn.

🏠 Orosí 📞 8706-6777

$$$

Giardino
This low-key restaurant serves tasty pizzas, pastas, and tiramisu.

🏠 Orosí 📞 2533-2022

$$$

Cafetería 1743
Tuck into moreish cakes, tasty sandwiches, and blackboard specials at this squareside café, an ideal spot for people-watching.

🏠 Orosí 📞 2201-6665

$$$

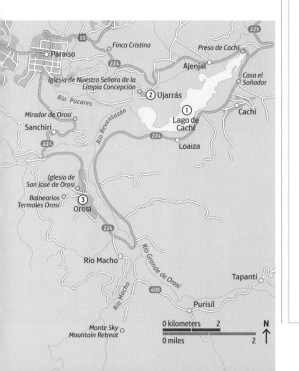

❸

BASÍLICA DE NUESTRA SENORA DE LOS ANGELES

🅰E4 🏠Calle 15/17 Ave Central/1, Cartago 🚌From San José (Calle 5) 🕐 6am–7pm daily
🌐 santuarionacional.org

Cartago's well-restored basílica, built in 1639 and partially destroyed by an earthquake in 1926, bears a unique mix of colonial architecture and 19th-century Byzantine style. The current building was built largely in 1939.

Named in honor of the country's patron saint, the Virgin of Los Angeles, Cartago's Cathedral of Our Lady of the Angels is Costa Rica's most important church. According to legend, in 1635 a peasant girl found a small figurine of a dark-skinned Virgin Mary on a rock. The statue, also called La Negrita, was moved twice and mysteriously returned to the rock both times. The statue, now an important pilgrimage shrine, is housed in the basílica, which was built to mark the spot. The church was destroyed by earthquakes so many times during its construction that the church was relocated to where the statue was found and the building was finally completed unscathed. The impressive Byzantine-style edifice features a decorated façade and is topped by a octagonal cupola.

WHAT ELSE TO SEE IN CARTAGO

Costa Rica's first city and original colonial capital, founded in 1563, has been plagued by earthquakes for much of its history. The town is not especially attractive, but the ruins of the Iglesia de la Parroquia are lovely. Originally built in 1575 and destroyed five times by earthquakes, the mossy ruins now form the centerpiece of a small, pretty garden that runs alongside the stark central plaza. The Museo Municipal de Cartago, in the former army barracks, hosts revolving art exhibitions and has become a place to learn more about the area's natural and cultural heritage.

↑ The vaulted octagonal cupola, ringed by stained-glass windows

↑ Bishops expressing penitence and devotion in one of the panels of modern stained glass

←
The gilt-painted Moorish-style arches and fluted pilasters of Cartago's well-preserved basilica

EXPERIENCE MORE

Parque Nacional Los Quetzales

E4 **Pan-Am Hwy, 47 miles (76 km) SE of San José** **To Km 80, then hike** **7:30am–3:30pm daily** **sinac.go.cr**

Bordering the Pan-American Highway is Parque Nacional Los Quetzales, created in 2005 from the Los Santos Forest Reserve, the Biological Reserve of Cerro de las Vueltas, and various state properties. Covering 19 sq miles (50 sq km) of cloud forest, the park spreads along the banks of the Río Savegre. This is one of the most biologically diverse regions in Costa Rica, with 116 species of mammals, mangroves, and lagoons of glacial origins. One of the highlights is the glorious emerald-green-and-garnet resplendent quetzal, for which the park is named.

Dantica Cloud Forest Lodge, southeast of the park's main entrance, has trails running through primary cloud forest in which peccaries, deer, tapir, otters, ocelots, and pumas have all been sighted.

Dantica Cloud Forest Lodge
2.5 miles (4 km) S of San Gerado de Dota
dantica.com

Jardín Botánico Lankester

E4 **4 miles (6 km) SE of Cartago** **From Cartago** **8:30am–4:30pm daily** **jbl.ucr.ac.cr**

Operated by the University of Costa Rica as a research center, these luxuriant botanical gardens were founded in 1917 by English horticulturalist and coffee-planter Charles Lankester West. They display almost 3,000 neotropical species in separate sections dedicated to specific plant families. The highlight – and the focus of conservation research here – is the sizable orchid collection spread throughout the garden. The 1,100 species are best seen in the dry season, especially from February to April.

Pathways wind through a bamboo tunnel, a swath of premontane forest, a cactus

↑ Lush neotropical plantings at the Jardín Botánico Lankester

garden, a butterfly garden, a medicinal plant garden, and a Japanese garden. Visitors are first given an orientation talk before setting out on a self-guided tour; alternatively, guided tours are available on Sundays: phone ahead to book a place.

San Isidro de Coronado

E3 **6 miles (10 km) NE of San José**

Clinging to the western slopes of Irazú volcano (p150), San Isidro de Coronado is an agricultural center boasting the largest Gothic church in the country. The **Parroquia de San Isidro**, which soars over the town's tree-shaded plaza, was pre-fabricated in Germany in 1930, erected in situ, and finally completed in 1934.

San Isidro is a gateway to Irazú Volcano National Park via an unbelievably scenic stretch of Rancho Redondo. The road snakes along the mountainsides, granting spectacular vistas over San José and the rolling Central Highlands.

Parroquia de San Isidro
Calle Polo Rodriguez
2771-4281

↑ A hummingbird perched on a spiny branch in Parque Nacional Los Quetzales

↑ Sorting coffee, from the ripe cherry to the roasted bean, for quality, size, and shape

COSTA RICAN COFFEE

Costa Rica's famous coffee was introduced to the country in 1779. For more than a century, beginning in the 1830s, the *grano de oro* (golden grain) was Costa Rica's foremost export, funding the construction of fine buildings and enriching a rising class of so-called coffee barons.

GROWING CONDITIONS

The nation's mountains provide ideal conditions for the coffee plant, which prefers consistent, warm temperatures, distinct wet and dry seasons, and fertile, well-drained slopes. Shade trees allow the ideal amount of sunlight to filter through, while volcanic soil contains the nutrients that coffee bushes require. More than 425 sq miles (1,100 sq km), concentrated in the Central Highlands at elevations between 2,650 and 4,900 ft (800–1,500 m), are dedicated to coffee production.

↑ A fresh, milky brew, made from fine Costa Rican coffee beans

FROM BERRY TO CUP

Typically it takes four years for the coffee bush to bear fruit. Small white blossoms appear with the rains in May, giving off a jasmine-like scent. The fleshy green berries containing the beans gradually turn red as they ripen. From November, the red berries are hand-picked and carried from the field in handwoven wicker baskets to be measured. The berries are cleaned at a *beneficio*, where the fleshy outer pulp is stripped off and returned to the slopes as fertilizer. The beans are dried, in the sun or in hot-air ovens, and the leathery skin removed before roasting. The roasted beans are sorted by quality, size, and shape. Export-quality beans are vacuum-sealed in foil bags. Lower grade beans are sold domestically as *café puro* (unadulterated) or *café tradicional* (mixed with sugar).

THE EARLY DAYS

Before the advent of the railway in the late 19th century, coffee beans were transported to port in carretas (oxcarts). Trains of carretas loaded with coffee traveled down the mountains in convoys. The beans were then shipped to Europe, a journey that took three months.

STAY

Tacacori Eco Lodge
Surrounded by coffee fields and forest, this hilltop eco-lodge features stand-alone villas with killer views.

🅐D3 🏠Tacacori
🌐tacacori.com

$$$

Poás Volcano Lodge
Deluxe boutique mountain lodge with glorious rooms on a working cattle farm.

🅐D3 🏠Vara Blanca
🌐poasvolcanolodge.com

$$$

Villa Blanca Cloud Forest Hotel
Chic remake of a colonial mountaintop hacienda in its own forest reserve. Chalets have whirlpool tubs.

🅐E3 🏠Los Angeles Norte 🌐villablanca-costarica.com

$$$

---

❼

Alajuela

🅐D3 🏠12 miles (19 km) NW of San José 🚗🚌

Sitting at the base of Volcán Poás, this busy market town is Costa Rica's third-largest city. The mango trees that shade the main square, Plaza del General Tomás Guardia, are the source of Alajuela's nickname, "City of Mangoes"; the fruit even has its own festival here, in July. Centered on a triple-tiered fountain with cherubs at its base, the plaza has a bandstand, and benches with built-in chess sets. It is dominated by the simple, domed Catedral de Alajuela, with a magnificent barrel-vaulted ceiling lavishly adorned with frescoes and a Classical façade. More interesting is the Baroque Iglesia Santo Cristo de la Agonía, five blocks east, which dates only from 1935. The interior boasts intriguing murals. The former jail, one block north of the main plaza, houses the **Museo Histórico Cultural Juan Santamaría**, honoring the local drummer-boy who gave up his life torching William Walker's hideout during the War of 1856. Call ahead to arrange a guided tour and a screening of a video about the event.

A bronze statue of Santamaría stands in cobbled Parque Juan Santamaría, which is two blocks south of the main plaza.

→

A peacock displaying its plumage to a peahen, Rescate Wildlife Rescue Center

Museo Histórico Cultural Juan Santamaría
🚫♿ 🏠Ave 1 and Calles Central/2 🕘9am–5:30pm Tue–Sun 🌐museojuansantamaria.go.cr

---

❽ ♿ 🍴 🏛

Rescate Wildlife Rescue Center

🅐D3 🏠Hwy 3, La Garita, 2 miles (3 km) E of Pan-Am Hwy 🚌From San José (Sat–Sun at 8am) & Alajuela 🕘9am–5pm daily 🌐rescatewildlife.org

This wildlife rehabilitation center has the largest collection of tropical birds in Central America, covering 34 acres (14 ha). The privately owned rescue center is one of only two in the world to display resplendent quetzals. More than 60 other native bird species can be seen in large flight cages. Mammals are represented by deer, peccaries, pumas, tapirs, and the four native monkey species. Crocodiles, caimans, and snakes are among the dozens of reptile species.

The animals and birds here were confiscated from poachers, or rescued by the National Wildlife Service. The sanctuary is also a breeding

←

Statue of Juan Santamaria, standing defiant in Alajuela

center and has successfully raised endangered species such as green and scarlet macaws.

A short distance away, the **Botanical Orchid Garden** delights with its walking trails, exhibitions, and hothouses where about 150 orchid species are grown. Bamboos, heliconias, and palms are also represented, and there's a macaw breeding facility. The peaceful water gardens offer a relaxed stroll with glimpses of koi carp and turtles.

Botanical Orchid Garden

📷 🕐 ♿ 🅰 1 mile (1.6 km) W of Autopista General Cañas 🕐 9am-4pm Tue-Sun 🌐 orchidgardencr.com

---

9

Grecia

🅰 D3 🅰 11 miles (18 km) NW of Alajuela 🚌

A tranquil market town first settled in 1864 and voted the nation's cleanest town several times since, Grecia's claim to fame is the Iglesia de Grecia, made of rust-red prefabricated steel plates. Trimmed in white filigree, the church has twin spires and a wooden interior with an elaborate marble altar.

Universidad de Paz

🅰 D3 🅰 8 miles (13 km) W of Escazú 🚌 To Ciudad Colón, then by taxi 🕐 Campus: 8am-4:30pm Mon-Fri; Recreation Park: 8am-4pm daily 🌐 upeace.org

A United Nations institution, the University of Peace (UPAZ) enjoys an idyllic setting on the Hacienda Rodeo, a cattle estate and forest reserve that donated the land for the purpose. Founded in 1980, the university is dedicated to research and education for the promotion of peace. The Recreation Park surrounding the campus contains busts of famed pacifists such as Mahatma Gandhi, novelist Alexsey Tolstoy, and Henry Dunant, founder of the Red Cross. Particularly moving is the life-size statue *Peace Pilgrim* by Fernando Calvo, dedicated to Mildred N. Ryder (1908–81), who, from the age of 44 until her death, walked for the cause of world peace. Trails lead into the Reserva Forestal el Rodeo, a 4.6-sq-mile (12-sq-km) primary forest reserve that shelters deer, monkeys, wild cats, and more than 300 species of birds.

Around a lake to the south of the university grounds is the roadside Monument for Disarmament, Work, and Peace, by Cuban artist Thelvia Marín. A series of majestic columns each depict a key moment and personality in Costa Rican history, striding towards peace.

↑ The stirring Monument for Disarmament, Work, and Peace at the Universidad de Paz

↑ Workshop in the town of Sarchí, famed for traditionally crafted and decorated wares

⓫ Sarchí

🅰D3 🏛18 miles (29 km) NW of Alajuela 🚍 🅸 Plaza de la Artesanía, Sarchí Sur

The country's foremost crafts center is set in the midst of coffee fields on the southern flank of Volcán Poás. The town is famous for its wooden furniture, leather rocking chairs, and hand-painted oxcarts, decorated with signature floral motifs and geometric designs. The whitewashed buildings of Sarchí Norte, the town center, are graced by similar motifs. Don't miss the pink-and-turquoise Iglesia de Sarchí in the town plaza. One of its twin spires is topped by a trademark oxcart wheel.

Craft stores and *mueblerías* (furniture workshops) are concentrated in Sarchí Sur, half a mile (1 km) east. A good place to buy souvenirs is **Fábrica de Carretas Joaquín Chaverrí**. Decorative oxcarts of various sizes are painted in *talleres* (workshops) at the rear. **Fábrica de Carretas Eloy Alfaro** is the only remaining *taller* in the country that actually makes oxcarts.

Fábrica de Carretas Joaquín Chaverrí

Ⓜ 🅰Sarchí Sur 📞2454-4411 🕒8am–5pm daily

Fábrica de Carretas Eloy Alfaro

Ⓜ🅹 🅰164 yd (150 m) N of Sarchí Norte 📞2215-1439 🕒8am–5pm daily

---

⓬ Atenas

🅰D3 🏛15 miles (24 km) W of Alajuela 🚍

Heralded for having the best climate in the world, this quiet mountain town was once an important way-stop on the old *camino de carretas* (oxcart trail). A century ago caravans of carts, laden with coffee beans, would begin their descent to Puntarenas from Atenas, which perches atop the westernmost ridge of the Cordillera Central. The Monumento a los Boyeros, by Manuel Torrecillas López, commemorates the carters, and the Museo Ferroviario, in the old railway station on Rio Grande, displays antique locomotives from the same era. Today, Atenas is still an important coffee-producing center – El Toledo organic coffee farm offers tours, and the local social initiative COOPEATENAS co-operative has tours of the processing mill. The town's palm-shaded central park is a peaceful and popular spot to relax and watch the world go by.

TRADITIONAL OXCARTS

The quintessential symbol of Costa Rica, the traditional solid-wheeled *carreta* (oxcart) was once used on farmsteads and for transporting coffee beans. In the mid-19th century, the carts began to be painted in brightly colored, stylized floral and geometric starburst patterns, with metal rings on the hubcaps that create a unique chime when in motion. Still traditionally made, today's *carretas* are largely decorative, and can cost as much as $5,000.

⓭ 🚴 🏍

Bosque de Paz Rain/Cloud Forest Biological Reserve

🅰D3 🏛9 miles (14 km) E of Zarcero 🚍To Zarcero, then by taxi 🕒6am–5pm daily, by prior arrangement only 🌐bosquedepaz.com

Set deep in the valley of the Río Toro on the northern slopes of Volcán Platanar, this 4-sq-mile (10-sq-km) reserve connects Parque Nacional Volcán Poás (*p145*) with remote Parque Nacional Juan Castro

Blanco. Some 14 miles (22 km) of trails lead through primary and secondary forest, from rain-sodden montane growth to cloud forest at higher levels. The prodigious rainfall feeds the reserve's many waterfalls, as well as the streams that rush past a hummingbird and butterfly garden.

On clear days, *miradores* (viewpoints) offer fabulous vistas, as well as a chance to catch sight of sloths, wild cats, and howler, capuchin, and spider monkeys. A favorite of bird-watchers, the reserve has more than 330 species of birds, including resplendent quetzals and the noisy three-wattled bellbirds.

Meals and accommodation are offered in a rustic log-and-riverstone lodge.

14

La Guácima

🅰D3 🏠7 miles (12 km) SE of Alajuela 🚌

The sprawling community of La Guácima is renowned for the murals of butterflies that adorn its walls. Horse-lovers will find a visit to **Rancho San Miguel**, on the outskirts of La Guácima, particularly interesting. This stable and stud farm raises Andalusian horses and

offers riding lessons, as well as a dressage and horse-manship show in the manner of the Lipizzaners of the Spanish Riding School at Vienna. It offers tours of its sustainable agriculture facility, including a bee farm.

Rancho San Miguel

👁👁 🏠3 miles (4.5 km) N of La Guácima 📞2439-0003 🕐9am–5pm daily, with prior reservation only

---

15

Zarcero

🅰D3 🏠15.5 miles (25 km) NW of Sarchí 🚌

This quiet mountain town, at an elevation of 5,600 ft (1,700 m), has a spectacular setting, with lush pastures and forest all around. It is renowned for its cheese, called *palmito*.

At the heart of the town, the main attraction is the Parque Francisco Alvardo, a spacious park with well-tended gardens and topiary features. Since 1960, gardener Don Evangelisto Blanco has been transforming the park's cypress bushes into various fanciful forms: an ox and cart, an elephant with lightbulbs for eyes, a helicopter and airplane, a bullfight with matador and charging bull, and even a monkey riding a motorcycle. An Art Nouveau-style

EAT

Chubascos

Hearty *gallotes* (large tortillas packed to the brim) are on offer here.

🅰D3 🏠Fraijanes de Poás 📞2482-2280

💲💲💲

Fiesta del Maíz

Popular local eatery serving all things *maíz* (corn), from fritters to tamales.

🅰D3 🏠La Garita 📞2487-5757

💲💲💲

La Lluna de Valencia

Fun-filled place known for its superb paella and its ebullient Catalan owner, Vicente Aguilar.

🅰D3 🏠San Pedro de Barva 🌐llalunade valencia.com

💲💲💲

topiary archway frames the central pathway, which leads to the 19th-century pink-and-blue Iglesia de San Rafael with its prettily painted interior.

↑ The surreal topiary in the Parque Francisco Alvardo

16 ⬡ ⬡ ⬡ ⬡

La Paz Waterfall Gardens

🅰 D3 📍 Montaña Azul, 20 miles (32 km) N of Alajuela 🚌 From San José 🕐 8am–5pm daily 🌐 waterfallgardens.com

This multifaceted attraction's main draw is five thunderous waterfalls plummeting down into deeply forested ravines on the northeast slopes of Volcán Poás. Paved pathways lead downhill through pristine forest to the cascades, where spray blasts visitors standing on viewing platforms. Access to the falls involves negotiating metal staircases, but there's a shuttle that runs visitors back uphill.

The landscaped grounds feature the Hummingbird Garden, which draws about 40 percent of the nation's 57 species. As many as 4,000 butterflies flit about the Butterfly Garden, including the owl butterfly. Scores of macaws, toucans, and other birds can be seen in a walk-through aviary enclosed by a massive netted dome, while grand jaguars are a highlight of a wild cat exhibition. Other attractions include a walk-in ranarium displaying poison-dart and other frog species; a serpentarium, with dozens of snake species; and a traditional farmstead with staff dressed in period costume. Renowned ornithologists lead birding tours.

The park's restaurant has a veranda with marvelous views. Deluxe accommodation is available at the Peace Lodge.

Did You Know?

The largest butterfly species in Costa Rica is the owl butterfly, with a wingspan of up to 8 in (20 cm).

17 ⬡ ⬡ ⬡

El Silencio de Los Angeles Cloud Forest Reserve

🅰 D3 📍 20 miles (32 km) NW of Sarchí 🚌 To San Ramón, then by taxi 🕐 6am–5pm daily 🌐 villablanca-costarica.com

Providing easy access to a cloud forest environment, this 3-sq-mile (9-sq-km) reserve reverberates with the raucous calls of aricaris, bellbirds, and three species of monkeys. Wild cats prowl the mist-shrouded forests, which reach as high as 5,900 ft (1,800 m) in elevation. Clouds swirl around the handsome colonial farmhouse here, which sits above the Continental Divide and houses

←

Reaching out to feel the spray from a voluminous La Paz waterfall the Villa Blanca Cloud Forest Hotel & Spa. From here, knowledgeable guides lead tours of the reserve along a network of trails; if you're not staying at the hotel, it's advisable to book your place in advance. There are also self-guided walks and, if you arrive early enough, you can even help milk the hotel's cows.

The hotel's tiny La Mariana chapel has a high ceiling covered with hand-painted tiles, each devoted to a different female saint. Outside, an effigy of the Black saint San Martín de Porres welcomes visitors.

Nearby **Nectandra Cloud Forest Garden** has well-kept trails and landscaped gardens exhibiting the rich flora and fauna of Costa Rica.

Nectandra Cloud Forest Garden

 9 miles (15 km) NW of San Ramón ⏱8am-3pm daily, by appointment only ⓦnectandra.org

Doka Estate

🅐D3 ⓐSabanilla de Alajuela, 7 miles (11 km) N of Alajuela ⏱ 9am-3pm daily 🚍From Alajuela ⓦdokaestate.com

Located on the lower slopes of Volcán Poás, this coffee *finca* was founded in 1929 by merchant Don Clorindo Vargas. The family-owned estate has some 6 sq miles (15 sq km) planted with coffee bushes.

The Doka Estate still follows the time-honored tradition of drying coffee beans by laying them out in the sun, and welcomes visitors eager to learn about coffee production, from cultivating *arabica* seedlings to processing the beans (*p139*). The guided tour (obligatory) of the historic site, which has National Historic Landmark status, starts on a delicious note with a fresh-roasted coffee-tasting. The tour demonstrates the various

↑ The volatile landscape at the summit of Volcán Poás, where an acidic lake steams

stages involved in coffee production and ends in the roasting room. Tours begin at regular intervals during the morning and early afternoon. The estate offers splendid views down the slopes and across the valley. There is also a small B&B nearby.

---

19 🄼 🄼
Parque Nacional Volcán Poás

🅐D3 ⓐ18 miles (30 km) N of Alajuela 🚍From Alajuela and San José ⏱ 8am-4pm daily ⓝDuring phases of volcanic activity ⓦsinac.go.cr

The nation's most visited national park was inaugurated on January 25, 1971. Covering 25 sq miles (65 sq km), the reserve encircles Volcán Poás (8,850 ft/2,700 m), a restless giant that formed more than one million years ago and is still volatile. Following strong eruptions in 2017, which closed the park completely for some time, it has now reopened with strictly controlled access and safety conditions. Tickets must be

purchased online in advance; your entry time is specified and visits are limited to 40 minutes only. Visits are not advised for young children or adults with limited mobility or heart or respiratory problems, in case an evacuation is necessary.

The gateway to the park is the mountain hamlet of Poasito. The summit of the volcano is reached by a scenic drive, with spectacular views back down the valley. From the parking lot, a short walk along a paved path leads to a viewing terrace that grants visitors an awe-inspiring vista down into the heart of the hissing and steaming crater, which is 895 ft (300 m) deep and a mile (1.6 km) wide. It contains an acidic lake, sulfurous fumaroles, and a 245-ft- (75-m-) tall cone that began to form in the 1950s. On clear days, it is possible to view the Caribbean Sea and the Pacific Ocean.

Clouds typically form by mid-morning, so it is best to book an early time-slot. Bring warm clothing: the average temperature at the summit is 12° C (54° F), but cloudy days can be bitterly cold.

> **The reserve encircles Volcán Poás (8,850 ft/2,700 m), a restless giant that formed more than one million years ago and is still volatile.**

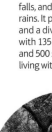

20

Parque Nacional Braulio Carrillo

🅰 E3 📍 Guápiles Hwy, 23 miles (37 km) N of San José 🚌 San José–Guápiles

Named for Costa Rica's third chief of state, this sprawling 185-sq-mile (480-sq-km) park climbs from 120 ft (36 m) at La Selva in the northern lowlands to 9,500 ft (2,900 m) at the top of Volcán Barva. It is bisected by the Guápiles Highway, which links San José with Puerto Limón. The park remains one of the nation's most rugged, with craggy mountains, dense rainforest cover, and numerous waterfalls, and is subject to torrential rains. It protects five ecozones and a diversity of wildlife, with 135 mammal species and 500 species of birds living within the park.

The main entrance is **Puesto Quebrada González** ranger station, 8 miles (13 km) north of the Zurqui ranger station (closed to visitors), near the Rainforest Aerial Tram (*p210*). The best hiking is around the summit of Volcán Barva, on the west side of the park and accessed by 4WD via the Puesto Barva ranger station above Sacramento. From here, a trail leads through the cloud forest to the crater. Dormant Barva has at least 13 eruptive cones. Hikers must report to the ranger stations when on the way in and out. Tour operators in San José offer half-day or full-day tours.

On the southern slopes, **Sibú Chocolate** offers its irresistible products for sale, a lovely garden café, and a fascinating tasting tour that shows how the chocolate is made.

Puesto Quebrada González

📍 Hwy 32 ☎ 2206-5000 🕘 8am–3:30pm daily

Professional actors dressed as *campesinos* (*inset*) leading Café Britt's tours, which end in the coffee bar

Sibú Chocolate

🌐 📍 200 yd (180 m) W of Hwy 32, 5 miles (8 km) S of Zurquí tunnel 🕘 11am–6pm Tue–Sat 🔗 sibuchocolate.com

---

21

Café Britt

🅰 D3 📍 Santa Lucía, 3 miles (5 km) W of Heredia 🚌 Tour buses from San José 🕘 9am–3pm daily 🔗 coffeetour.com

A mecca for coffee lovers, this *beneficio* (processing mill) roasts and packs gourmet coffees. Entertaining guided tours are led by *campesinos*, played by professional actors in period costume. Their homespun repartee unfolds a spellbinding love story along with a fascinating educational narrative on the history and production cycle of coffee, from the plantation to the cup, as well as highlighting the role of the *grano de oro* (golden bean) in cultivating Costa Rican democracy and investigating its importance in molding a national identity. Visitors are led through the coffee estates before taking a hard-hat tour of the packing facility, where they breathe in the aroma of roasting beans. The tour ends in the coffee bar where a delicious brew awaits. The factory store sells coffees, chocolates, souvenirs, and local crafts, and you can buy sandwiches in the canteen.

↑ Barva's pretty 1867 church, built on the site of two earlier churches felled by earthquakes

22
Barva

🅐 D3 🕐 2 miles (3 km) N of Heredia 🚌 From Heredia

One of the country's oldest settlements, this quaint town was founded in 1613. Located at the base of Volcán Barva, the green town contains many simple 18th-century adobe houses with red-tiled roofs.

The flower-filled and palm-shaded town square, laid out in 1913, is graced by the pretty Iglesia de San Bartolomé de Barva, erected in 1867 on the site of an Indian burial ground.

The **Museo de Cultura Popular**, on the outskirts of Barva, provides a portrait of late 19th-century life, with period pieces laid out in the fashion of the times. The building is a former home of ex-president Alfredo González Flores. The kitchen serves traditional meals.

Museo de Cultura Popular

🅐 Santa Lucía de Barva, just S of Barva 🕐 8am-4pm Mon-Fri (groups only), 10am-5pm Sun 🅦 museo.una.ac.cr

23
Heredia

🅐 D3 🕐 7 miles (11 km) NW of San José 🚌

A peaceful and orderly town founded in 1706, Heredia has a smattering of important colonial buildings at its heart and a bustling student life, owing to the presence of a branch of the University of Costa Rica (p118). It is centered on Parque Nicolás Ulloa, popularly called Parque Central. Shaded by large mango trees, the park contains numerous busts and monuments. Dominating the park is the squat, weathered cathedral, La Parroquia de la Inmaculada Concepción. Built in 1797, it has lovely stained-glass windows, and a two-tone checkerboard floor of marble.

On the north side of Parque Central, the forecourt of the municipality office features the Monumento Nacional a la Madre, an endearing bronze sculpture of a mother and child by Miguela Brenes. Next door, the colonial-era **Casa de la Cultura** occupies the home of former president Alfredo González Flores (1877–1962). It is now an art gallery and a tiny museum. Nearby is an interesting circular fortress tower, El Fortín, built in 1876.

A popular attraction in the lively town of Santa Barbara de Heredia, northwest of Heredia, is the **Ark Herb Farm** with its extensive orchards and gardens. The farm is also an exporter of medicinal herbs.

Casa de la Cultura

🅐 Calle and Ave Central 📞 2261-4485 🕐 8am-5:30pm Mon-Fri, 9am-5pm Sat

Ark Herb Farm

♦ ✪ 👜 🅐 Santa Barbara de Heredia, 3 miles (5 km) NW of Heredia 🕐 7am-4pm Mon-Sat, 9am-3pm Sun 🅦 arkherbfarm.com

STAY

Finca Rosa Blanca
Comfort and high sustainability, overlooking coffee estates.

🅐 D3 🅐 Santa Bárbara de Heredia 🅦 fincarosablanca.com

💲💲💲

Hotel Chalet Tirol
Chalet-style villas amid centuries-old cypresses and beautiful gardens.

🅐 D3 🅐 San Rafael de Heredia 📞 2267-6222

💲💲💲

Dantica Cloud Forest Lodge
Cute, eco-friendly bungalows, perfectly located for birders.

🅐 E4 🅐 San Gerardo de Dota 🅦 dantica.com

💲💲💲

Cooling off at a Tapantí-Macizo National Park wild swimming spot

24

Parque Nacional Tapantí-Macizo la Muerte

E4 **5.5 miles (9 km) S of Orosí** **2771-3155** **To Orosí, then by jeep-taxi** **8am–4pm daily**

South of the Orosí Valley, the vibrantly green Tapantí-Macizo National Park protects 225 sq miles (583 sq km) of the Talamanca Mountains. Ranging in elevation from 3,950 ft to 8,350 ft (1,200–2,550 m), it features diverse flora, from lower montane rainforest to montane dwarf forest on the upper slopes. The park is deluged with rains for most of the year, which feed the fast-flowing rivers rushing through it; February to April are the least rainy months. Spectacularly rich in wildlife, the park has animals such as anteaters, jaguars, monkeys, tapirs, and even otters. More than 260 bird species inhabit its thick forests. Resplendent quetzals frequent the thickets near the ranger station, which has a small nature display.

Well-marked trails lace the rugged terrain. A particularly pleasant and easy hike is

WHITE-WATER RAFTING

Costa Rica boasts perfect white-water-rafting rivers. The best of the runnable rivers churn between the mountainous Central Highlands to the Caribbean, interspersed by stretches of calm water.

Across the country professional operators guide groups downstream in large rubber dinghies on trips lasting half a day to a week. Whether expert or novice, trips make lots of stops to refuel, explore, or break overnight.

→ Adrenaline junkies paddling the rapids on an organized rafting trip

Sendero La Catarata, which leads to a waterfall. Fishing in the park is permitted from April to October.

25

Turrialba

△E3 🚗27 miles (44 km) E of Cartago 🚌

This pleasant regional center squats in a broad valley on the banks of the Río Turrialba at 2,130 ft (650 m) above sea level, against the base of Volcán Turrialba *(p151)*. It was once an important transportation hub midway between San José and the Caribbean; rusting railroad tracks serve as reminders of the days when the Atlantic Railroad thrived. There is little of special interest in the town, but it

Did You Know?

Visitors can swim under the 130-ft- (40-m-) high Aquiares waterfall in Turrialba.

↑ Rappelling down one of the many waterfalls around Turrialba

serves as an agreeable base for exploring the surrounding area, and for kayaking and rafting trips on the Río Reventazón and Río Pacuare. The valley bottom southeast of Turrialba is filled by the 1-sq-mile (2.5-sq-km) Lake Angostura, created by the building of a hydroelectric dam. It lures varied waterfowl and is a water sports center, although it is gradually being choked by water hyacinths. Below the dam, Class III–IV rapids run the Río Reventazón (Exploding River). It is fabulously scenic, as is the nearby Río Pacuare, which is also favored by rafters. East of the town, there are good hiking trails through forest.

SHOP

Señor y Señora Ese
A huge artisan store where most of the handcrafted items, including jewelry, are made on site.

△D3 🏠Villa Bonita de Alajuela 📞2441-8333

Molas y Café
This well-stocked souvenir shop sells its own Trilogy brand of coffee.

△D3 🏠Hwy 3 near Farmer and Oxcart, Atenas 📞8348-2121

Dantica Galerí de Arte
Located in the lodge of the same name *(p138)*, this well-lit gallery sells high-quality Indigenous crafts from across Central America.

△E4 🏠San Gerardo de Dota 🌐dantica.com

Two of the finest rafting destinations are the Río Reventazón and Río Pacuare. Flowing through the Orosí and Turrialba Valleys, the Río Reventazón has separate sections ranging from Class II (easy) to V (very difficult). In the east, torrential Río Pacuare takes thrillseekers on adrenaline-packed rides along wildlife-rich gorges and pounding rapids.

↑ Rafting past forested banks on both sides in a calmer section of the river

TOP 3 WHITE-WATER RIVERS FOR BEGINNERS

Río Sarapiquí
Ideal for all levels, these rapids go through lush tropical rain forest.

Río Corobicí
Easy rapids and lengthy still sections make it perfect for bringing the kids.

Río Reventazón
Something for everyone, with calm stretches and long, roiling rapids runs.

26

Parque Nacional Volcán Irazú

🅰 E3 📍19 miles (30 km) N of Cartago 🚌 From Ave 2, Calles 1/3, San José (8am daily) 🕐 8am–4pm daily 🌐 sinac.go.cr

Encircling the upper slopes of Volcán Irazú, this 7-sq-mile (18-sq-km) park was established in 1955. The name Irazú is derived from the indigenous word *istarú*, which means "mountain of thunder" – an appropriate moniker for Costa Rica's historically most active volcano. The first written

↑ Views of Irazú's crater lake, reached by rail-lined paths *(inset)*

reference to an eruption was in 1723. Several devastating explosions occurred between 1917 and 1921, and the volcano famously erupted on March 13, 1963, when US President John F Kennedy was in the country to attend the Summit of Central American Presidents.

At 11,260 ft (3,430 m), the cloud-covered Irazú is also Costa Rica's highest volcano. At the summit a viewing platform lets visitors gaze into a 985-ft (300-m) deep, 0.5-mile (1-km) wide crater, containing a pea-green lake (which sometimes dries up). Four other craters can be accessed, but there are active fumaroles, and the marked trails should be followed.

The lunar landscape of the summit includes a great ash plain called Playa Hermosa. Hardy vegetation, such as myrtle and the large-leaved "poor man's umbrella," maintains a foothold against acidic emissions in the bitter cold. Wildlife is scarce, although it is possible to spot birds such as the sooty robin and endemic volcano junco. The **Museo**

Vulcanológico, below the park, has displays that explain the action of volcanoes and profile the activity and ecology of Irazú.

Museo Vulcanológico

 📍1 mile (1.6 km) below the park entrance 🕐 9am–3:30pm daily 🌐 noche buenacr.com

---

27

San Gerardo de Dota

🅰 E4 📍5.5 miles (9 km) W of Pan-Am Hwy at Km 80 🚌 to Km 80, then hike or arrange a transfer (call 8367-8141)

One of the best sites in Costa Rica for quetzal-watching, this small community is tucked into the bottom of a steep valley furrowed by Río Savegre. Go down a switchback from the Pan-Am

---

GREAT VIEW
Peak Viewing

Although Volcán Irazú is often blanketed by fog, the cloud line tends to hover below the summit, which basks in brilliant sunshine. Arriving early increases the likelihood of clear weather and good views.

Gerardo de Dota. Various fruits grow in profusion in orchards, interspersed by meadows and centenary oaks.

About 22 miles (35 km) of graded trails crisscross the forest, with options from very easy to technically challenging. Activities include guided treks from the frigid heights of Cerro Frío (Cold Mountain) at 11,400 ft (3,450 m) to San Gerardo de Dota at 7,200 ft (2,200 m). Other trails lead along the banks of the gurgling river, stocked with rainbow trout.

Savegre Hotel Natural Reserve

Ⓢ ☺ ⏹ 7 miles (12 km) S of Pan American Hwy ⓦ savegre.com

---

28 ⌖

Parque Nacional Volcán Turrialba

Ⓐ E3 ⏹ 21 miles (34 km) NW of Turrialba 🚌 To Santa Cruz, then by taxi 🕐 Dec-Apr: 5am-10am daily; May-Nov: 8am-noon daily ⓦ sinac.go.cr

Established in 1955, the Turrialba Volcano National Park protects 5 sq miles (13 sq km) of cloud-forest-covered land. The easternmost volcano in Costa Rica, the 10,950-ft- (3,340-m-) high Turrialba was dormant for more than a century following a period of violent activity in the 1860s. In January 2010, it became active again. The park was closed to visitors between 2014 and 2020 because of eruptions. Some areas of the park near the volcano are still sometimes off-limits to visitors; check the website before visiting. The exclusion zone can vary in radius depending on the level of activity.

The volcano's name comes from the Huetar Indian words *turiri* and *abá*, which together mean "river of fire." Local legend says that a girl named Cira, lost while exploring, was found by a young man from a rival tribe, and they fell in love. When the girl's enraged father eventually discovered the two lovers and prepared to kill the young suitor, a tall column of smoke plumed from Turrialba, signifying divine assent.

Dirt roads go to within a few miles of the summit, which is then accessible by trails. Stamina is required for the switchback hike to the top. From there, in clear weather, it is possible to see the Cordillera Central and the Caribbean coast. A trail also descends to the floor of the largest crater. Access is granted only during inactive phases.

There are no public facilities or transportation in the park, but travel agencies in the town of Turrialba can provide transfers and guided tours.

VOLCANIC ACTIVITY AT TURRIALBA

The Turrialba volcano has a long history of intermittent activity. In 2010 it broke a century-long slumber and has been active ever since. Emissions of ash and lava occur daily, and have forced periodic evacuations of nearby settlements and long-term closure of the Parque Nacional Volcán Turrialba. After closing early in 2014, the park was finally reopened to visitors in December 2020.

Highway to reach the hamlet, which was first settled in 1954 by Don Efraín Chacón and his family. Today, the Chacóns' **Savegre Hotel Natural Reserve** protects around 1.5 sq miles (4 sq km) of cloud forest and houses the Quetzal Education Research Center (QERC). This study center for quetzal ecology is the tropical campus of the Southern Nazarene University of Oklahoma. Quetzals are most abundant in April to May, their nesting season. More than 170 other bird species are present seasonally.

Dramatic scenery, crisp air, and blissful solitude reward the few travelers who take the time to make the sharp descent into San

A DRIVING TOUR
LA RUTA DE LOS SANTOS

CENTRAL HIGHLANDS

La Ruta de los Santos

Locator Map
For more detail see p128

Length 95 miles (153 km) **Stopping-off points** Stop for a coffee at the well-run Beneficio Coopedota in San Marcos de Tarrazú or La Casona de Sara in Santa María

South of San José, the Cerro de Escazú rises steeply from Desamparados to the town of Aserrí. Twisting roads then pass through San Gabriel, San Pablo de León Cortés, San Marcos de Tarrazú, Santa María de Dota, and San Cristóbal Sur in the steep-sided coffee country known as Tarrazú. These off-the-beaten-track villages – named for saints Gabriel, Paul, Mark, Mary, and Christopher – give this fabulously scenic drive through verdant landscapes its apt name, "Route of the Saints."

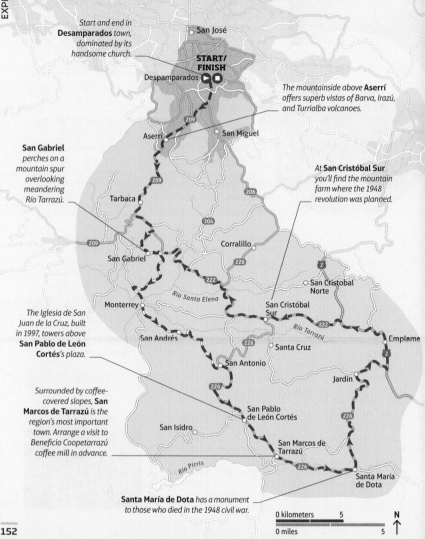

Start and end in **Desamparados** town, dominated by its handsome church.

START/FINISH

The mountainside above **Aserrí** offers superb vistas of Barva, Irazú, and Turrialba volcanoes.

San Gabriel perches on a mountain spur overlooking meandering Río Tarrazú.

At **San Cristóbal Sur** you'll find the mountain farm where the 1948 revolution was planned.

The Iglesia de San Juan de la Cruz, built in 1997, towers above **San Pablo de León Cortés**'s plaza.

Surrounded by coffee-covered slopes, **San Marcos de Tarrazú** is the region's most important town. Arrange a visit to Beneficio Coopetarrazú coffee mill in advance.

Santa María de Dota has a monument to those who died in the 1948 civil war.

0 kilometers 5
0 miles 5

N ↑

Spreading coffee berries to dry
in the heat of the day outside ↑
San Marcos de Tarrazú

CENTRAL PACIFIC AND SOUTHERN NICOYA

The Nicoya Peninsula and central Pacific coastline were settled by the Indigenous Matambú people around 500 AD. Escaping slavery from southern Mexico, they were drawn to the area by the wealth of the ocean and fertile hills. Spanish conquistadors explored the region in the early 16th century and established short-lived settlements. These fell victim to tropical disease and the ferocious resistance of the Matambú. However, the Indigenous population was ultimately overwhelmed by Spanish forces. Founded in 1522, Puntarenas was the principal city of the region by the early 1800s. It flourished due to the 19th century coffee trade, and developed into the nation's main port for coffee exports to Europe. In the early decades of the 20th century, bananas were planted along the narrow coastal plain farther south. They were replaced in the 1970s by African oil palms, which extend for miles between the shore and forested mountains. Much of the region, notably Southern Nicoya, was heavily denuded during the last century, but major conservation and reforestation efforts are now extending the protected areas.

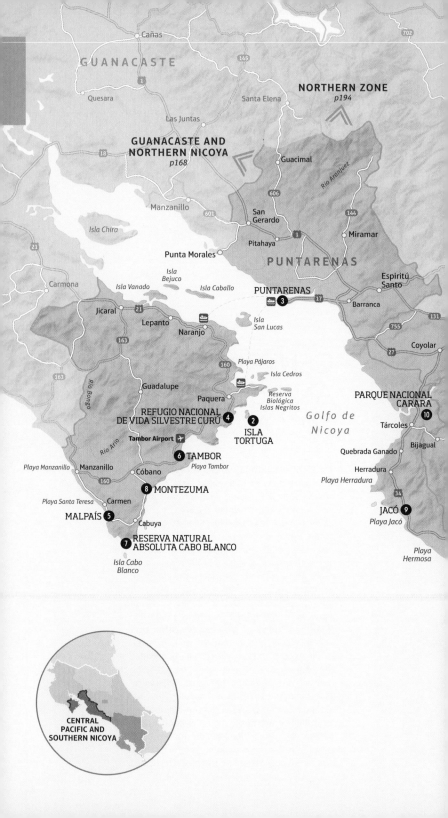

CENTRAL PACIFIC AND SOUTHERN NICOYA

Must See
① Parque Nacional Manuel Antonio

Experience More
② Isla Tortuga
③ Puntarenas
④ Refugio Nacional de Vida Silvestre Curú
⑤ Malpaís
⑥ Tambor
⑦ Reserva Natural Absoluta Cabo Blanco
⑧ Montezuma
⑨ Jacó
⑩ Parque Nacional Carara
⑪ Boca Damas
⑫ Santa Juana Mountain Tour
⑬ Valle del Río Savegre
⑭ Quepos

❶ ⊗ ⊗ ⊡

PARQUE NACIONAL MANUEL ANTONIO

🗺D5 🚗100 miles (160 km) S of San José and 5 miles (8 km) S of Quepos
📞2777-5185 🕐7am–4pm Wed-Mon (limited to 600 visitors a day)

Established in 1972, Parque Nacional Manuel Antonio is Costa Rica's smallest national park, covering a mere 6 sq miles (16 sq km). It is also the country's most popular, with five equally beautiful beaches which are safe for swimming.

Named for a Spanish conquistador, and flanked by the ocean and forested hills, this beautiful park has remarkable biodiversity, with flowing rivers, abundant wildlife, and magnificent beaches. Clearly marked trails crisscross the rainforest and rocky headlands that back the white-sand beaches, and visitors are almost guaranteed to spot cute coatis, trees hung with sloths, and raucous toucans and scarlet macaws flitting about the canopy. This is one of the most visited parks in the nation: although there is a limit on the daily number of visitors, tour-bus loads of people often pack out the park by midmorning.

Enjoying an evening paddle as the sun sets over the park ↑

Wildlife spotting in an organized group along one of the well-marked hiking trails ↑

← A tiny squirrel monkey, native to the park, peeking over a branch

THE MANCHINEEL

Called *manzanillo*, or "beach apple," by locals, the manchineel tree is quite common on the beaches at Manuel Antonio National Park and can be rather unpleasant for unwary visitors seeking its shade. This evergreen species (*Hippomane manicinella*), identified by its short trunk and bright green elliptical leaves, is very toxic. Contact with the sap and bark will inflame the skin, leaving welts in more serious cases, while the small yellow apple-like fruit is poisonous. Moreover, if its wood is burnt, the smoke is an irritant to the lungs, and causes respiratory problems.

Did You Know?

Crocodiles swim across the bay when they migrate between the park's estuaries.

The park's idyllic white sands and turquoise sea backed by rainforest ↑

EXPERIENCE MORE

2 🍴 🍽

Isla Tortuga

🅰C4 🚤2 miles (3 km) SE of Curú 🚢From Puntarenas

This sun-bleached island – actually twin islets, Isla Tolinga and unoccupied Isla Alcatraz – offshore from Curú is run as a privately owned nature reserve of just over 1 sq mile (3 sq km). Isla Tolinga, which has no overnight accommodation, is very popular for day visits.

Isla Tortuga is rimmed by sugar-white sands lapped by startlingly blue waters and fringed by coconut palms that lend their shade over the beach. The hilly interior is covered by deciduous forest, accessed by a short, steep trail leading to the highest point of the island (570 ft/175 m). Signs point out rare hardwoods, such as cholo pelao trees.

The preferred activity here is to laze in a hammock while sipping the island cocktail, *coco loco*, a heady mix of rum,

coconut milk, and coconut liqueur, served in a hand-cut coconut shell. The warm waters are great for snorkeling. There are no jet skis to break the blissful silence, but visitors can choose from an array of other water sports.

Trips out to the island were pioneered in 1975 by Calypso Cruises, which now operates a 70-ft (21-m) motorized, high-speed catamaran that departs from Puntarenas. A number of other companies offer similar excursions, and typically also provide hotel transfers, round-trip transportation, and a tasty buffet lunch. The 90-minute journey is its own reward – dolphins and whales can be frequently spotted. Try to visit midweek, as weekends can get crowded.

3

Puntarenas

🅰C3 🚤75 miles (120 km) W of San José 🚌

Often seen as a provincial backwater, the sleepy city of Puntarenas (Sandy Point) was once an important port. First settled in 1522 by the Spanish, Puntarenas later became the main shipping point for coffee beans, brought from the highlands in *carretas* (oxcarts). City fortunes waned in 1890, once the Atlantic Railroad was built, and many of its wooden structures are now dilapidated. Today this slightly down-at-heel town exists on fishing, as attested to by rows of well-worn fishing boats moored at the wharves.

> The preferred activity here is to laze in a hammock while sipping the island cocktail, *coco loco* (rum, coconut milk, and coconut liqueur).

←

Arriving at Isla Tortuga, an almost picture-perfect island paradise

It remains the main gateway for excursions to Isla Tortuga, as well as for ferries to Paquera and Naranjo, on the Peninsula de Nicoya.

The town occupies a 3-mile-(5-km-) long, thin peninsula fringed on the south by a beach. A broad estuary runs along the north shore, where extensive mangrove forests are home to waterfowl, such as roseate spoonbills, storks,

↑ Pelicans against the setting sun in Puntarenas harbour

🔍 HIDDEN GEM
Isla San Lucas

From afar, this idyllic palm-shaded isle belies a grim history as a penal colony. Hop on a boat from Puntarenas (www.bayislandcruises.com) and spend a day pondering carefully preserved prison-era graffiti as well as spotting wildlife.

---

pelicans, and frigate birds. Puntarenas is favored as a *balneario* (bathing resort) by Josefinos who flock to the seafront boulevard, Paseo de los Turistas. The main draw in town is the **Museo Histórico Marino**, situated in the former 19th-century city jail. The museum has displays on Indigenous cultures, maritime history, and the coffee era.

Museo Histórico Marino

☺ 🅿 🚹 Paseo de los Turistas
☎ 2661-1394 ⏰ 9am–4:30pm Tue–Sun

4

Refugio Nacional de Vida Silvestre Curú

🅰 C4 🚗 2 miles (3 km) S of Paquera 🚌 Paquera-Cobano ⏰ 7am–4pm daily, by appt only 🌐 curu.org

Part of a much larger privately owned hacienda, the seldom-visited Curú National Wildlife Refuge has been set up to protect five distinct habitats that extend inland from Golfo Curú.

The majority of the hilly reserve is tropical deciduous and semi-deciduous forest populated by capuchin and howler monkeys, anteaters, agoutis, and sloths, as well as several species of wild cats and more than 220 species of birds. Endangered spider monkeys have also been successfully reintroduced. Since the number of visitors is low, it is possible to spot

---

animals more easily than at many other refuges. Marked trails provide access.

Three beautiful beaches – Playa Colorada, Playa Curú, and Playa Quesera – are tucked inside the fold of green headlands and extend along 3 miles (5 km) of coastline. Hawksbill and olive ridley turtles crawl ashore at night to nest in the sand. Whales and dolphins can sometimes be seen swimming in the warm offshore waters, while the mangrove swamps and lagoons along the Río Curú are good for spotting caimans.

SHOP

Dantica Gallery

Remarkable jewelry, hammocks, and crafts made by Indigenous peoples from across the Americas, including Boruca masks and Wounaan baskets.

🅰 C4 🚹 Plaza Jacó Walk, Jacó 🌐 danticagallery.com

The Cigar Shop

Locally grown Costa Rican tobacco and a Cuban-born *torcedora*'s skill combine to produce fine hand-rolled cigars. As well as the cigars made on site, you can find Cuban cigars here.

🅰 D4 🚹 Quepos
☎ 2777-2208

Regáleme

This gallery at Hotel Sí Como No offers a fine selection of quality art, crafts, and tchotchkes, including gorgeous hardwood bowls, naïve art, and gold jewelry.

🅰 D5 🚹 Manuel Antonio
☎ 2777-7707

5

Malpaís

Ⓐ B4 **Ⓐ** 6 miles (10 km) NW of Montezuma **🚌** From Cóbano **Ⓦ** malpais.net

Its name may mean "bad land," but the Malpaís area's Pacific shoreline is unsurpassed for its rugged beauty. Two decades ago, the region was unknown, but today it has become a famed surfers' paradise.

Named for their respective beaches, three contiguous communities are strung along the dirt road that fringes the shore. Relaxed to a fault, they are characterized by colorful hotels, restaurants, and bars. The main hamlet is Carmen, from where the road runs 2 miles (3 km) south to the fishing hamlet of Malpaís itself. Beyond Malpaís, where vultures perch on fishing boats, the beach ends amid tidepools and fantastically sculpted rocks near the entrance to Cabo Blanco. A 4WD is required.

The best surf beach is Playa Santa Teresa, north of Carmen and merging with *playas* that are virtually uninhabited: Los Suecos, Hermosa, and Manzanillo.

6

Tambor

Ⓐ C4 **Ⓐ** 11 miles (18 km) SW of Paquera **🚌**

A small, laid-back fishing village with a wide silver-gray beach, Tambor lines the aptly named Bahía Ballena (Whale Bay), where whales gather in mid-winter. Palm-fringed sands extend from the bay north to mangrove swamps. The village itself can be sleepy, but two upscale resorts just outside town attract a large number of foreign beachgoers and Josefinos, most of whom fly in to the local airstrip. Visitors can play golf or tennis for a fee at the **Tango Mar Resort**, which has a 9-hole golf course, or at the **Los Delfines Golf and Country Club**, which has an 18-hole course. **Seascape Kayak Tours** offers guided sea kayaking trips of the bay and coastal mangroves from October to May.

Tango Mar Resort

Ⓣ Ⓓ **Ⓐ** Quizales Beach, Tambor **Ⓦ** tangomar.com

Los Delfines Golf and Country Club

Ⓣ Ⓓ Ⓖ **Ⓐ** 1 mile (1.6 km) E of Tambor **Ⓦ** delfines.com

Seascape Kayak Tours

Ⓦ seascapekayaktours.com

7

Reserva Natural Absoluta Cabo Blanco

Ⓐ B4 **Ⓐ** 6 miles (10 km) W of Montezuma **Ⓒ** 2642-0093 **🚌** Montezuma-Cabuya **Ⓞ** 8am–4pm Wed–Sun and public hols

Established in 1963 as the nation's first protected area, the 4-sq-mile (10-sq-km) Cabo Blanco reserve owes its genesis to the tireless work of the late Olof Wessberg and his wife, Karen Morgenson; they

↓ The serene Playa Santa Teresa, Malpaís, a popular destination for surfers *(inset)*

↑ Cooling off in one of the waterfall basins at Montezuma

also helped set up the Costa Rican National Park Service. Cabo Blanco was initially an "absolute" reserve, off-limits to all visitors, but today there is access to the eastern part of the tropical forests that cover the hilly tip of the Nicoya Peninsula. About 85 percent of the reserve is covered by rejuvenated secondary forest and pockets of lowland tropical forest. Here, there are many monkeys, as well as anteaters, coatis, and deer. The 3-mile- (5-km-) long Sendero Sueco trail leads to beautiful Playa Cabo Blanco and other beaches along the shore. Cabo Blanco is accessed from the community of Cabuya, a mile (1.6 km) along a rough road. It can also be entered at Malpaís. Tour operators nationwide offer excursions to the reserve.

___

8

Montezuma

🅰️B4 🄰20 miles (32 km) W of Paquera 🚌From Paquera

A favorite with budget travelers, this offbeat beach community has a laidback lifestyle, ocean vistas and beaches, and hip yet unpretentious bars. The compact village is tucked beneath precipitous hills and opens onto a rocky cove. Two superb beaches – Playa Montezuma and Playa Grande – can be found to the east, shaded by tall palms and backed by thickly forested mountains. Swimmers should be aware that there are dangerous riptides. Sliding between treetops on the **Sun Trail Tour** is a safe, fun, and adrenaline-boosting activity. Sun Trails, who run the tour, also offer activities such as fishing, ATV riding, hikes, and scooter racing. Clambering up the waterfalls to the west of the village is unsafe; instead, cool off in the pools at the base of them. **Rainsong Wildlife Sanctuary** rehabilitates confiscated illegal pets and injured animals, and reintroduces endangered species to the wild. Volunteers are welcome.

Sun Trail Tour
🄰1 mile (1.6 km) W of Montezuma 🄰Entry by tour only: 9am, 1pm, & 3pm daily 🆆suntrails.com

Rainsong Wildlife Sanctuary
🄰5 miles (8 km) W of Montezuma 🆆rainsong sanctuary.com

EAT

Néctar
Gourmet Asian-Pacific-inspired dishes.

🅰️B4 🄰Santa Teresa 🆆florblanca.com/nectar

💲💲💲

___

Taco Bar
Tacos and more, plus super lemonades.

🅰️C4 🄰Jacó 📞2203-6989

💲💲💲

___

El Gran Escape
Popular with locals for its seafood and live music.

🅰️D4 🄰Quepos 🆆elgranescape quepos.com

💲💲💲

___

Arbol
Divine fusion dishes in a romantic setting.

🅰️D5 🄰Manuel Antonio 🆆arbolrestaurant.com

💲💲💲

STAY

Villa Caletas
Deluxe boutique stays in a sublime mountaintop setting with sea views.

C4 **Playa Herradura** **hotelvillacaletas.com**

$$$

Ylang Ylang Resort
Beachfront romance with a pool and a fabulous restaurant.

B4 **Montezuma** **ylangylangbeach resort.com**

$$$

El Mono Azul
Popular budget hotel in a great ridgetop location.

D5 **Manuel Antonio** **hotelmonoazul.com**

$$$

Hotel Sí Como No
Whimsical hilltop hotel with a pool and a movie theater.

D5 **Manuel Antonio** **sicomono.com**

$$$

9
Jacó

C4 **40 miles (65 km) S of Puntarenas**

Thriving on the surfer trade and flocks of Canadian "snowbirds" that descend each winter, Jacó has evolved as the nation's largest and most party-oriented beach resort – even though its gray sands are rather unremarkable, the sea is usually a murky brown from silt washed down by rivers, and riptides make swimming unsafe. There's no shortage of things to do, however – from hiking to all-terrain vehicle (ATV) tours – and the nightlife is lively. Many of the nation's top surfers live here, although as a surf center, Jacó is best for beginners. Many surf shops supply rent out boards and the Jacó Surf School offers one-off lessons, surf camps, and packages.

Outside town, the **Pacific Rainforest Aerial Tram** takes you on a 90-minute guided ride through the treetops on silent open-air gondolas. The modified ski lifts skim the forest floor, soar above giant trees, pass waterfalls, and give fabulous views along the Pacific coast. There are four departures daily, and booking ahead is

> **Species from as far afield as the Amazon are abundant, including the endangered spider monkey and the poison-dart frog.**

advisable. Guided nature walks such as the Poison-Dart Frog Trail, are also offered.

There's safe swimming, plus snorkeling, scuba diving, and sportfishing at quieter Playa Herradura, a broad bay north of Jacó. South of Jacó, Playa Hermosa is served by dedicated surf hostels. Sand bars provide consistently good breaks swelling in from deep waters offshore.

Pacific Rainforest Aerial Tram
 2 miles (3 km) E of Jacó **9am-5pm daily** **rainforestadventure.com**

10
Parque Nacional Carara

C4 **31 miles (50 km) SE of Puntarenas** **From San José and Jacó** **May-Nov: 8am-4pm daily; Dec-Apr: 7am-4pm daily** **sinac.go.cr**

Despite its relatively small size – 20 sq miles (52 sq km) – Carara National Park offers some of the most diverse wildlife viewing in Costa Rica. Species from as far afield as the Amazon are abundant, including the endangered spider monkey and the poison-dart frog. The birding here is spectacular, and the near-ubiquitous scarlet macaw is a major draw. They can be seen on their twice-daily migration between the

← Sportfishing boats moored at the Playa Herredura, marina north of Jacó

↑ Looking for macaws *(inset)* from a canopy bridge in the Carara national park

of local tour operators offer crocodile safaris by boat from Tárcoles, 2 miles (3 km) south-west of Carara.

forest and nearby coastal mangroves. Carara's lower elevation forests have easy-to-walk trails that begin at the roadside visitor center; the longest is 5 miles (8 km). Guides can be hired to access more remote pre-Columbian sites and several tour operators in San José arrange day visits.

Carara is a Huetar word for crocodile, and these reptiles are easily seen from the high-way as they bask on the banks of the Río Tárcoles. A number

INSIDER TIP
Croc Your World

Avoid crocodile safaris that lure the crocodiles with chicken; this disrupts the animals' behavior. Eco-Jungle Cruises *(www.eco junglecruises.com)* respect the animal's natural ways.

⑪

Boca Damas

🄰D4 **🄰43 miles (70 km) SE of Jacó** ▣

Crisscrossed by countless sloughs and channels, this vast *manglare* (mangrove) complex extends along the shoreline between the towns of Parrita and Quepos, at the estuary of Río Damas. Coatis, pumas, white-faced monkeys, and several species of snakes inhabit the dense forests. Crocodiles and caimans lurk in the tannin-stained waters. Stilt-legged shorebirds and boat-billed herons, with their curious keel-shaped beaks, pick among the mudflats in search of molluscs.

Tour operators in Quepos offer kayaking excursions. Guides offer boat trips from the small dock at Damas.

⑫

Santa Juana Mountain Tour

🄰D4 **🄰8 miles (11 km) SE of Hwy 34, 32 miles (50 km) S of Jacó** ▣ **Organized transfers** ⓦ **sicomono. com/toursantajuana**

This educational tour travels deep into the Fila Chonta Mountains inland of Quepos. It departs early in the morning from the Sí Como No wildlife resort in Manuel Antonio National Park, although pickups can be arranged from other hotels. The tour centers on a remote rural community at the heart of an ecological project to engage local families in ecotourism while preserving rural customs.

There are hiking trails and a river walk, with waterfalls and pools for bathing and cooling off. Participants visit animal-husbandry, butterfly-breeding, and reforestation projects; learn about snakes at a serpentarium; and visit an authentic sugar mill powered by oxen. You can even help pick coffee and citrus, or fish for tilapia. A guided horseback ride is another option. A hearty lunch is served at a restaurant offering sensational views.

13

Valle del Río Savegre

🅰E4 🚗41 miles (66 km) E of Quepos 🚌From Quepos

Cutting inland into the Fila San Bosco Mountains, the Río Savegre Valley is covered by plantations of African oil palms at its lower levels. Farther up the valley lies the rural community of El Silencio, where the local farmers' cooperative operates the **El Silencio Rural Tourism Lodge**. It offers cabin-style accommodation, plus horses for rides down rustic trails, and has a wildlife rescue center with macaws, deer, and monkeys.

Farther along the same road, up a rugged track where a 4WD is needed, **Rafiki Safari Lodge**, set atop a ridge over-looking the Savegre, makes a great base for hiking, birding, horseback riding, and exhila-rating white-water rafting and kayaking trips on stretches of the Río Savegre.

El Silencio Rural Tourism Lodge
🕒 🚗25 miles (40 km) SE of Quepos 🌐turismoruralcr. com/el-silencio/

Rafiki Safari Lodge
🕒 🚗34 miles (55 km) E of Quepos 🌐rafikisafari.com

14

Quepos

🅰D4 🚗34 miles (55 km) SE of Jacó 🚕🚌 🌐quepo landia.com

Traditionally a game fishing base and center for the production of African palm oil, Quepos has blossomed as a tourist center and a gateway to Manuel Antonio National Park. The town buzzes both by day and at night, when its numerous bars and restau-rants come alive.

South of Quepos, a road winds over headlands to the hamlet of Manuel Antonio, fronted by Playa Espadilla, a wide scimitar of gray sand. Restaurants and hotels line the route, including El Avión, a lively bar set inside and under the wings of a Fairchild C-123 transport plane. Nearby, **Greentique Wildlife Refuge**, run by the Sí Como No hotel (p164) opposite, offers easy walks and is teeming with different animals and phenom-enal birdlife.

The Río Naranjo Valley runs east of Quepos into the Fila Nara Mountains. The ruins of a Spanish mission stand by the roadside. White-water rafting trips are a popular excursion from Quepos. **Tucanes Tours** offer a range of adventure

programs including rafting, kayaking, horseriding, whale-watching, and snorkeling.

Greentique Wildlife Refuge
🕒🚶 🚗1 mile (1.6 km) S of Quepos 🕗8am–4pm daily (night tour at 5:20pm) 🌐sicomono.com/tours

Tucanes Tours
🕒 🚗Marina Pez Vela, Quepos 🌐tucanestours.com

DRINK

Habaneros
Sunset spot with great Margaritas and tacos.

🅰B4 🚗Playa Santa Teresa 📞2640-1106

Cuban Republik Disco Lounge
Cocktails galore, plus DJ anthems after 11pm.

🅰D4 🚗Quepos 📞2777-7438

Jacó Blu Beach Club
Right on the sand, with DJs, amazing cocktails, and a great atmosphere.

🅰C4 🚗Ave Pastor Diaz, Jacó 📞2643-1179

← A laid-back day on palm-shaded Playa Espadilla

Settling in for the day on →
a small sportfishing boat
in the turquoise-colored seas

SPORTFISHING ON THE PACIFIC COAST

The ultimate draw for the game-fishing enthusiast, Costa Rica's Pacific waters witness new International Game Fish Association records every year.

A wide variety of game fish await the keen angler on Costa Rica's Pacific coast year-round. In the wet season (May-November), fishing is best off Northern Nicoya. In the dry season (December-April), head farther toward the south to the sholes of Southern Nicoya and around Quepos. Apart from hiring out boats, charter shops and fishing lodges can also arrange fishing licenses for visiting anglers. Sportfishing vessels often travel 20 miles (32 km) or more from shore to find game fish, and a strict catch-and-release policy is usually followed by operators in Costa Rica.

↑ An angler holstered to the
boat catching a big one

DEEP SEA FISH

Yellowfin Tuna
These extremely powerful, warm-water fish weigh in at up to 350 lb (160 kg).

Wahoo
Long, sleek, and explosively fast fish found in northern waters.

Dorado
Also called dolphinfish or mahimahi, their scales flash in a spectrum of colors.

Sailfish
These hard-fighting giants leap spectacularly when hooked.

Blue Marlins
The "Bull of the Ocean": females can weigh up to 1,000 lb (455 kg).

GUANACASTE AND NORTHERN NICOYA

A chain of volcanoes runs across this region, creating vast fertile plains to the east, while the rugged Pacific shore to the west is serrated by deep bays. Attracted by the abundance of natural resources, the matriarchal Matambú people established fishing communities around 500 AD; they later moved inland, leaving a legacy of superb artisan pottery that continues in the Guaitíl area. Guanacaste was colonized by Spanish *sabaneros* (cowboys) in the mid-1500s, under the rule of Nicaragua, marking the start of a proliferation of grand haciendas, many of which can still be seen around Santa Cruz and Liberia. In 1825 Guanacaste seceded from Nicaragua and joined Costa Rica; the resulting border disputes remained unresolved until the boundary treaty of 1896. Cattle culture caused heavy deforestation throughout the 20th century. A slow trickle of conservation efforts, beginning in the 1970s, became a flood by the 1990s; the region now contains four national parks, as well as wildlife refuges and other nature reserves.

GUANACASTE AND NORTHERN NICOYA

Must Sees

① Monteverde and Santa Elena
② Parque Nacional Santa Rosa

Experience More

③ Tilarán
④ Cañas
⑤ Reserva Biológica Lomas Barbudal
⑥ Zona Protectora Volcán Miravalles
⑦ Parque Nacional Palo Verde
⑧ Parque Nacional Rincón de la Vieja
⑨ Bahía Salinas
⑩ Liberia
⑪ Parque Nacional Guanacaste
⑫ Bahía Culebra
⑬ Playa Flamingo
⑭ Tamarindo
⑮ Nosara
⑯ Playas del Coco
⑰ Islita
⑱ Refugio Nacional de Vida Silvestre Ostional
⑲ Sámara
⑳ Nicoya
㉑ Santa Cruz
㉒ Guaitíl
㉓ Parque Nacional Barra Honda

Pacific Ocean

GUANACASTE AND NORTHERN NICOYA

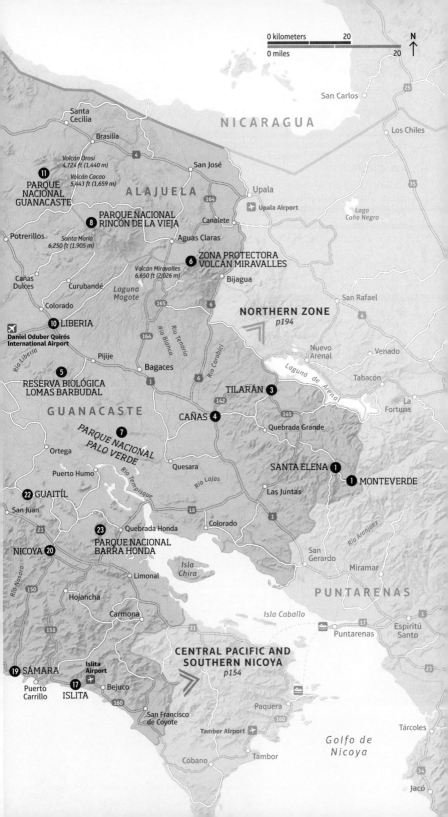

MONTEVERDE AND SANTA ELENA

🅰C3 🏠42 miles (68 km) N of Puntarenas, 22 miles (35 km) uphill from the Pan-Am Hwy 🚌To Santa Elena and up to Monteverde Cloud Forest Biological Reserve

Cool and verdant Monteverde has its fair share of interesting sights, many of which are spread out along the winding dirt road that slopes gently upward from the surprisingly bustling town of Santa Elena and into the Monteverde Cloud Forest Biological Reserve, with other smaller reserves tucked away off side roads.

Known worldwide for its unique cloud forest reserve, which helped promote Costa Rica's reputation for ecotourism, Monteverde boasts a pastoral alpine setting at an elevation of 4,600 ft (1,400 m), high up in the heart of the Cordillera de Tilarán. To the northwest is Santa Elena, which is the main commercial center. Several other reserves, incorporated within the Zona Protectora Arenal-Monteverde, are to be found in the area. Monteverde's fame has spawned all manner of "green" initiatives, including a variety of tours that permit visitors a monkey's-eye view of the forest canopy, which remains pristine, even in the face of these ever-increasing services and attractions. Walking is a pleasure, but heavily trafficked roads can be muddy or dusty, depending on the weather. Hotels and restaurants line the steeper dirt road to Santa Elena Cloud Forest Reserve, with key attractions along the route, such as the Bat Jungle (p175) and Sky Walk/ Sky Trek (p176).

A footbridge over Reserva Biologica Bosque Nuboso Monteverde and (inset) a zipline through the canopy providing two ways to travel ↑

1. A vibrant flower in the Cloud Forest, which is known for having the most unique species of flora and fauna.

2. The colorful male orange-bellied trogon is just one of the many species that attract birdwatchers to this protected area.

3. A sleek mountain lion finds a shady crook in a tree to relax in, to ward off the heat of the day.

GREAT VIEW
Viewing Portal

As you head up the Sendero Bosque Nuboso (Cloud Forest Trail), look out for La Ventana (the Window). Aptly named, it opens onto stunning views of the Continental Divide, where the slopes of the Atlantic and Pacific converge.

A hiker sizing up some of the ancient growth in the Monteverde cloud forest ↑

EXPLORING MONTEVERDE AND SANTA ELENA

①

Reserva Biológica Bosque Nuboso Monteverde

🚶🚴🍽️🏠 🅿 4 miles (6 km) SE of Santa Elena ⏰ 7am–4pm daily 🌐 cct.or.cr

The dirt road that winds uphill from Santa Elena ends at this

THE GOLDEN TOAD

In 1964 a tiny new species of toad was found in Monteverde's cloud forest, inhabiting an area of just 8 sq km (3 sq miles). The bright orange creature was named *sapo dorado* (golden toad), for the colour of the male. It is now considered extinct.

40-sq-mile (105-sq-km) jewel in the crown of the vast Arenal-Monteverde Protection Zone, which is owned and operated by the Tropical Science Center of Costa Rica. It straddles the Continental Divide and has six distinct ecological zones. The high forests are smothered by near-constant mists fed by the Atlantic trade winds, and on exposed ridges, trees are stunted by those same winds.

Wildlife, though elusive, is plentiful: here there are over 150 species of amphibians and reptiles; over 500 species of butterflies; and more than 100 mammals, including jaguars, jaguarundis, pumas, margays, and ocelots. The quetzals, hummingbirds, and endangered three-wattled bellbirds are among the more than 400 bird species. There are 75 miles (120 km) of trails, and a booklet details the most popular routes, which have wooden boardwalks. More challenging trails extend down the Caribbean slopes to the lowlands; these involve a full day's hike, with mud oozing underfoot. Rubber boots can be rented.

Did You Know?

Bosque Nuboso Monteverde houses 2.5 percent of worldwide biodiversity.

②

Reserva Bosque Nuboso Santa Elena

🚶🚴🍽️🏠 🅿 4 miles (6 km) NE of Santa Elena ⏰ Park: 7am–3pm daily; tours: 4:50am, 7:30am, 9:15am, 11:30am, 1pm, & 4:50pm 🌐 reservasanta elena.org

Funded and run by the local community, this 2-sq-mile (5-sq-km) reserve and educational centre is higher and cloudier than the more famous Bosque Nuboso Monteverde. Spider and howler monkeys, trogons, quetzals, and agoutis are often seen. More scarce are tapirs, jaguars, and pumas. There are great views of Volcán Arenal too.

→

A shy jaguar prowling one of the remote areas of Monteverde's reserves

③
Monteverde Butterfly Garden

🦋🐞🏛 📍1 mile (2 km) S of Santa Elena 🕐8:30am-4pm daily 🌐monteverde butterfly garden.com

With educational exhibits as well as a large butterfly enclosure housing 40 species, this nature center is an ideal place to learn about the life cycle of the butterfly. It also has stick insects, tarantulas, giant rhinoceros beetles, and 5-in- (13-cm-) long caterpillars. Visitors can also view leaf-cutter ants in their nest.

---

④
Frog Pond of Monteverde

🦋🐞🏛 📍330 yd (300 m) SW of Santa Elena 📞2645-6320 🕐9:30am-8:30pm daily

Visitors can come face-to-face with about 28 species of frogs and other amphibians, as well as snakes, lizards, and salamanders. Several of Costa Rica's most intriguing species can be seen, including poison-dart frogs, transparent frogs, endearing red-eyed tree frogs, and marine toads. Visit in the evening for best viewing.

⑤
Herpetarium Adventures

🦋🐞 📍550 yd (500 m) S of Santa Elena 🕐9am-8pm daily (phone to reserve a guided tour) 🌐sky adventures.travel

More than 20 species of snakes are on display here, as well as an array of other reptiles and amphibians turtles, frogs, iguanas, and chameleons.

---

⑥
Bat Jungle

🦋🐞 📍2 miles (3 km) S of Santa Elena 🕐9am-6pm daily 🌐batjungle.com

Costa Rica is home to 109 species of bats (Monteverde alone has 65 of them), and you can learn all about these fascinating creatures here.

There's a glass-walled flyway that is a habitat for eight bat species, documentary films are shown, and you can don giant ears to experience an idea of the bat's phenomenal acoustic abilities.

⑦
Monteverde Orchid Garden

🦋🐞 📍54 yd (50 m) S of Banco Nacional in Santa Elena 🕐9am-5pm daily 🌐monteverdeorchid garden.net

More than 500 local species line a winding trail here. Use a magnifying glass to see the tiniest ones up close.

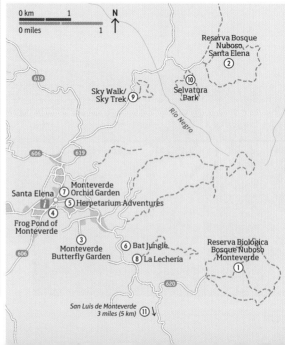

⑧

La Lechería

🚲🚶🅿️ 🅰️C3 🅾️2 miles (3 km) SE of Santa Elena
☎️2645 6889 🕐9am-5pm Mon-Sat, 10am-4pm Sun

Founded by Quaker settlers in 1953, this cheese factory now produces more than 2,200 lb (1,000 kg) of pasteurized cheese a day. The more than 20 types include Gouda, parmesan, and the bestselling Monte Rico. A video relates company history, and there's a cheese and ice cream shop.

⑨

Sky Walk/SkyTrek

🚲🚶😊🅿️ 🅰️C3 🅾️3 miles (5 km) NE of Santa Elena
🕐7am-3pm daily
🆆skyadventures.travel

With high walkways, ziplines, and suspension bridges, this project on the edge of the Reserva Bosque Nuboso Santa Elena offers a variety of ways to explore the cloud forest. The two-hour SkyTrek takes securely harnessed visitors between treetop platforms on a mile (1.6 km)

of ziplines. Two observatory towers offer panoramic views. The more sedate Sky Walk, with 3,300 ft (1,000 m) of meandering aerial pathways and bridges, is just as good for seeing wildlife.

⑩

Selvatura Park

🚲🚶🚻🅿️ 🅰️C3 🅾️4 miles (6 km) NE of Santa Elena
🕐7am-5pm daily
🆆selvatura.com

Selvatura Park boasts 2 miles (3 km) of treetop walkways with suspension bridges winding through the cloud forest canopy, as well as an adrenaline-fuelled, 14-platform zipline tour. On the ground, a hummingbird garden and domed butterfly garden are full of colorful delights.

The Ecological Awareness Center features the largest private insect collection in the world, with stick insects, butterflies, wasps, beetles, moths, and other insects. It also has giant crustaceans and a collection of human skulls from Australopithecus to Homo sapiens. There's also a video link to view scientists at work.

THE QUAKERS

A group of 44 Quakers, the pacifist Protestant group, comprised Monteverde's original settlers. Hailing from Alabama, USA, where they had been jailed for refusing to be drafted, they arrived in Costa Rica in 1951, drawn by the fact that the country had abolished its army after the 1948 Civil War. They settled in the Cordillera de Tilarán to raise dairy cattle. Since then, the Quakers have been at the forefront of local conservation efforts.

⑪

San Luis de Monteverde

🚲🚶😊🅿️ 🅰️C3 🅾️5 miles (8 km) SE of Monteverde
🆆ugacostarica.org

The University of Georgia's scientific research facility offers an immersive educational experience and great birding, as well as stays at its Ecolodge San Luis.

← Soaring above the Nuboso Santa Elena reserve with SkyTrek

↑ Rolling mists lying in
a blanket across the top
of the cloud forest

CLOUD FORESTS OF COSTA RICA

Named for the ephemeral mists that always envelop them, Costa Rica's cloud
forests are typically found at elevations above 3,500 ft (1,050 m). More properly
called montane tropical rainforests, they are extraordinarily biodiverse.

Cloud forests produce an astounding
array of flora. On wind-swept, exposed
ridges, trees and shrubs grow close to the
ground as a form of protection, forming
elfin forest with a primeval quality. In
these dense forests, epiphytic plants such
as orchids and bromeliads cling to sodden
branches, which also drip with lichen,
fungi, mosses, and liverworts. The lush
canopies rarely reach 100 ft (30 m),
although massive trees occasionally
break through.

Fauna is equally abundant, with herds
of chattering peccaries and tayras, which
belong to the same family as otters. The
mists and thick foliage often prevent
sightings, but the telltale yodel of prong-
billed barbets and booming packs of
howler monkeys are frequently heard.

↑ Dripping umbrella mushrooms clinging
to a moss-covered tree trunk

> **INSIDER TIP**
> **What to Wear**
>
> Cloud forests are
> cooler than those at
> lower elevations.
> Wear layers and light-
> weight long pants
> when hiking. It's also
> a good idea to carry a
> poncho or raincoat
> and pack an inexpen-
> sive backpack cover,
> in case of a downpour.

← A male mantled howler
monkey, mid-
call, high up in
the canopy

PARQUE NACIONAL SANTA ROSA

⚑ A1 **🚗 22 miles (35 km) N of Liberia** **🚌 Santa Rosa Sector: from Liberia; Murciélago Sector: from Santa Rosa park entrance, via Cuajiniquíl** **🕐 8am–3:30pm daily for vehicles; 24 hrs for campers** **🌐 acguanacaste.ac.cr**

The country's first national park, inaugurated in 1971, Santa Rosa National Park covers 190 sq miles (492 sq km) of the Santa Elena Peninsula and adjoining land. It is divided between the untouched Murciélago Sector (Bat Sector) and the popular Santa Rosa Sector, which is of great historical importance.

Santa Rosa National Park protects some of the last remaining tropical dry forest in the world, as well as nine other distinct habitats. It was established to provide safe territory for wide-ranging species such as jaguars and mountain lions To the north is the Murciélago Sector, full of hidden beaches – notably Playa Blanca – accessed by a rugged dirt track. The much larger Santa Rosa Sector, in the south, was the site of several battles for national independence, and features most of the sights of interest. The highlight is La Casona Hacienda, where the Battle of Santa Rosa was fought in 1856. All along the coast are great opportunities for surfing, especially around Witch's Rock, where a sandbar creates waves as long as 3 miles (5 km).

With 115 mammal species, including 20 types of bats, and 250 species of birds, the park is also a superb wildlife-viewing area.

↑ An iguana attempting to blend in, despite its iridescent blue and shimmering gray markings

↑ The mystically named Witch's Rock, standing in the swells off Playa Naranjo

THE CONTRA CONNECTION

During the 1980s, the remote northern coast-line of the park's Murciélago Sector (Bat Sector) was utilized as a secret training ground for the CIA-backed Nicaraguan Contras in their battle to topple the Sandinista government. An airstrip was illegally established here under the orders of Colonel Oliver North *(pictured),* himself a key player in the Iran-Contra scandal that shook the US in 1983-8. The road to the park entrance runs along-side the airstrip, which occupies land that was confiscated from Nicaraguan strongman Anastasio Somoza.

EXPERIENCE Guanacaste and Northern Nicoya

Did You Know?

According to legend, a witch living on the rock creates the whistle that sounds when the wind blows.

The calm waters around the rising ↑ archipelago of the Murciélago Islands in the northern sector of the park

The expanse of Laguna de Arenal's sloping shore, lined with beaches ↑

EXPERIENCE MORE

③
Tilarán

🅰C2 🕐14 miles (22 km) E of Cañas 🚌

This neat little town, at an elevation of 1,800 ft (550 m) on the Continental Divide, has crisp air and a pretty plaza shaded by pines and cypress trees. It makes a delightful stop en route to and from Lake Arenal (p198), although the only sight of note is the modern-looking 1960s cathedral, decorated with marquetry. An agricultural town surrounded by undulating fields, Tilarán is known for its annual livestock show and rodeo.

④
Cañas

🅰B2 🕐53 miles (86 km) N of Puntarenas 🚌

This dusty cowboy town is set dramatically in the lee of the Cordillera de Guanacaste.

Surrounded by cattle haciendas in the baking Tempisque basin, the town of Cañas is most appealing for its lively *sabanero* (cowboy) culture. It sits astride the Pan-Am Highway, and serves as the gateway to Lake Arenal and Parque Nacional Palo Verde.

To the north, the **Centro de Rescate y Santuario Las Pumas** (Puma Rescue Shelter) is a private facility for rescued wild cats. Some of the cats – which include jaguars, pumas, ocelots, margays, jaguarundis, and oncillas – are quite tame, having been raised from cubs by the late founder, Lilly Bodmer de Hagnauer. There are no guard rails to prevent visitors from going up to the cages but due caution is nonetheless required – these animals are wild at heart.

Nearby, the winding Río Corobicí is popular for guided rafting trips offered by Rincón Corobicí Rafting, as well as for gentler adventures floating downriver in inflatable rings: small rapids add touches of excitement.

Centro de Rescate y Santuario Las Pumas

🕸 🚩Pan-Am Hwy, 3 miles (5 km) N of Cañas 🕐8am–4pm daily 🌐centrorescate laspumas.org

⑤
Reserva Biológica Lomas Barbudal

🅰C2 🕐4 miles (6 km) SW of Pan-Am Hwy, 10 miles (16 km) SW of Bagaces 📞2200-5336 🚐To Bagaces, then by jeep-taxi 🕐8am–5pm daily (subject to change)

Famous for its plentiful insect population, not least the 250 species of bees, the seldom-visited Lomas Barbudal Biological Reserve protects rare tropical dry forest that hosts a similar array of wildlife to the Parque Nacional Palo Verde. Well-marked trails lace the 9-sq-mile (23-sq-km) reserve from the Casa de Patrimonio visitor center on the banks of the Río Cabuyo.

6

Zona Protectora Volcán Miravalles

🅰B2 📍16 miles (26 km) N of Bagaces 🚌From Bagaces

This active volcano rises some 6,650 ft (2,000 m) above the Guanacaste plains. Peaceful hiking trails lace the 42-sq-mile (109-sq-km) Miravalles Forest Reserve on the upper slopes, but the main draw here is Las Hornillas (Little Ovens), an area of steam vents and mud pools bubbling and hissing on the western slopes. The Institute of Electricity (ICE) produces power from the super-heated water vapor at Proyecto Geotérmico Miravalles; local operators can arrange tours of this facility. The fumaroles and mud pools are best viewed at **Las Hornillas Volcanic Activity Center**, where a short trail leads into an active crater. You can even wallow in warm, therapeutic mud before diving into a swimming pool. There is also a thrilling thermal water-slide that plunges into a pool with awesome volcano views.

Las Hornillas Volcanic Activity Center
🕸🛍🍴 📍1 mile (1.6 km) SE of Proyecto Geotérmico Miravalles 🕗8am–5pm daily 🌐hornillas.com

---

7 🕸 🛍 🍴

Parque Nacional Palo Verde

🅰B2 📍26 miles (42 km) W of Cañas 🚌To Bagaces, then by jeep-taxi 🕗8am–4pm daily 🌐sinac.go.cr

Palo Verde spreads over 50 sq miles (130 sq km), protecting a mosaic of mangrove swamps, marshes, savanna, and tropical dry forest at the mouth of silt-filled Río Tempisque. Shade here is provided by drought-tolerant trees such as ironwood and sandbox, as well as the ubiquitous evergreen *palo-verde* (greenstick) trees, which give the park its name.

During the dry season, from December to April, the trees burst into a riot of vibrant bloom. Ripening fruits draw monkeys, coatis, white-tailed deer, peccaries (wild hogs), pumas, and other mammals. In the wet season, much of the area floods and draws flocks of waterfowl to join herons, jabiru storks, ibis, roseate spoonbills, and other waders. Palo Verde has more than 300 species of birds, including a large population of scarlet macaws and curassows. Isla de Pájaros, in the middle of Río Tempisque, is a major nesting site.

Wildlife viewing is best in the dry season, when the deciduous trees lose their leaves and animals collect near water holes. Well-maintained trails lead to lookout points. The simple restaurant here can provide lunch if booked at least a day ahead.

> The main draw here is Las Hornillas (Little Ovens), an area of steam vents and mud pools bubbling and hissing on the western slopes.

SHOP

Talabartería La Estrella
Buy hand-stitched cowboy boots and more.
🅰B2 📍Calle 9 & Ave 3, Liberia 📞8837-4388

Hidden Garden Art Gallery
Around 70 Costa Rican artists show here.
🅰B2 📍10 miles (16 km) W of Liberia 🌐hiddengardenart.com

Oven Store
A family-run pottery, in the Chorotega tradition.
🅰B3 📍Guaitíl 📞2681-1696

Nativa Gallery
Handmade accessories by Jennifer Stone.
🅰A3 📍Nosara 🌐jenstonesonline.com

→ A flock of whistling ducks in the Parque Nacional Palo Verde

← Adventurers in Rincón de la Vieja national park, watched by capuchin monkeys *(inset)* and other local wildlife

19th-century Hacienda Santa María, and at Las Pailas ranger station. They lead past mud pools, hot sulfur springs, waterfalls, and fumaroles.

Hikers must report to one of the two ranger stations before setting out and on return. Both can be reached from Liberia by jeep-taxi, and they are linked by a trail. Nature lodges on the slopes of the volcano also operate as activity centers. On its southwestern flanks, Hacienda Lodge Guachipelín, accessed from Liberia via Curubandé, is a working cattle ranch, that specializes in horseback rides. Nearby, Rincón de la Vieja Lodge has a 1.5-sq-mile (3.5-sq-km) private forest reserve. Both lodges offer canopy tours. From Liberia, a road leads via Cañas Dulces to Buena Vista Mountain Lodge and Adventure Center on the northwestern slopes. It offers riding, a canopy tour, and a 1,300-ft- (400-m-) long water slide. **Hotel Borinquen Mountain Resort and Spa** nearby has bubbling mud pools and spa treatments.

Hotel Borinquen Mountain Resort and Spa
⊕ ⊕ ♿ 19 miles (30 km) NE of Liberia via Cañas Dulces
Ⓦ borinquenresort.com

8

Parque Nacional Rincón de la Vieja

Ⓐ B1 ♿ 19 miles (30 km) NE of Liberia 🚌 To Liberia, then by jeep-taxi Ⓞ 8am–3pm Tue–Sun Ⓦ acguanacaste.ac.cr

The dramatically beautiful Rincón de la Vieja volcano is studded with nine craters, of which only Rincón de la Vieja crater (5,900 ft/1,800 m) is active. The highest is Santa María (6,250 ft/1,900 m), while Von Seebach crater is filled with an acidic turquoise lake. The park protects an area of 55 sq miles (140 sq km). The eastern slopes of the volcano are rain-soaked all year round; in contrast, the western side has a distinct dry season, and the landscape ranges from deciduous forest at lower levels to cloud forest below the stark moonscape summit.

Visitors can spot capuchin, howler, and spider monkeys, anteaters, sloths, kinkajous, and more than 300 species of birds, including quetzals and three-wattled bellbirds. Pea-green Lago Los Jilgueros is visited by tapirs.

The park offers some superb hiking. Trails start at the park headquarters, the

STAY

Casa Rural Aroma de Campo

This is a welcoming and good-value B&B near Rincón de la Vieja.

🅰B2 🏠Curubandé
🌐aromadecampo.com

$(S)(S)(S)$

Hotel Río Perdido

Expect stunning contemporary design at this nature lodge, with its deluxe spa.

🅰B2 🏠San Bernardo de Bagaces
🌐rioperdido.com

$(S)(S)(S)$

Hacienda Lodge Guachipelín

A working cattle ranch with cosy rooms - a perfect base for exploring the Rincón de la Vieja national park.

🅰B2 🏠Curubandé
🌐guachipelin.com

$(S)(S)(S)$

---

⑨
Bahía Salinas

🅰A1 🏠38 miles (62 km) NW of Liberia 🚌To La Cruz, then by jeep-taxi

Framed by cliffs to the north, salt pans to the east, and mangrove-fringed beaches to the south, this flask-shaped bay is swept by breezes from December to April. Fishing hamlets line its shores. Hotels at La Coyotera and Playa Copal serve as surfing centers. The Costa Rican Tourism Board visitor center in La Cruz has great views.

Frigate birds use the drafts around the Refugio Nacional de Vida Silvestre Isla Bolaños to take off. As a protected nesting site for pelicans and American oystercatchers, this island is off-limits to visitors.

---

⑩
Liberia

🅰B2 🏠20 miles (32 km) N of Bagaces 🚗🚌

Guanacaste's charming historic capital is often overlooked as merely the main gateway to the Parque Nacional Rincón de la Vieja and the beaches of northern Nicoya (p191). Yet the town is an attractive locale in its own right. Founded in 1769, it is known as the White City for its whitewashed adobe houses with terracotta-tiled roofs. The loveliest houses are on Calle Real. The city is also known for its *puertas del sol* – double doors, one on each side of a corner, to catch both morning and afternoon sun. Liberia's cowboy tradition is celebrated at the Monumento Sabanero, on the main boulevard, at the **Museo de Guanacaste**, housed in a former jail, and during a raucous festival each March. The main plaza has the modern Iglesia Inmaculada Concepción de María. Next door,

COWBOY CULTURE

Many Guanacastecos make their living as *sabaneros* (cowboys). Proud, folkloric figures, they ride straight-backed in elaborately decorated saddles, leading their horses in a high stepping gait. The most important days of the year in Guanacasteco culture revolve around *topes* (horse shows) and *recorridos de toros* (bullfights), in which bulls are rather controversially ridden and baited.

the *ayuntamiento* (town hall) flies Guanacaste's flag, the only provincial flag in the country. Each July 25, locals celebrate Guanacaste's 1824 separation from Nicaragua with colorful parades and, unsurprisingly, a rodeo.

Museo de Guanacaste
🏠Ave 1, Calles 2 and 4
📞2665-7114 🕗8am–4pm Mon–Sat

←
The wedding-cake tiers of the Iglesia de la Agonía in Liberia

↑ A dreamy bend of Río Celeste as it meanders through Guanacaste park

EAT

Restaurante Sofia

Nuevo Latin fusion food to the sounds of live jazz.

⌂C3 ⌂Cerro Plano, Monteverde
☎8315-5652

$$ $($)

Tierra Mar

Zingy fish and seafood dishes at a friendly joint.

⌂B2 ⌂Liberia
☎6335-5407

$$ $($)

Ginger

Asian-inspired dishes in a sleek open tree house.

⌂A2 ⌂Playas Hermosa
🌐gingercostarica.com

$$ $($)

Lola's

Local fare at a laid-back beach restaurant.

⌂A3 ⌂Playa Avellanos
🌐lolascostarica.info

$$($)($)

11

Parque Nacional Guanacaste

⌂A1 ⌂22 miles (35 km) N of Liberia 🚌To Liberia, then by jeep-taxi
🕐8am–5pm daily, with advance notice only
🌐acguanacaste.ac.cr

Thanks largely to the efforts of ecologist Daniel H. Janzen, this park was created in 1989. It links Santa Rosa National Park to the cloud forest atop Volcán Cacao and Volcán Orosí. The "biological corridor" created allows wildlife to roam freely and extends the territory available for wide-ranging mammals, such as jaguars. This remote reserve now encompasses over 325 sq miles (840 sq km) of reforested woodland and pasture. Facilities are few, but the rewards are many, with superb opportunities for viewing wildlife. Biological stations Cacao, Pitilla, and Maritza offer spartan lodgings; though Cacao and Maritza are accessible only on foot or horseback.

A two-hour trek from Maritza is an array of pre-Columbian petroglyphs at Llano de los Indios, carved into volcanic stone on the lower western flanks of Volcán Orosí.

> This remote reserve now encompasses over 325 sq miles (840 sq km) of reforested woodland and pasture. Facilities are few, but the rewards are many.

12

Bahía Culebra

⌂A2 ⌂19 miles (31 km) W of Liberia

Ringed by dramatic cliffs and fringed by beaches of varying hues, Bahía Culebra (Snake Bay) is the setting for a controversial tourism project. Proyecto Papagayo, as it is called, has restricted access to the bay's sparkling waters. Spilling down the cliffs are big hotels, including the Four Seasons Resort. In the surrounding dry forest canopy, **Witch's Rock Canopy Tour** has ziplines and a walkway. In the bay below, pre-Columbian settlements still await excavation.

Witch's Rock Canopy Tour
⊛ ⌂23 miles (37 km) W of Liberia 🕐8am–3pm daily
🌐witchsrockcanopy.com

COSTA RICA'S DRY FORESTS

Dry tropical forests withstand a dry season that lasts as long as eight months, yet are still home to diverse plant- and wildlife.

The northwestern province of Guanacaste is home to one of the largest areas of dry tropical forest in the Americas. This habitat once swathed the lowlands of the Pacific littoral from Mexico to Panama. By the 1980s, it had been nearly decimated to create pastureland for cattle, resulting in tinder fires in the arid dry season. Conservation efforts, spearheaded by biologist Dr Daniel Janzen, led to the creation of the Guanacaste Conservation Area and expanded Santa Rosa National Park *(p178)*, to return savanna and ranchland to their original ecosystems.

↑ A lone guanacaste tree rising from the brush-covered dry forest

DRY FOREST FLORA

Guanacaste Trees
Wide-reaching branches provide precious shade in the searing midday heat.

Indio desnudo
Also called the gumbo-limbo, the copper-red bark peels to reveal an olive-colored trunk.

Acacia
Thorny scrub, such as acacia, have long spines to prevent birds and animals from gorging on their flat leaves and seeds.

Purple Jacaranda
The dry season sees these sweet-smelling trees explode in an outburst of color, attracting many birds.

Flamboyán
Startlingly red spoon-shaped petals hang from this tree's wide-spreading umbrella-like canopy from March to September.

Dry forest running along the wave-lapped shores of Santa Rosa National Park ↑

↑ Riding a wave on a shortboard at popular Playa Nosara

SURFING BEACHES OF NORTHERN NICOYA

Acclaimed as the "Hawaii of Latin America," Costa Rica offers world-class surfing and warm waters year-round. The greatest concentration of surfing beaches is in Northern Nicoya, where Pacific breakers pump ashore all year. Dozens of beaches guarantee that surfers will find a fairly challenging ride on any day, while extremely varied tidal conditions provide breaks for every level of experience.

REMOTE BEACHES

Remote Playa Naranjo in the Golfo de Papagayo has a superb beach break, called Witch's Rock after the island that sits in the bay. Naranjo is accessed by 4WD or by boat from the resorts of Northern Nicoya. Further south, Playas Bongo, Arío, and Manzanillo are as off-the-beaten-track as is possible in Costa Rica. Just getting there is half the fun. Cracking waves, combined with the solitude, guarantee surfer bliss.

RELIABLE SURF SPOTS

Consistently high waves pump ashore onto Tamarindo's (p187) Playa Grande. This accessible beach is protected as part of a prime nesting site of the leatherback turtle. Also popular among surfers, the mangrove-backed beach at Nosara (p188) has a fine beach break and warm tidepools.

BUDGET FRIENDLY

Long slivers of silvery sand are washed by good surf at Playas Bejuco and San Miguel. These remote beaches are oriented toward budget-conscious travelers, with cheap B&Bs and sodas among the otherwise few facilities.

↑ The waves crashing off Playa Naranjo in the Golfo de Papagayo

COSTA RICA'S SURF HISTORY

Despite the epic waves around the coast, surfing only arrived in Costa Rica in the 1960s, brought by American tourists. It soon took off. The Costa Rica Surfing Association was founded in 1999 supporting pro-surfers and hosting annual surf championships.

⑬ Playa Flamingo

🅐A2 **⏱46 miles (74 km)**
SW of Liberia 🚌

With gently curving white sands forming a gleaming crescent between rugged headlands, the gorgeous Playa Flamingo justifies its official, yet less common name, Playa Blanca (White Beach). The large bay is a popular anchorage. Deluxe villas dot the rocky headlands, and most of the hotels are upscale timeshare resorts. As a result, despite its fine beach, Flamingo is shunned by the offbeat and party crowd.

North of Playa Flamingo, Punta Flamingo has surprisingly good point breaks, especially at mid-tide, and few crowds. Carry along to find the estuary of the Río Salinas opening out at Playa Penca, where egrets, roseate spoonbills, and a rich variety of other birdlife can be spotted weaving among the roots of the mangrove trees.

Southwest of Flamingo is Playa Conchal (Shell Beach), with its shining sands; the diamond-like sparkle of the sand is caused by crushed seashells. The beach slopes gently into turquoise waters, which are ideal for snorkeling and other water sports.

⑭ Tamarindo

🅐A3 **⏱14 miles (23 km)**
S of Flamingo 🚗🚌

Once a sleepy fishing village, Tamarindo has developed into the region's premier resort. This popular surfers' haven is a great place to learn how to ride the waves. Well-regarded surf schools, such as **Witch's Rock Surf School** teach novices, including young children, taking advantage of the consistent waves and winds that sweep the bay.

Tamarindo is also a world-renowned center for diving, snorkeling, and sportfishing. Popular with backpackers, it has a cosmopolitan selection of cafés, restaurants, and boutique hotels. The area lies within the pristine **Parque Nacional Marino Las Baulas** (Leatherback Turtle Marine National Park), which protects 85 sq miles (220 sq km) of ocean, as well as 1.5 sq miles (4.5 sq km) of beach – Playa Grande. This beach is a prime nesting site of leatherback turtles, and Pacific ridley, green, and hawksbill turtles occasionally nest here too. During the nesting season, nobody is permitted on the beach after sundown, except for guided groups. The timing of these visits is tide-dependent and so varies from day to day. Places must be booked ahead, by phone or at the park office. Groups are only permitted onto the beach if the turtles are spotted by the guards there; if none appear, you have to try another night.

Witch's Rock Surf School
🆆 witchsrocksurfcamp.com

Parque Nacional Marino Las Baulas
♿🚸 📞 2653-0470
🕐 Mar–Sep: 6am–6pm daily (Oct–Feb: to 5pm)

DRINK

Volcano Brewing Company
Located at the Witch's Rock Surf Camp, this is the ultimate surfers' pub, spilling out onto the beach.

🅐A3 🏠Tamarindo
🆆volcanobrewing company.com

Lo Que Hay
This welcoming beach bar offers regular two-for-one specials.

🅐A3 🏠Sámara
📞2656-0811

La Luna
Sitting atop a beach and river estuary, this cosy bar is a great spot for a sundowner.

🅐A3 🏠Nosara
📞2682-0122

La Bodega
Offering top-notch coffee and breakfast, this place is a great stop after a big night out.

🅐A3 🏠Tamarindo
📞8395-6184

Safe swimming and a beautiful beach at the idyllic Playa Flamingo

→ Pausing to watch the spectacular sunset at Nosara beach

15

Nosara

🔺A3 🅰3 miles (5 km) S of Ostional 🚗🚌
🌐nosara.com

This isolated community on the Nicoya coast comprises twin villages. Bocas de Nosara, 3 miles (5 km) inland on the banks of the Río Nosara, is a peasant hamlet where oxcarts still creak along dusty lanes. To the south, the predominantly expat settlement of Beaches of Nosara is all contemporary homes amid forest groves near the shore. It backs the stunning Playa Guiones, a long, calm stretch of white sand and sun-warmed tide-pools in which monkeys can sometimes be seen having a soak. Strong tides rule out swimming, but the breakers are perfect for surfing. Farther

---

ARRIBADAS OF OLIVE RIDLEY TURTLES

Synchronized mass nestings called *arribadas* (arrivals) are unique to the ridley turtle, and occur regularly at three beaches in Costa Rica – Playa Nancite, Playa Ostional, and Playa Camaronal. On any one night, as many as 20,000 turtles congregate just beyond the breakers.

↑ Olive ridley hatchlings emerging from nest and making their way to the sea

ARRIVING EN MASSE

Taking place between April and December, peaking in September and October, these mass arrivals last three to eight days, in two- to four-week intervals that usually coincide with the last quarter of the moon's cycle. Turtles storm ashore, climbing over one another in a single-minded effort to nest on the crowded sands.

THE NESTING PROCESS

Turtles seek sandy sites above the high-water mark in which to nest. Millions of eggs are laid during each *arribada*, believed to be an evolutionary adaptation to ensure survival in the face of heavy predation. Each individual female lays an average of 100 eggs. Nests are scooped out to a depth of about 3 ft (1 m) using their rear flippers. Flippers then scatter sand

↑ An octopus, found beneath the waves at Playas del Coco

north, small Playa Pelada is encircled by steep cliffs. **Reserva Biológica Nosara**, nearby, protects the tropical forest along the Río Nosara estuary. Over 250 bird species nest here, including wood storks, and frigate birds. Crocodiles can also be seen in the estuary.

Reserva Biológica Nosara

🌐🌐🌐 🏠 Bocas de Nosara
Ⓦ lagartalodge.com

---

⑯

Playas del Coco

🅰 A2 📍 22 miles (35 km) SW of Liberia 🚌

This wide beach combines the allure of a traditional fishing community with the benefits of a no-frills resort. Although the pelican-patrolled beach is not especially attractive, it is a favorite with Costa Rican families, and has a buzzy nightlife. A party atmosphere erupts at the weekends, when music (and revellers) spills from every bar on the beach.

A number of local outfitters offer sportfishing and scuba excursions to nearby Islas Murciélagos and Isla Catalina, where schools of rays can be seen gently soaring under the waves. Secluded Playa Ocotal,

west of Playas del Coco, has the region's best dive site and world-class sportfishing.

Head to Playas Hermosa and Panamá, curving north of Coco in bite-shaped coves, to enjoy exquisite vistas, with Isla Catalina silhouetted dramatically at sunset.

DRINK

Coconutz Sports Bar
This lively microbrewery has a great selection of beers and the best brew-brined chicken in town.

🅰 A2 📍 Playas del Coco
Ⓦ coconutzbar.com

Cerveceria Independiente
Serving awesome craft brews, this place also has a street food garden next to the tap room.

🅰 A2 📍 1 mile (2 km) NE of Playa Flamingo
Ⓦ independiente.cr

---

over the nest to disguise it from raccoons, coatis, and other animals who dig up turtle nests to feast on the eggs; less than 10 percent of turtle eggs hatch.

HATCHLINGS

Incubation typically takes around 50 days. The temperature of the nest affects the sex of the hatchling - cooler nests produce males, while warmer ones produce females. Hatchlings emerge together at night for the dangerous run to the safety of the sea. Only about 1 percent survive to adulthood.

→ An olive ridley turtle pulling herself out of the sea and onto the sands of Playa Ostional

↑ Decorated trees and buildings in the "art village" of Islita

17 Islita

A B4 **⊙** 13 miles (21 km) E of Sámara **↕** 🚌 To Sámara, then by jeep-taxi

Set in the lee of the soaring Punta Islita, this charming village is known for its remote, palm-fringed beaches and the Hotel Punta Islita, a hilltop resort home to the Galería de Arte Contemporáneo Mary Anne Zürcher. Artworks in various media by both well-established artists and local hobbyists are available at this delightful spot. The hotel also supports the Museo de Arte Contemporáneo al Aire Libre (Open Air Museum of Contemporary Art). Spread around the village, the "collection" consists of houses, individual trees, and even the soccer field, all decorated with murals and other forms of spontaneous aesthetic expressions. The hotel also hosts the Lapa Lookout education and viewing center, an important breeding center and release site for the Macaw Recovery Network, which works tirelessly to conserve green and scarlet macaws. You can visit the center to learn about their work and watch their released flock swoop in at snack time.

18 Refugio Nacional de Vida Silvestre Ostional

A A3 **⊙** 34 miles (55 km) S of Tamarindo **☎** 2682-0400 🚌 From Santa Cruz and Nicoya via Nosara

The setting for one of the most remarkable occurrences in nature, Ostional National Wildlife Refuge protects 4 sq miles (10 sq km) of land and sea around Playa Ostional. The beach is one of only a dozen worldwide where Pacific ridley turtles nest in synchronized *arribadas*. Green and leatherback turtles also nest here in smaller numbers. Ostional is the only place in Costa Rica where residents are legally allowed, under strict guidelines, to harvest eggs during the first 36 hours of an *arribada*. Visitors, may not access the beach at nesting times unless escorted by a guide. Close contact with the turtles is forbidden, as are flashlights and flash photography.

Ostional is accessed by dirt roads that require 4WD during the muddy wet season. The remote setting and the vast surrounding forests have largely shielded the area from development, though now there are a few hotels.

INSIDER TIP
Conservation

There are numerous conservation efforts to help sea turtles across the country. The Refugio Nacional de Vida Silvestre Ostional, near Nosara, is one of the world's best breeding grounds of the olive ridley sea turtle. Get involved by signing up to join a tagging team, which tags nesting turtles, counts eggs, and protects the site with its very presence.

→

Palm trees swaying above the white sands of Playa Carrillo, just south of Sámara

19 Sámara

A A4 **⊙** 16 miles (26 km) S of Nosara **↕** Carrillo 🚌

Popular with backpackers, surfers, and middle-class Costa Ricans, Sámara is the most southerly of the beach resorts developed for tourism, where life revolves around lazing on the gray sands, or going surfing and riding. At the southern end of Playa Sámara, at Matapalo, villagers eke out a living from the sea. Playa Carrillo, 2 miles (3 km) south of Sámara, is a sportfishing center, while to the north, the **Flying Crocodile Lodge and Flying Center** sends visitors into the air in an ultralight plane.

Flying Crocodile Lodge and Flying Center

🛏️ 🍴 📶 🅰 Esterones, 3 miles (5 km) N of Sámara 📞 8988-6368 🕖 7am–3pm daily

---

⑳

Nicoya

🅰 B3 🅰 50 miles (80 km) SW of Liberia 🚌

Nicoya is a sleepy little town that dates back to the mid-1600s, and is named after the Chorotega *cacique* (chief), who greeted the Spanish conquistador Gil González Davila in 1523. A blending of the indigenous and Catholic belief systems culminate today in the annual Fiesta de la Yegüita, held on December 12. The administrative center and gateway for the Nicoya Peninsula, the town bustles with the comings and goings of *campesinos* (rural workers) and cowboys. Here life centers around the old plaza, Parque Central. Built in 1644, the intimate, wood-beamed Iglesia Parroquia San Blas, in the northeast corner, has a small museum has a display of religious memorabilia and historical artifacts.

Nature lovers can head about 17 miles (27 km) northeast to Puerto Humo, an affable riverside port town from where boats depart for Parque Nacional Palo Verde *(p181)*. Buses operate from Nicoya. Nearby, Rancho Humo Estancia is a nature conservancy that has superb bird-watching in the wetlands adjoining Palo Verde. It offers hiking and guided tours, on land or by boat.

FIESTA DE LA YEGÜITA

Also known as the Festival of the Virgin of Guadalupe, this fiesta blends Chorotega and Catholic traditions. According to legend, twin brothers were battling to the death for the love of a Chorotega princess. As onlookers prayed to the Virgin to stop the violence, a *yegüita* (little mare) suddenly appeared and intervened to stop the fight. The festival features traditional Costa Rican food, bullfights, rodeos, street processions, fireworks, music, dance, and ancient rituals.

↑ Chorotega motifs adorning a canopy in Plaza Bernabela Ramos

㉑ Santa Cruz

🅐A3 📍14 miles (22 km) NW of Nicoya 🚌

Steeped in local tradition, Santa Cruz is Costa Rica's official La Ciudad Folklórica (National Folkloric City). Connected by Highway 160 to Tamarindo and the beaches of the north-central Nicoya Peninsula, famous for their surfing (p186), the city was founded in 1760. Many of the wooden colonial edifices that once graced its historic core were destroyed in a fire, but the overall ambience is still charming. Plaza de los Mangos serves as a focal point for the city's festivals, which draw visitors from miles around to enjoy traditional *marimba* music and dance. *Topes* (horse shows) and *recorridos de toros* (bullfights) also take place here.

The architectural highlight of Santa Cruz is the landscaped Plaza Bernabela Ramos. On its eastern flank is a modern church with fine stained-glass windows. Next to it is the ruined bell tower of a colonial-style church, which was destroyed by an earthquake in 1950. The plaza is a pleasant spot to relax and admire the statues, including that of Chorotega *cacique* (chief) Diría in the southwest corner, and a *montador* (bull-rider) on a bucking bull in the northeast.

㉒ Guaitíl

🅐B3 📍7 miles (11 km) E of Santa Cruz 🚌

This small village offers the most authentic display of traditional culture in Costa Rica, with virtually the entire community involved in making ceramics in pre-Columbian style. Even the contemporary pieces draw inspiration from traditional Chorotega designs.

Most households have a traditional wood-fired, dome-shaped *horno* (oven) for firing potted objects. The town is lined with thatched stores where finished items are displayed. Visitors can watch artisans work the red clay dug from nearby riverbanks, and can even try to make their own in some workshops. In nearby San Vicente, the tiny **Ecomuseo de la Cerámica Chorotega** has a fine collection of original and replica pottery, and visitors can watch new pieces being made.

Ecomuseo de la Cerámica Chorotega
⊛ 📍1 mile (1 km) E of Guaitíl ⏰8:30am–4pm Mon–Sat 🆆eco museosanvicente.org

CHOROTEGA POTTERY

Guaitíl artisans use the same simple tools and techniques perfected by their ancestors to craft decorative bowls, pots, and clay figures, bringing their own creative flair to traditional designs. The finished pieces are polished with *zukias* (ancient grinding stones) and blessed by shamans, after which totemic animal motifs in black, red, and white are painted on ocher backgrounds. The quintessential Guaitíl piece is a three-legged vase in the form of a cow.

23 ✦ Ⓜ Ⓨ

Parque Nacional Barra Honda

🅐 B3 ⌂ 9 miles (14 km) E of Nicoya ☎ 2659-1551 🚍 Nicoya–Santa Ana village (half a mile/1 km from park entrance), then by jeep-taxi 🕐 Park: 8am–4pm daily (last admission 2pm); caving: 8am–1pm daily

One of the best spots in Costa Rica for caving, this national park was established in 1974, and spreads over 9 sq miles (23 sq km). A tropical dry forest area, Barra Honda was used for raising cattle, but is now in the process of being reforested.

Best accessed using a 4WD, the park is well known for its excellent hiking, with trails leading up to the Mirador Nacaome lookout points atop Cerro Barra Honda (1,450 ft/ 440 m), a massif lifted up by powerful tectonic forces. Cerro Barra Honda is riddled with limestone caverns formed by erosive torrents of water over millions of years. Of the 40 caves discovered so far, only 20 have been explored. Although indigenous artifacts have been found in some of the caves, evidence of pre-Columbian cave art has yet to be discovered.

Most of the caves boast dramatic stalactites and stalagmites, but each has its own appeal. Santa Ana, the largest cave, soars to a height of 790 ft (240 m). A dripstone formation called El Órgano (The Organ) produces musical tones when struck inside Cueva Terciopelo. El Pozo Hediondo (Stinking Well) is named for the droppings of the bats roosting here, while other caves are inhabited by blind salamanders and fish.

It is compulsory to use a licensed guide for descents into the Cueva Terciopelo, which is entered via a 100-ft (30-m) ladder. Access to the other caves requires prior permission. Spelunking equipment can be hired.

Guides are also compulsory when hiking on Las Cascadas trail, which leads to a series of spectacular waterfalls. Hikers must report to the ranger station before embarking into the park, whether or not they plan to follow Las Cascadas.

← Access ladder leading down into the Terciopelo cave, Parque Nacional Barra Honda

NORTHERN ZONE

The northern provinces are Costa Rica's flatlands –
a gentle landscape quilted in pastures, fruit plantations, and humid rainforest dominated by Volcán
Arenal, the youngest of Costa Rica's volcanoes. The
Corobicí peoples are thought to have settled the
lower flanks of the mountains around 1000 AD.
By the time the Spanish arrived 500 years later,
they were at war with their Nicaraguan neighbors.
During the colonial era, Spanish settlements pro-
liferated along the main river courses, and were
subject to constant plundering by pirates. The
region remained aloof from the rest of the country
until the early 19th century, when a trade route
was laid linking highland towns to a wharfside
settlement – today's Puerto Viejo – which gave
access to the Caribbean. Founded around that
time, Ciudad Quesada grew to become the region's
administrative center. The settlement campaign
initiated in the 1950s led to the decimation of
huge tracts of forest to make room for cattle farms
as well as banana and citrus plantations, although
efforts to re-forest the region are underway.

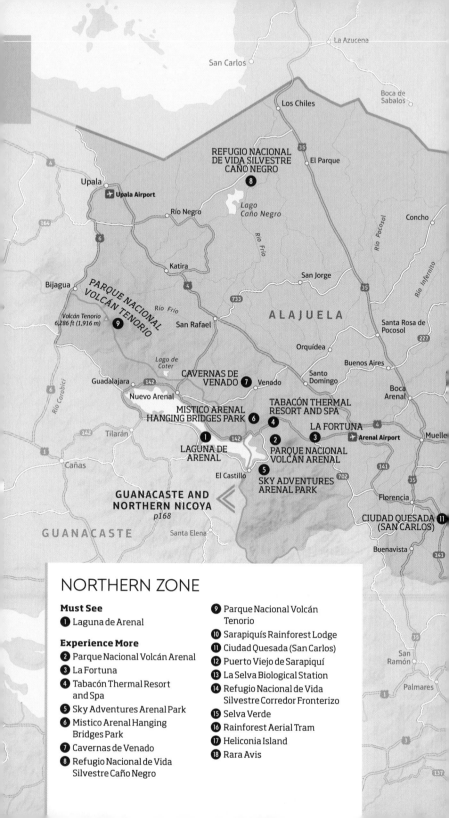

NORTHERN ZONE

Must See
1 Laguna de Arenal

Experience More
2 Parque Nacional Volcán Arenal
3 La Fortuna
4 Tabacón Thermal Resort and Spa
5 Sky Adventures Arenal Park
6 Mistico Arenal Hanging Bridges Park
7 Cavernas de Venado
8 Refugio Nacional de Vida Silvestre Caño Negro
9 Parque Nacional Volcán Tenorio
10 Sarapiquís Rainforest Lodge
11 Ciudad Quesada (San Carlos)
12 Puerto Viejo de Sarapiquí
13 La Selva Biological Station
14 Refugio Nacional de Vida Silvestre Corredor Fronterizo
15 Selva Verde
16 Rainforest Aerial Tram
17 Heliconia Island
18 Rara Avis

①

LAGUNA DE ARENAL

⚠ C2 📍 11 miles (18 km) E of La Fortuna along Hwy 142
🚌 From La Fortuna

Costa Rica's largest lake, sited beneath the Arenal volcano, attracts anglers and watersports enthusiasts; yet its waters have also been used to create clean energy in a hydroelectric power plant at Presa Sangregado.

Ringed by hills, with Volcán Arenal standing tall to the east, Lake Arenal has a breathtaking setting at an elevation of 1,800 ft (540 m). Created in the 1970s when the Instituto Costarricense de Electricidad (ICE) dammed the eastern end of the valley, the 48-sq-mile (124-sq-km) lake fills a tectonic depression that forms a gap between Tilarán and the Cordillera de Guanacaste.

Archaeologists have identified the remains of pre-Columbian settlements in the area. Today, the lake is ringed by small hamlets; the sole township is Nuevo Arenal *(p200)*, on the lake's north shore. The hotels and restaurants lining this side of the lake make a pleasant break from driving. The easternmost shores are forest-clad, while huge swaths of verdant pasture lie to the south and west.

Lake Arenal is encircled to the west and north by the winding Route 142, which links Tilarán with La Fortuna. East of Nuevo Arenal, the road deteriorates and is frequently blocked by landslides.

The lake is swept by near-constant winds, providing windsurfers with world-class conditions. However, the greatest attractions of the area are the picture-postcard vistas of majestic Arenal volcano reflected in the lake, which are best appreciated from the southwest shore.

Volcán Arenal, which dominates the landscape, adds another element to the attractions around the lake, in the form of bubbling hot springs. These range from low-key pools, ideal for an informal soak, to luxurious spa resorts, and can be the perfect end to a day of hiking or lake activities.

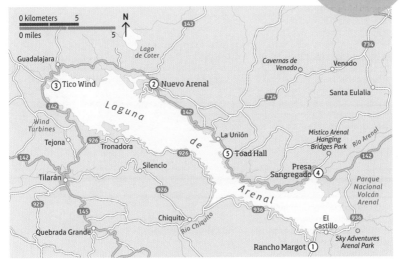

①
Rancho Margot

🏠 2 miles (3 km) W of El Castillo 🚌 To La Fortuna, then by jeep-taxi ⏱ 7am–9pm daily 🌐 rancho margot.com

The dirt road along the southeastern shore of Lake Arenal leads past Parque Nacional Volcán Arenal to Rancho Margot, a self-sustainable organic farm, hotel, and activity center beside the Río Caño Negro. Educational tours of the eco-oriented farm, including cow milking, give fascinating insights into sustainable agriculture. Visitors can also enjoy the wildlife rescue, rehabilitation, and breeding center. Many sporting enthusiasts come here for activities such as kayaking, fishing, and hiking in Rancho Margot's forest reserve. There are also twice-daily yoga sessions, spa treatments, and Spanish classes on offer. Meals are served in a historic farmstead.

↑ Stunning scenery of the mighty Volcán Arenal towering over Lake Arenal

WIND TURBINES

Rising over emerald pastures on the western shores of Lake Arenal, two parallel ridge crests are dotted with over 100 wind turbines, each 120 ft (35 m) high. Situated near the village of Tejona, which has some of the highest average wind speeds in the world, this wind farm is the largest in Central America, with a projected annual production of up to 70 MW. Electricity is sold to the state-owned ICE (Instituto Costarricense de Electricidad), adding to the country's admirable levels of sustainable energy.

Windsurfers skimming the
suitably windswept waters
of picturesque Lake Arenal ↑

② Nuevo Arenal

🏠 28 miles (46 km) W of
La Fortuna

Replacing the old village,
which was flooded in 1973 by
the formation of the lake, this
orderly town is a service center
for the lake region. It has the
area's only fuel station as well
as a number of good restaurants. A dirt road leads north
through the valley of the
Río Quequer, linking Nuevo
Arenal to San Rafael on
scenic Highway 4.

③ Tico Wind

🏠 10 miles (16 km) SW of
Nuevo Arenal 🌐 tico
wind.com

Swept by steady, strong
northeasterly winds between
November and March, Lake
Arenal is rated as one of the
finest windsurfing sites in
the world. The Tico Wind,
located southwest of Nuevo
Arenal, caters for all levels of
windsurfers and kitesurfers. In
addition to renting out sail-
boards and stand-up paddle-
boards, it offers multiday
packages and beginners' and
advanced lessons between the
months of November and April.
As water levels fluctuate during
the year, islands appear and
disappear, making navigation
part of the fun during low-
water level periods.

④ Presa Sangregado

🏠 4 miles (6 km) NW of
Nuevo Arenal

This 288-ft- (88-m-) long,
184-ft- (56-m-) high earthen
dam was completed in 1979
across the path of Río Arenal
in order to create the lake.
Today the dam generates
12 percent of the country's
clean energy.

> 💬 INSIDER TIP
> ### Cute Coatis
>
> Although they are
> adorable, resist the urge
> to feed the coatis that
> often wait along the
> roadside for tourists
> to stop. Not only is it
> illegal, it is dangerous
> to the animals' health.

⑤ Toad Hall

🏠 4 miles (6 km) SE of
Nuevo Arenal

This well-restored hacienda
has reaching views across
the lake and the surrounding
forest. Tours of the area
and into Parque Nacional
Volcán Arenal (p202) can be
arranged, and art supplies
are left out for visitors
in the popular café.

The colorful entrance to
Toad Hall, an ideal stop
off point for a bit of art →

VOLCANOES IN COSTA RICA

Located in one of the world's most volcanic zones, Costa Rica has seven active volcanoes and at least 60 that are either dormant or extinct. Concentrated in the northwestern and central regions, most are steep-sided cones formed by silica-rich magma, and are highly explosive. Arenal is the most active.

Volcanoes are created by plate tectonics, the movement of the interlocking plates that make up the earth's crust riding on the magma (molten rock) in the mantle. Most volcanoes occur at the boundaries where plates meet or move apart, with magma bursting through cracks.

Lying between 100 and 150 miles (160–240 km) inland of the subduction zone of the Cocos and the Caribbean plates, Costa Rica's landmass sits on the Caribbean plate, beneath which the thinner east-moving Cocos plate is being forced down. This intense pressure melts the rocks and magma wells up to create volcanoes.

Smoke and ash are often steadily emitted by active volcanoes, such as Volcán Arenal, even when "resting", and smoking cinder blocks sometimes roll down the slopes. During its active phase, Arenal will erupt every few hours, with hot lava oozing down its slopes and superheated avalanches of gas, ash, and rock moving at astonishing speeds.

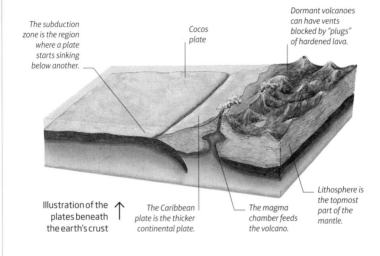

The subduction zone is the region where a plate starts sinking below another.

Cocos plate

Dormant volcanoes can have vents blocked by "plugs" of hardened lava.

Illustration of the plates beneath the earth's crust ↑

The Caribbean plate is the thicker continental plate.

The magma chamber feeds the volcano.

Lithosphere is the topmost part of the mantle.

↑ Clouds of steam puffing atmospherically from vents around the lake-filled crater of Volcán Poas, which has erupted 40 times since 1828

The perfectly conical peak of once active *(inset)* Volcán Arenal ↑

EXPERIENCE MORE

2

Parque Nacional Volcán Arenal

⬛C2 **⬛11 miles (18 km) W of La Fortuna** **⬛To La Fortuna, then by jeep-taxi** **⬛8am–4pm daily (last admission 2:30pm)** **⬛sinac.go.cr**

Encircling the country's most historically active volcano, Arenal Volcano National Park spreads over 45 sq miles (120 sq km). Rising from the San Carlos Plains, the majestic Arenal was thought by local Indigenous cultures to be the sacred "Home of the Fire God." Arenal ceased activity between the 13th and 16th centuries, and stayed inactive until July 29, 1968, when an earthquake re-awakened it. The perfectly conical 5,400-ft-(1,650-m-) high volcano ceased erupting in 2010 and remains inactive, but not extinct.

Visitors can walk or drive close to the base of the volcano and then follow trails across an old lava flow and into the rainforest. At the westernmost edge, next to Lake Arenal, there is a paved trail (suitable for wheelchairs) through forest with lookout points and an observation tower, from where you can see the volcano and lake. The ranger station at the park entrance has restrooms and sells maps, while tour companies and hotels in La Fortuna offer guided tours.

The park also includes the dormant Volcán Chato to the east. Arenal Observatory Lodge and volcanology museum, midway up the western flank of Chato, has stunning views of Volcán Arenal and Lake Arenal. Trails from here lead through forest to Chato's summit, where a jade-colored lake in the crater shimmers with opportunities for canoeing.

3

La Fortuna

⬛C2 **⬛81 miles (131 km) NW of San José** **⬛**

Volcán Arenal towers over this agricultural community and tourist hub, officially known as La Fortuna de San Carlos. Situated on a gentle slope, the picturesque town is laid out on a grid around a broad, landscaped plaza. A modern church stands on the plaza, its tall bell tower contrasting with Arenal behind. Restaurants and hotels cater to tourists and several agencies offer riding, caving, fishing, biking, and rafting. A popular horse-back trip is to Monteverde *(p172)*, but the ride is quite taxing for the horses, so take care to check that the animals are well looked after.

Southeast of the town, an educational and surprisingly fun-filled introduction to sustainable organic farming is on offer at **Finca Educativa Don Juan**, which ends with a typical *campesino* lunch. Head westward to **Natura Eco Park** for a fantastic frog garden and reptile house, as well as great dawn birdwatchers' tours and night walks at 6pm. Also in the vicinity, the "wild" **Arenal Mundo Aventura** is a petite 2-sq-mile (5-sq-km) wildlife refuge and ecotour center

Natura Eco Park

♨ 🦋 🚗 **☐** 4 miles (6.5 km) W of La Fortuna ☐ 8am–8pm daily ⊠ arenalnatura.com

Arenal Mundo Aventura

♨ 🦋 🚗 **☐** 1 mile (1.6 km) S of La Fortuna ☐ 2479-2190 ☐ 8am–5pm daily

Baldi Hot Springs Hotel Resort and Spa

♨ 🦋 🚗 **☐** 3 miles (5 km) W of La Fortuna ☐ 9am–10pm daily ⊠ baldihotsprings.cr

The Springs Resort and Spa

♨ 🍴 **☐** 6 miles (10 km) W of La Fortuna ☐ 8am–10pm daily ⊠ thespringscostarica.com

---

4 ♨ 🍴 🛍

Tabacón Thermal Resort and Spa

🅰 C2 **☐** 8 miles (13 km) W of La Fortuna 🚌 From La Fortuna ☐ 10am–10pm daily ⊠ tabacon.com

Steaming-hot waters pour out from the base of Volcán Arenal and tumble through this lush, landscaped *balneario* (bathing resort). The Río Tabacón feeds a series of therapeutic mineral pools with temperatures that range from 27° to 39° C (80° to 102° F). The main pool has a swim-up bar, and there is a splendid restaurant *(p204)*. The *balneario*'s Grand Spa is a sumptuous alfresco full-service spa. Try a volcanic mud wrap, a local specialty treatment.

with trails, rappeling, and canopy tours. Less energetic visitors can soak in thermal waters at **Baldi Hot Springs Hotel Resort and Spa**, which has landscaped outdoor pools and a swim-up bar and restaurant, or **The Springs Resort and Spa**, which also has thermal pools and cascades.

Finca Educativa Don Juan

♨ 🦋 **☐** 1 mile (1.6 km) SE of La Fortuna ☐ 2479-1130 ☐ 8am–5pm daily

←
Enjoying the cascading thermal waters at the Tabacón Thermal Resort

EAT

Don Rufino

Organic fusion dishes are served at this rustic yet elegant restaurant.

🅰C2 🅰La Fortuna
🆆donrufino.com

$$$⑤

Pizza John's Jardin Escondido

Feast alfresco on delicious stone-baked pizza and homemade ice cream.

🅰C2 🅰El Castillo
📞8801-0967

$$⑤⑤

Tom's Pan

This German bakery serves homemade strudels and Costa Rican classics.

🅰C2 🅰Nuevo Arenal
📞2694-4547

$$⑤⑤

Gingerbread

Israeli chef Eyal creates delicious fusion dishes, from duck quesadillas to shrimp risotto.

🅰C2 🅰Nuevo Arenal
🆆gingerbread arenal.com

$$$⑤

Ave

Costa Rican staples are served alongside volcano views. Try the corvina fish.

🅰C2 🅰Tabacón
🆆tabacon.com

$$$⑤

→ Following the trail through the canopy at Mistico Arenal park

---

⑤

Sky Adventures Arenal Park

🅰C2 🅰El Castillo, 14 miles (22 km) W of La Fortuna 🚌To La Fortuna, then by jeep-taxi ⏰7:30am–5pm daily 🆆skyadventures. travel

Teleféricos (aerial trams) whisk visitors up the northern slopes of the Cordillera de Tilarán at this private facility southeast of Lake Arenal. At the top, a series of 2-mile- (3-km-) long ziplines connect the canopies, sending adrenaline junkies on exhilarating rides across broad ravines. There is also mountain biking and canyoning.

A little further west along the lakeside road is the turnoff to the Butterfly Conservatory, which has a small, fascinating display of insects, scorpions, and snakes, as well as a butterfly garden and a medicinal herb garden. Tours take in the atrium habitats, labs, and glasshouses.

---

⑥

Mistico Arenal Hanging Bridges Park

🅰C2 🅰12 miles (19 km) W of La Fortuna 🚌To La Fortuna, then by jeep-taxi ⏰6:15am–4:30pm daily (night tour at 6:30pm) 🆆mistico park.com

A self-guided trail meanders through pristine primary forest, punctuated by a series of 14 bridges suspended over ravines. The relatively easy, 2-mile (3-km) trail clings to the mountainside and offers close-up views of every level of the tropical forest, from ground to canopy. Among the tours available are the Spider Monkey Canyon Tour, which includes abseiling, and a twilight birding tour.

---

⑦

Cavernas de Venado

🅰C2 🅰1 mile (1.6 km) W of Venado, 24 miles (39 km) NW of La Fortuna 🚌From Ciudad Quesada ⏰8am–3pm daily 🆆cavernasdel venadocr.com

Bioluminescent fungi light the way for visitors scrambling through the underground passageways of these limestone caverns to the north of Lake Arenal. Ten chambers, accessible by a dirt road that begins at Hotel La Mansion Inn, extend almost 2 miles (3 km). Exquisite stalagmites and stalactites fill the labyrinthine and narrow chambers, many of which contain marine fossils. Cascada de La Muerte is an underground waterfall that gushes during the wet season from May to November, and after heavy rain. Bats flit about, blind fish swim in the underground streams, and small transparent frogs hop around in the ooze.

Guides, whose services can be arranged in La Fortuna,

↑ The brilliant Pozo Azul on the Río Celeste, Parque Nacional Volcán Tenorio

lead two-hour-long explorations through the caves, offering a fascinating commentary of the different rock formations. Wilbert Solis, who owns the land under which the caves are located, supplies safety helmets, flashlights, and rubber boots. Come prepared to get covered in mud, and bring a change of clothes. Venado is also accessible by a dirt road that begins at Hotel La Mansion Inn, on the north shore of Lake Arenal.

8

Refugio Nacional de Vida Silvestre Caño Negro

🅰 C1 🕐 65 miles (105 km) NW of La Fortuna 📞 2471-1309 🚌 From Upala 🚢 From Los Chiles 🕐 8am–4pm daily

One of Costa Rica's main wetland conservation areas, Caño Negro Wildlife Refuge protects over 38 sq miles (98 sq km) of marshlands, lagoons, and *yolillo* palm forest. Most visitors come to fish for snook and tarpon, which thrive in the Río Frío and other watercourses that feed Lago Caño Negro, a 3-sq-mile (9-sq-km) seasonal lake. Rare ancient garfish, usually found in the Atlantic Ocean, also inhabit the lake's tannin-stained waters. The short dry season (December–April) is best for viewing crocodiles, caimans, and the large mammals that gather near permanent bodies of water.

Monkeys and tapirs are numerous, while jaguars and other cats are more elusive. Lucky visitors may also see large flocks of jabiru storks, Nicaraguan grackles, roseate spoonbills, and the largest colony of neotropic cormorants in Costa Rica, passing through during migration.

Caño Negro village, on the west bank of Lago Cano Negro, is the only community within the reserve. The park headquarters is located here, as are several lodges that arrange guided tours and fishing licenses. Boats can also be rented in the nearby town of Los Chiles, and several agencies in San José offer tours, especially during the fishing season (July–March). Much of the area floods in the wet season. Access along the dirt roads can be a challenge, so 4WD is recommended.

9 ✍ ⛰

Parque Nacional Volcán Tenorio

🅰 C2 🕐 7 miles (11 km) E of Bijagua 📞 2200-0135 🚌 From Upala, then by jeep-taxi 🕐 8am–4pm daily

Several nature lodges offer easy access to this 71-sq-mile (184-sq-km) park. Trails lead through montane rainforest to thermal springs and the Pozo Azul, a teal-blue pool at the base of the volcano. Local guides lead hikes in search of tapirs and other wildlife, but the summit trail is closed to all but scientists.

🔍 HIDDEN GEM
Iguana Encounters

A sea of green iguanas sprawl in the bamboo and branches at the Centro Turístico Iguana Azul on Ruta 35, just north of the Muelle junction. A bridge offers eye-to-eye views of the lazing reptiles. At the adjacent restaurant, they hang around for tidbits of tossed fruit.

10 (symbols)

Sarapiquís Rainforest Lodge

D2 **La Virgen de Sarapiquí, 29 miles (47 km) N of Alajuela** **From San José to Puerto Viejo de Sarapiquí** **9am–5pm daily** **sarapiquis.com**

This broad-ranging ecological center on the banks of the Río Sarapiquí offers an enriching insight into Indigenous cultures. The state-of-the-art Museo de Cultura Indígena is a fantastic museum, dedicated to Costa Rica's Indigenous communities and the preservation of their artifacts.

The Parque Arqueológico Alma Alta, set in an orange grove, is centered around four Indigenous tombs, dating from the 15th century, and a re-created pre-Columbian village. Local Indigenous guides offer tours of Chester's Field Botanical Gardens. Named for the naturalist Chester Czepulos (1916–92), the gardens have about 500 native species of plants renowned since pre-Columbian times for their medicinal use. The center also has a top-notch restaurant and hotel, as well as a library and conference center.

The center adjoins the **Tirimbina Rainforest Reserve**, which protects just over 1 sq mile (3 sq km) of mid-elevation premontane forest. It can be reached from Sarapiquís Rainforest Lodge by an 855-ft- (260-m-) long suspension bridge across the Río Sarapiquí. A 325-ft (100-m) canopy walkway features among Tirimbina's 5 miles (8 km) of trails. Guided tours include a special "World of Bats" night walk. Adjoining Tirimbina, **Dave and Dave's Nature Park** (that's Dave Landos Sr. and Dave Jr.) is a supreme birding venue, with observation decks, trails, and guided tours. Five minutes south, **Hacienda Pozo Azul** is a working cattle ranch that offers white-water rafting trips and canopy tours. Some 22 miles (35 km) north of here, the **Cinco Ceibas Rainforest Reserve and Adventure Park** is part of a vast farm that can be toured in an ox-pulled cart. It also offers hiking and kayaking. The boardwalks are wheelchair accessible, and there are also plenty of options for children and families.

Tirimbina Rainforest Reserve

(symbols) **7am–5pm daily** **tirimbina.org**

Dave and Dave's Nature Park

(symbols) **La Virgen de Sarapiquí** **7am–5pm daily** **eco-observatory.com**

Did You Know?

When you're on the Río San Juan, you're officially in Nicaragua.

Hacienda Pozo Azul

⊛ⓨⓢ⑩ 🚗 La Virgen de Sarapiquí ⏱9am–6:30pm daily 🌐pozoazul.com

Cinco Ceibas Rainforest Reserve and Adventure Park

⊛⑩ 🚗20 miles (32 km) NW of La Virgen via San Miguel 📞2476-0606 ⏱10am–5pm daily

⓫ Ciudad Quesada (San Carlos)

🅰D3 🚗59 miles (95 km) NW of San José 🚌 ℹICT, 75 yards N of Universidad Católica, 2461-9102

An important market center serving the local dairy and cattle industries, Ciudad Quesada is set amid pastures atop the mountain scarp of the Cordillera de Tilarán, at an elevation of 2,130 ft (650 m). The town, known locally as San Carlos, is the administrative center for the region, and is famous for its annual cattle fair. The town's numerous *talabarterías* (saddle-makers' workshops) and *heladerías* (ice cream shops) make a visit here well worthwhile.

Highway 140 slopes east out of town, passing **Termales del Bosque**, where visitors can soak in thermal mineral springs and have mud baths. Hiking trails lace botanical gardens, while the adventurous can take a zipline canopy tour. Nearby, **La Marina Wildlife Rescue Center** is a non-profit zoo that takes in rescued animals. Its numerous inhabitants include jaguars, agoutis, monkeys, peccaries, and snakes, as well as macaws,

← Kayaking at the Cinco Ceibas Rainforest Reserve and Adventure Park

↑ Warm thermal pools of mineral-rich waters at Termales del Bosque

toucans, and other bird species. Tapirs are also bred for release into the wild.

Termales del Bosque

⊛ⓨⓢ 🚗4 miles (6 km) E of Ciudad Quesada ⏱7am–10pm daily 🌐hoteltermales delbosque.com

La Marina Wildlife Rescue Center

⑩⊛ 🚗6 miles (10 km) E of Ciudad Quesada ⏱8am–4pm daily 🌐zoocostarica.com

⓬ Puerto Viejo de Sarapiquí

🅰E2 🚗52 miles (84 km) N of San José 🚌🚌

Positioned at the base of the Cordillera Central, on the banks of the Río Sarapiquí, Puerto Viejo has functioned as an important river port since colonial days.

Banana trees cover most of the Llanura de San Carlos flat-lands around Puerto Viejo. Head 12 miles (20 km) southwest to **Finca Ecoorganica Sarapiquí** to learn more about the region's banana and other crops.

Finca Ecoorganica Sarapiquí

⊛ⓢ 🚗La Virgen de Sarapiquí ⏱7am–5pm daily 🌐sarapiquiecoorganico.com

DRINK

Cafe y Macadamia

Fantastic rich coffees and fresh smoothies, plus tasty dishes, vie with epic views.

🅰C2 🚗1 mile (1.6 km) E of Guadalajara 📞8635-8235

Hotel Lake Arenal and Brewery

Enjoy superb brews and gorgeous views of the lake at this hotel's micro-brewery.

🅰C2 🚗3 miles (5 km) N of Tilarán 🌐lakearenalhotel.com

Rain Forest Café

At this café, choose from a range of superb espressos, cappuccinos, and lattes made from beans grown on the slopes of Volcan Poás.

🅰C2 🚗La Fortuna 📞2479-7239

La Fortuna Pub

A great range of Costa Rican craft brews, plus tasty burgers, chicken wings, and nachos are served at this lively pub.

🅰C2 🚗La Fortuna 📞2479-1511

Lava Lounge Bar and Grill

This no-frills open-air bar hosts great live music nights and raises money for a local dog rescue.

🅰C2 🚗La Fortuna 📞2479-7365

470

The number of bird species found at La Selva.

13 🏊 🎣 🍴 🏛

La Selva Biological Station

🅰 E2 🚗 2 miles (3 km) S of Puerto Viejo 🚌 From San José to Puerto Viejo de Sarapiquí, then by jeep-taxi 🕐 8am–5pm daily, by appt only 🌐 ots.ac.cr

Created by scientist Dr. Leslie Holdridge in 1954, La Selva Biological Station has been run as a private research facility by the Organization of Tropical Studies (OTS) since 1968. Scientific research at this 6-sq-mile (15-sq-km) reserve

spans physiological ecology, soil science, and forestry, with over 1,000 tree species in the Holdridge Arboretum.

The predominant habitat is a vast swath of lowland and premontane rainforest at the base of the Parque Nacional Braulio Carrillo (p146). Snakes, although abundant, are rarely seen. More noticeable are poison-dart frogs, enameled in gaudy colors, and more than 500 species of butterflies, including neon-blue morphos. Elusive jaguars and other big cats prowl the forests, preying on monkeys, coatis, and deer, which are among La Selva's 120 mammal species, and little peccaries are commonly seen around the facility. About half of Costa Rica's bird species have been sighted here; as a result, the annual 24-hour La Selva Christmas Bird Count has become a pilgrimage for ornithologists from around the world. A basic bird-watching course is offered on Saturdays. Although it is open to the public access to the

reserve is restricted to just 65 people, with scientists and students getting priority, so it's important to book your visit in advance.

OTS offers guided tours from San José that include transportation, but the gift shop has self-guiding booklets that cover the 31 miles (50 km) of boardwalk trails crisscrossing La Selva. Precipitation here can exceed 157 inches (400 cm) in a year, so expect to get muddy on many of the trails. Dormitory lodging is offered depending on whether space is available.

14

Refugio Nacional de Vida Silvestre Corredor Fronterizo

🅰 C1 🚗 Bahía Salinas to Punta Castillo 📞 2471-2191 (Los Chiles)

The 230-sq-mile (590-sq-km) Frontier Corridor National Wildlife Refuge protects a wide strip of Costa Rican territory along the border with Nicaragua, from Bahía Salinas on the west coast to Punta Castillo on the east. The eastern part of the refuge runs along the Río San Juan. Lined with virgin rainforest, this broad river flows 120 miles (195 km) east from Lake Nicaragua to Punta Castillo, and has long been disputed by the two nations.

Water-taxis link Puerto Viejo de Sarapiquí to Trinidad village, where the Ríos San Juan and Sarapiquí meet. The river trip through the reserve is splendid for spotting sloths, crocodiles, and myriad birds, including oropendolas.

Boca San Carlos, 24 miles (39 km) upstream of Trinidad on the Río San Juan, has an airstrip and can also be

←

Observing what's beneath the currents at La Selva Biological Station

Awaiting a weary hiker, a
hammock on the balcony
at Selva Verde lodge ↑

reached by a dirt road. It is a gateway for river journeys into Nicaragua. Nearby, **Laguna del Lagarto** is a private reserve protecting 2 sq miles (5 sq km) of virgin rainforest and swamp, and lagoons inhabited by elusive manatees. A nature lodge offers excellent wildlife viewing. Also worth a visit is the 17th-century Fortaleza de la Inmaculada Concepción, a restored mossy hilltop fort near the Nicaraguan hamlet of El Castillo, 25 miles (40 km) upstream of Boca San Carlos. Its small museum recounts when Spanish defenders fought back pirates and an English invasion fleet led by Lord Nelson.

Laguna del Lagarto

⊗ ⍟ ⌂ 10 miles (16 km) S of Boca San Carlos 🅦 laguna lagartoecolodge.com

15 ⊗ ⍟ ⍟ ⍟

Selva Verde

🅐 D2 ⌂ 5 miles (8 km) W of Puerto Viejo de Sarapiquí 🚌 From San José to Puerto Viejo de Sarapiquí ⏰ 6am–7pm daily 🅦 selva verde.com

One of the country's best private reserves, Selva Verde

(Green Forest) lies alongside the Parque Nacional Braulio Carrillo *(p146)*. A prime destination for birders, the virgin low-elevation rainforest is home to over 420 bird species, including eight species of parrots. Ocelots, sloths, cheeky capuchin monkeys, and vocal mantled howler monkeys are among the 120 species of mammals to be seen. Poison-dart frogs are numerous, as are snakes, although these are difficult to spot. Several of Selva Verde's 500 species of butterflies can be seen in a netted butterfly garden.

Guided canoe trips are offered on the Río Sarapiquí, which runs through Selva Verde. Naturalist guides can be hired, and maps are provided for the well-maintained trails.

The reserve also has a lodge offering comfortable rooms. Staff are happy to help guests arrange excursions to other local attractions; the nearest, only a 10- to 15-min drive away, is a fun tractor-trailer tour of an organic pineapple plantation, where you can also see how peppercorns are grown, harvested, and dried.

POISON-DART FROGS

The rainforests of Central and South America are inhabited by poison-dart frogs, so named because their poison was used to tip arrows and blow-darts. About 65 species exist, although only three are deadly to humans (none found in Costa Rica). The frogs, no more than 2.4 inches (6 cm) long, produce the bitter toxin in their mucous glands and advertise this with flamboyant colors – mostly vivid reds, greens, and blues – to avoid being eaten by predators. Thus, unusually for frogs, they are active by day among the moist leaf litter. Several species of non-toxic frogs mimic their coloration. In captivity, poison-dart frogs tend to lose their toxicity, which they derive from their principal diet of ants and termites.

↑ Spotting wildlife high in the forest canopy on the Rainforest Aerial Tram

⑯ Rainforest Aerial Tram

E3 **Hwy 32, 30 miles (48 km) NE of San José** **From San José to Guápiles** **7:30am–2pm daily** **rainforestadventure.com**

Offering an alternative view of the forest canopy, this automated exploration system was conceived by American naturalist Dr. Donald Perry while he was involved in scientific investigation at Rara Avis. Inaugurated in 1994, the Rainforest Aerial Tram, also called "El Teleférico," is the highlight of a 1.5-sq-mile (3.5-sq-km) private nature reserve on the eastern edge of the Parque Nacional Braulio Carrillo. Visitors ride in open gondolas that silently skim the floor of the rainforest and then soar above the trees on a 90-minute, 2-mile (3-km) circuit. A naturalist guide accompanies each gondola to assist visitors in spotting and identifying wildlife. Howler and white-faced monkeys are occasionally seen at close quarters, as are iguanas, sloths, and snakes. While the views are fabulous, and the photo opportunities come thick and fast, visitors should keep in mind that the main aim of the journey is to learn about rainforest ecology.

Trails lead to the Río Corinto, and guided birding sorties, and frog and butterfly exhibits, are offered. Accommodation are in the form of cabins. Tour agencies nationwide offer package excursions.

INSIDER TIP
Bird's-Eye View

Early morning and late afternoon are the best times to spot wildlife on the Rainforest Aerial Tram. There's a 7:30am departure that's too early for the tour buses bringing visitors from San José, but perfect if you're staying locally.

⑰ Heliconia Island

E2 **5 miles (8 km) S of Puerto Viejo** **From San José to Puerto Viejo de Sarapiquí via PN Braulio Carrillo** **8am–5pm daily** **heliconiaisland.com**

This beautifully laid-out garden on the banks of the Río Puerto Viejo was created in 1992 by American naturalist Tim Ryan. Hundreds of tropical plant species grow amid lush lawns. The garden specializes in heliconias, of which it has more than 80 species from around the world. Various species of ginger thrive here, plus a superb collection of bamboos and orchids. Equally impressive are the palms, which include the Madagascan traveler's palm, so named because in an emergency, travelers can drink the water that is stored in its stalk. More than 200 species of birds are drawn to the exotic flora. Hummingbirds hover about vibrant flowers as they sip nectar, while violaceous trogons and orange-chinned parakeets compete to be heard, and rare green macaws nest in *almendro* (almond) trees.

Knowledgeable tour guides impart fascinating facts on tropical plant ecology. The torchlit nighttime tours are especially rewarding. The river has calm stretches safe for swimming, and the island has a restaurant, plus B&B rooms.

⑱ Rara Avis

D3 **17 miles (27 km) S of Puerto Viejo** **From San José to Las Horquetas** **rara-avis.com**

This world-famous rainforest reserve was among the first private reserves in Costa Rica.

→

A violet sabrewing hummingbird sipping nectar on Heliconia Island

STAY

Celeste Mountain Lodge

Located on the slopes of Volcán Tenorio, this airy, stylish eco-lodge provides comfortable en-suite rooms with sweeping views of the Tenorio and the Miravelles volcanoes and surrounding tropical jungle.

🅰B2 🏠Bijagua
🆆celestemountain
lodge.com

$$$ $$$ $$$

Selva Verde

Hidden away in a rainforest reserve, this much-loved family-friendly lodge offers a tremendous array of wildlife-focused activities, tours, and programs. It is a perfect retreat for nature lovers and adventure seekers.

🅰D2 🏠Chilamata
🆆selvaverde.com

$$$ $$$ $$$

→
Pristine wilderness at its most spectacular at the Rara Avis reserve

Adjoining the Parque Nacional Braulio Carrillo and La Selva, the diminutive 4-sq-mile (10-sq-km) Rara Avis is quietly perched on the remote northeast slopes of the extinct Volcán Cacho Negro, at an elevation of 2,300 ft (700 m).

The brainchild of biologist Amos Bien, who created it in 1983, Rara Avis pioneered the notion of generating income through ecologically sustainable ventures in protected primary forests. Its selective farming projects include a butterfly farm, and philodendron and orchid cultivation.

Trails wander through pristine mid-elevation rainforest. The biodiversity is impressive; the eagle-eyed may spot everything from spider monkeys to boa constrictors. Elusive jaguars and pumas stalk silently through the undergrowth, while as many as 400 species of birds create a cacophony of sound, among them the umbrella bird, sunbitterns, and the endangered great green macaw. The park has several waterfalls; caution is recommended when swimming in the pools at their base.

This is not a destination for a casual day trip: the journey to get here is lengthy and quite challenging. Rara Avis is accessed by a daunting track, often knee-deep in mud. Transfers from Las Horquetas, on Highway 4, are by tractor-drawn canopied trailer, a bumpy 9-mile (14-km) journey that can take over two hours, followed by a one-hour hike to the lodge. Come prepared for heavy rainfall, which averages more than 200 inches (500 cm) per year, making rubber boots a must for hikers. Accommodation (two nights minimum) is in rustic lodges. Only the main office and dining room has electricity (pack a flashlight), but the jungle-backed rooms are clean and cosy, with private bathrooms and plenty of hot water.

> **Elusive jaguars and pumas stalk silently through the undergrowth, while as many as 400 species of birds create a cacophony of sound, among them the umbrella bird.**

THE CARIBBEAN

One of Costa Rica's wettest regions, the Caribbean extends along 125 miles (200 km) of the coastline between the Nicaraguan and Panamanian borders. The first inhabitants of the islands just off the coast were the Taínos, part of the Arawak nation, who were skilled agriculturists, fishermen, and potters. In 1502, Christopher Columbus landed in Costa Rica's Caribbean, specifically Playa Uvita, on his fourth voyage. After the closure of the port of Puerto Limón to trade in 1665, the Spanish made little attempt to settle the region. This drew pirates and smugglers, who induced the enslaved population to cut precious hardwoods for illicit trade. In the late 19th century, Jamaican and Chinese laborers and their families arrived to build the Atlantic Railroad and work on banana plantations. Succeeding generations adopted a subsistence life of farming and fishing, which continues in today's Creole culture. A network of canals, created in the 1960s to link Puerto Limón with Barra, immediately opened up this otherwise virtually inaccessible region to both trade and tourism, and led to the creation of several important conservation areas.

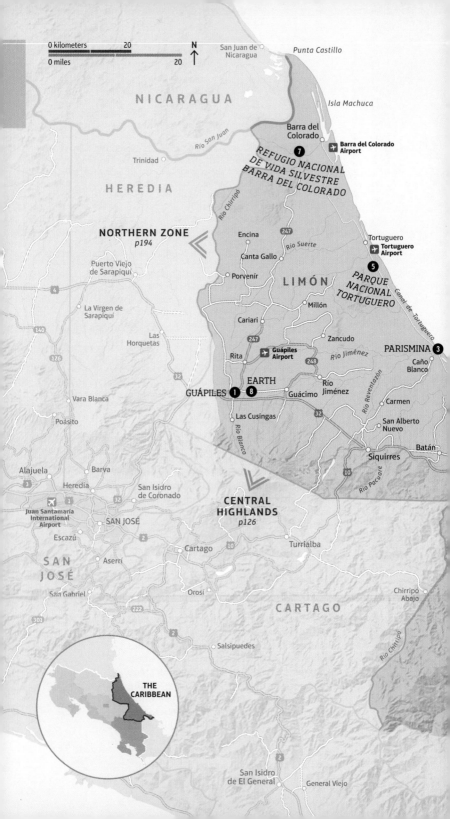

0 kilometers 20
0 miles 20

San Juan de
Nicaragua

Punta Castillo

NICARAGUA

Isla Machuca

Río San Juan

Barra del
Colorado

Barra del Colorado
Airport **7**

REFUGIO NACIONAL
DE VIDA SILVESTRE
BARRA DEL COLORADO

Trinidad

HEREDIA

Río Chirripó

Encina

247

NORTHERN ZONE
p194

Canta Gallo

Río Suerte

Tortuguero

Tortuguero
Airport

Puerto Viejo
de Sarapiquí

Porvenir

LIMÓN

5

PARQUE
NACIONAL
TORTUGUERO

4

La Virgen de
Sarapiquí

Millón

140

Las
Horquetas

Cariari

247

Zancudo

PARISMINA **3**

Caño
Blanco

126

Rita

Guápiles Airport

248

Río Jiménez

Río Reventazón

Canal de Tortuguero

32

GUÁPILES **1** **8**

EARTH

Guácimo

Río
Jiménez

Carmen

Vara Blanca

Las Cusingas

Río Blanco

32

San Alberto
Nuevo

Batán

Poásito

Siquirres

Alajuela

Barva

10

Río Pacuare

Juan Santamaría
International
Airport

Heredia

3

32

San Isidro
de Coronado

CENTRAL
HIGHLANDS
p126

1

Escazú

SAN JOSÉ

2

SAN
JOSÉ

Aserrí

Cartago

10

Turrialba

Chirripó
Abajo

San Gabriel

301

Orosí

CARTAGO

222

Río Chirripó

2

Salsipuedes

THE
CARIBBEAN

2

San Isidro
de El General

General Viejo

THE CARIBBEAN

Experience

1. Guápiles
2. Veragua Rainforest Eco-Adventure
3. Parismina
4. Puerto Limón
5. Parque Nacional Tortuguero
6. Sloth Sanctuary
7. Refugio Nacional de Vida Silvestre Barra del Colorado
8. EARTH
9. Cahuita
10. Parque Nacional Cahuita
11. Reserva Biológica Hitoy-Cerere
12. Refugio Nacional de Vida Silvestre Gandoca-Manzanillo
13. Bribri and Cabécar Indigenous Reserves
14. Puerto Viejo de Talamanca

Caribbean Sea

Punta de Riel

Matina

32

Moín

4 PUERTO LIMÓN

VERAGUA RAINFOREST ECO-ADVENTURE 2

Trébol

Limón International Airport

Aguas Zarcas

Finca Banaga

36

SLOTH SANCTUARY 6

Penshurst

Río Banano

Pandora

234

CAHUITA 9

PARQUE NACIONAL CAHUITA 10

Cuen

Vesta

11 RESERVA BIOLÓGICA HITOY-CERERE

PUERTO VIEJO DE TALAMANCA

Reserva Indígena KéköLdi

14

256

Manzanillo 12

REFUGIO NACIONAL DE VIDA SILVERSTRE GANDOCA-MANZANILLO

Bribri

Teliré

Río Telire

Shiroles

BRIBRI AND CABÉCAR INDIGENOUS RESERVES 13

Bambú

Las Tablas

36

Reserva Indígena Talamanca-Cabécar

San José Cabécar

Río Coén

Reserva Indígena Yorkín

Reserva Indígena Talamanca-Bribri

Sixaola

Changuinola

SOUTHERN ZONE
p226

PANAMA

La Gloria

←

Passing thundering cascades on the Puma Trail at Veragua Rainforest Eco-Adventure

EXPERIENCE

① Guápiles

🅰E3 ⏱41 miles (66 km) NE of San José 🚌From San José

The most westerly and largest town on Hwy 32, Guápiles lies in the heart of a banana-producing zone, and is known as a center for flowers and ornamental plant farms. The gateway town for the region, it's a popular local shopping destination without being too touristy, and has plenty of homely, traditional Tico restaurants. With a range of accommodation, it makes a good base for trips to nearby attractions such as the Parque Nacional Tortuguero (p218).

② Veragua Rainforest Eco-Adventure

🅰F3 ⏱18 miles (28 km) SW of Puerto Limón 🚌From Puerto Limón to Liverpool, then by jeep-taxi ⏰May-Dec: pre-booked groups only; Nov-Apr: 8am-3pm Thu-Sun 🌐veragua rainforest.com

This 5-sq-mile (13-sq-km) reserve is used for ecological research by INBio, whose laboratory is open to visitors.

You can wander through peaceful butterfly and frog gardens, view snake and insect exhibits, and hop aboard an aerial tram for a ride downhill to riverside trails, where poison-dart frogs hop about in the undergrowth. For the more energetic, there is a hike to a spectacular cascading waterfall, where the thundering spray can be felt. Try out the canopy zipline tour or visit the restaurant with its rainforest views. The entry fee includes a guided tour. Visitors driving themselves to the park may need a 4WD vehicle.

③ Parismina

🅰F3 ⏱30 miles (48 km) E of Guápiles 🚌From Guápiles via Siquerres to Caño Blanco, then 2 mile (3 km) by boat 🚌From Puerto Limón

This landlocked village at the mouth of the Río Parismina, 28 miles (45 km) north of Moín, is the only community along the canal linking Puerto Limón to Tortuguero. The humble fishing hamlet is a major center for tarpon and snook sportfishing, with two dedicated lodges: Jungle Tarpon and Río Parismina Lodge. Elsewhere, simple guest-houses and restaurants serve adventurous travelers seeking a slice of local life. The silvery beach is one of the most important nesting sites in the western hemisphere for leatherback turtles, and has taken on added importance with the recent crash in the leatherback population at Nicoya's Playa Grande. The **Association Save the Turtles of Parismina** has a reserve and hatching station, and is always looking for volunteers to assist during nesting season (February to October); accommodation with host families can be arranged.

Association Save the Turtles of Parismina

⊗ 🏠Barra del Parismina 🌐parisminaturtles.org

④ Puerto Limón

🅰G3 ⏱100 miles (160 km) E of San José 🚆🚌🚍

Located in the bay where Christopher Columbus and his son Fernando anchored in

---

📷 PICTURE PERFECT
Riot of Color

Walk down many Limón streets and you'll find wooden houses with broad balconies held up by stilts, all painted in tropical pastels. These classics of the Caribbean vernacular style will add a riot of color to any photo album.

→

New Orleans-style houses lining the water in Puerto Limón

1502, the port town of Puerto Limón had its origins in early colonial days. Used by pirates and smugglers for trading mahogany and other tropical hardwoods, the settlement thrived on this illicit traffic under the nose of the Spanish authorities. By the 1880s, the town had garnered a large Chinese population, who came in the 1880s as indentured laborers for the construction of the Atlantic Railroad. A small Chinese cemetery at the entrance to the town honors this heritage. Today, the port handles most of the nation's sea trade, and cruise ships dock regularly here. During the day the main highway into town is crowded with container trucks.

Columbus supposedly landed at Isla Uvita, half a mile (1 km) offshore. His landfall is commemorated by a bronze bust, unveiled in 1992 for the 500th anniversary of his arrival in the Americas. The bust faces Parque Vargas, at the east end of the pedestrian-only Avenida 2 (also known as El Bulevar). Nearby, a beautiful mural by artist Guadalupe Alvarez depicts local history since pre-Columbian days.

Puerto Limón has some intriguing architecture, with pretty filigreed iron balconies in the style of New Orleans, under which locals gather to play dominoes. To the west of Parque Vargas, the cream-colored stucco belle époque Alcaldía (the old Town Hall) is a fine example. There's a lively daily market, the Mercado Central, to the north of the museum, offering everything from pigs' heads to freshly caught fish. Opposite the market is the Casa de la Cultura. This House of Culture hosts exhibitions of local artists' works, as well as a film night every Thursday. A dramatic post-modernist concrete cathedral, La Catedral del Sagrado Corazón rises over the center of town with its unusual crystal-shaped 154-ft (47-m) spire.

Just outside of town, local surfers find their fun off Playa Bonita. This golden-sand beach gets crowded on weekends with Limonenses, as the town's inhabitants are known. Note that swimming at the south end of the bay is dangerous due to riptides.

CARNAVAL

In the second week of October, Puerto Limón erupts into color for Carnaval, a week-long Caribbean Mardi Gras that culminates on Día de las Culturas (Day of Cultures). Buses bring revelers from San José, and the city packs in as many as 100,000 visitors. Live reggae, salsa, and calypso get everyone dancing. Other events at Carnaval include beauty contests, *desfiles* (parades), street fairs, and firework displays. The highlight is the Gran Desfile, a huge parade of flamboyant costumes and floats.

↑ Wildlife-spotting on Tortuguero National Park's waterways

STAY

Tortuga Lodge
Gorgeous nature lodge with an infinity pool, above a tranquil lagoon.

🅐F2 🏠Tortuguero
🌐tortugalodge.com

$$$

Alby Lodge
Simple, well-tended thatched cottages on the edge of the park.

🅐G4 🏠Cahuita
🌐albylodge.com

$$$

Shawanda Ecolodge
Romantic bungalows, a spa, and gourmet alfresco dining.

🅐G4 🏠Playa Chiquita
🌐shawandha.com

$$$

5 ⊘ ⓂS

Parque Nacional Tortuguero

🅐F2 🚗32 miles (52 km) N of Puerto Limón 📞2709-8086 or 2710-2929 🚢From Pavona, Moín, and Caño Blanco ⏰6am–noon & 1–4pm daily

Created to protect the most important nesting site of the green turtle in the western hemisphere, the 297-sq-mile (770-sq-km) Tortuguero National Park extends along 14 miles (22 km) of shoreline and 19 miles (30 km) out to sea. The Canal de Tortuguero, which runs through the park, connects a labyrinth of deltas, canals, and lagoons, allowing visitors to get unusually close to the fauna.

With 11 distinct life zones, ranging from raffia palm forest to swamps, the park offers one of the most rewarding nature experiences in the country. This watery world is best seen by boat: the wide canals and the silent approach on the water allow grandstand wildlife watching, although

hiking trails start from the ranger stations at the northern and southern ends of the park. A huge array of wildlife are easily sighted – river otters, caimans, and howler, spider, and white-faced monkeys especially, as well as birds such as toucans and jacamars – but a guide is strongly recommended, both to avoid getting lost in the waterways and to identify wildlife that might otherwise be missed. The star attractions are the turtles, in particular the green turtle, which nests between June and November. Entry to the beach is strictly regulated after dark – only two escorted groups are allowed each night.

There are no roads to the park; access is by boat or small planes that land at Tortuguero village, to the north of the park. Local lodges organize guided tours through the park.

The villagers of Tortuguero traditionally made their living by lumbering or by culling turtles. Today, tourism is the major source of employment, and locals have learned a new ethic as conservationists. The

> **This watery world is best seen by boat: the wide canals and the silent approach on the water allow for grandstand wildlife watching.**

Sea Turtle Conservancy Visitor Center at the John H. Phipps Biological Station has excellent displays on local ecology, especially turtles.

Sea Turtle Conservancy Visitor Center

⊛ 🏠550 yd (500 m) N of Tortuguero village 📞2767-1576 🕐10am–noon & 2–5pm daily

---

6

Sloth Sanctuary

🅰G4 🏠7 miles (11 km) N of Cahuita 🚌From Puerto Limón to Cahuita, then taxi 🕐8am–2pm Tue–Sun 🌐slothsanctuary.com

This is one of the world's only centers devoted to sloth research and rescue. The facility began in 1992 with the adoption of an orphaned three-toed sloth. Many more sloths followed, and the Sloth

Sanctuary has now become a leading research center on sloth ecology, though it has faced some criticism for the way it cared for the sloths in the past.

Injured sloths, including those electrocuted while crawling along power lines, are treated at a "slothpital." Many are released into the wild, while others can be seen in enclosures. Visitors are led on guided tours that include the sloth nursery and the exercise facilities where sloths are rehabilitated. A guided canoe ride to observe tropical lowland rainforest flora and fauna is also included.

Trails lead into the wildlife refuge, dense rainforest and marshland where caimans, otters, and other creatures can be spotted.

7

Refugio Nacional de Vida Silvestre Barra del Colorado

🅰E2 🏠21 miles (34 km) N of Tortuguero 📞2709-8086 🚢From Tortuguero, Puerto Viejo de Sarapiquí, and Pavona 🕐8am–4pm daily

Connected to the Parque Nacional Tortuguero by the Caño de Penitencia, this 350-sq-mile (910-sq-km) refuge extends north to the border with Nicaragua. The flooded marshes, teeming rainforest, and vast raffia palm forests are home to abundant wildlife, but despite this the refuge is virtually untapped as a wilderness destination. Crocodiles as well as birds such as jabiru storks and endangered great green macaws can be spotted, while tapirs, jaguars, and manatees inhabit the deep forests and swamps. The refuge's many rivers have populations of

---

←

A three-toed sloth just hanging around at the Sloth Sanctuary

> **NICARAGUA**
>
> Marking the northern boundary of the Barra del Colorado reserve, and the border with Nicaragua, the Río San Juan has caused tensions between the two countries for 150 years. The area became politically sensitive again during the Contra-Sandinista conflict *(p178)*, making it dangerous to travel. These days it's safe to cross the border, but re-entry may be tricky, as there is a Costa Rican police checkpoint but no immigration office on the way back in.

tarpon, snook, and garfish. Lodges catering to fishing enthusiasts are centered around Barra del Colorado at the mouth of the Río Colorado.

8

EARTH

🅰E3 🏠1 mile (1.6 km) E of Guácimo 🚌From San José to Puerto Limón 🕐8am–5pm Mon–Fri, 8am–noon Sat & Sun 🌐earth.ac.cr

One of the world's leading tropical research centers, the Escuela de Agricultura de la Región Tropical Húmeda (Agricultural College of the Humid Tropical Region) focuses on ecologically sustainable practices. EARTH operates its own experimental banana plantation, banana processing plant, and paper-making plant that uses banana skins. There are guided tours and nature trails through the rainforest.

⑨
Cahuita

**▲G4 🏠 27 miles (43 km)
S of Puerto Limón** 🚌

With its rich African-Caribbean heritage, Cahuita (meaning "mahogany point") is one of Costa Rica's most attractive villages. Its residents live in brightly painted wooden houses, some of which stand on stilts. Unlike many other beach-focused villages, such as nearby Puerto Viejo, Cahuita has largely been skipped by the tourist boom and stays true to its laid-back island roots. Come here in July, when the energetic Festival Internacional de Calypso Walter Ferguson celebrates the town's musical and cultural traditions. The festival is named after the famous town resident

singer-songwriter Walter Gavitt Ferguson Byfield, also known as the "king of calypso".

North of the village are the black sands of palm-fringed Playa Negra, extending north to the Río Estrella estuary and perfect for tidepooling. A relaxing way to explore the surrounding beaches and jungle is by joining one

of the many tours that are offered at **Brigitte Ranch**. These include visits to a nearby chocolate finca, guided hikes, and kayaking and snorkeling trips in the national park. There are also yoga sessions and Creole cookery classes.

Brigitte Ranch
🐴⌚ 🏠 Playa Negra, Cahuita
🌐 brigittecahuita.com

> ### CARIBBEAN CULTURE
>
> Distinct in many respects from other parts of the country, the culture of the Caribbean coast has close affinities with the English-speaking Caribbean islands. About one-third of the population are descended from Black Jamaicans who arrived in Costa Rica's Caribbean lowlands in the late 19th century to work on the Atlantic Railroad and banana plantations. Many people still use colloquial phrases familiar to the West Indies. The Latin music of the highlands here is replaced by the mellow riffs of reggae, and many people are Rastafarian. The local cuisine is also deliciously distinct, not least for its use of tongue-searing chillies and spices.

10 Parque Nacional Cahuita

G4 **27 miles (43 km) S of Puerto Limón** **From Puerto Limón to Cahuita** **Puerto Vargas: 8am–4pm daily; Playa Blanca: 6am–5pm daily** **sinac.go.cr**

Wildlife abounds at this 4-sq-mile (10-sq-km) park adjacent to Cahuita. Lie on the beach here and you might see toucans and green macaws, or sloths hanging in the trees above. Foraging in the undergrowth are armadillos, rodent-like agoutis, and anteaters. Crocodile-like caimans can be seen in freshwater rivers, while parrot fish, lobsters, and green turtles swim around a depleted coral reef off Playa Blanca. A well-marked 4-mile (6-km) trail, with boardwalks over boggy patches connects Cahuita village's Kelly Creek ranger station to the one at Puerto Vargas. Riptides make the sea very dangerous in places here, especially at Playa Vargas, so check with rangers before swimming. A guide is obligatory for snorkeling.

11 Reserva Biológica Hitoy-Cerere

F4 **28 miles (45 km) S of Puerto Limón and 12 miles (20 km) SW of Hwy 36 at Penshurst** **From Puerto Limón to Finca 12, then by jeep-taxi** **8am–4pm daily** **sinac.go.cr**

Lying near the head of the Río Estrella valley and extending up the western flanks of the Talamanca Mountains, the 38-sq-mile (100-sq-km) Hitoy-Cerere Biological Reserve offers hardy hikers and nature lovers pristine rainforest habitats fed by heavy rainfall. July, August, November, and December are the wettest months, when rivers thunder down the steep slopes. Large mammals thrive amid the dense forests, including all six of Costa Rica's cat species.

The nearby **Reserva Selva Bananito**, on the border of Parque Internacional La Amistad (*p238*), protects 5 sq miles (13 sq km) of ecologically sustainable farmland and rainforest at the foothills of the Talamanca Mountains. It offers guided hikes, birdwatching, and tree-planting sessions, as well as more adrenaline-charged activities, such as tree climbing, gyrocopter trips, ziplining, and rappeling down waterfalls. A 4WD vehicle is required to get here, and overnight stays in the lodge are recommended.

Reserva Selva Bananito
22 miles (35 km) SW of Puerto Limón **selva bananito.com**

← Colorful toucans (*inset*) perching in the rich forest that lines idyllic Playa Blanca, Cahuita

EAT

Miss Junie's
Caribbean classics at this family-run spot.
F2 **Tortuguero** **2709-8029**
$ $ $

Cocoricó
Great pizzas and pastas, plus film nights.
G4 **Cahuita** **2755-0409**
$ $ $

Taylor's Place
A local favorite.
F2 **Tortuguero** **8468-6795**
$ $ $

Café Rico
Fantastic healthy-but-hearty breakfasts at this colorful café with a lean-to library.
G4 **Puerto Viejo** **2750-0510**
$ $ $

12 Ⓜ Ⓨ

Refugio Nacional de Vida Silvestre Gandoca-Manzanillo

🅰F4–G4 🚗8 miles (13 km) S of Puerto Viejo 📞2759-9001 or 2755-0302 🚌From Puerto Viejo de Talamanca 🕐8am–4pm daily

Enclosing a mosaic of habitats, Gandoca-Manzanillo Wildlife Refuge is a mixed-use park with settlements whose inhabitants live in harmony with the environment. Created in 1985, this 32-sq-mile (83-sq-km) reserve extends out to sea, protecting a coral reef and 17 sq miles (44 sq km) of marine habitat in which several species of turtles breed. The Costa Rican conservation body Asociación ANAI runs a volunteer program for those keen to assist with research and protection of turtles. On land, the refuge has mangrove swamp, rare raffia palm swamp and *cativo* forest, and tropical rainforest, all swarming with wildlife. Manatees and *tucuxí* inhabit the lagoons and estuaries. The waters are also important breeding grounds for sharks, game fish, and lobsters.

A coastal trail and several inland ones – often overgrown and muddy – give unparalleled opportunities for spotting mammals and an astounding diversity of birds, amphibians,

Did You Know?

Raffia palms have the largest leaves in the plant kingdom, up to 80 ft (25 m) long and 10 ft (3 m) wide.

and reptiles. The coast trail leads to Punta Mona (Monkey Point) and Punta Mona Center, an educational institution and thriving organic farm.

13

Bribri and Cabécar Indigenous Reserves

🅰G4 🚌To Bribri, then by jeep-taxi 🅦ATEC: atec cr.org; COOPRENA: turismoruralcr.com

The Indigenous Bribri and Cabécar peoples live in a series of fragmented reserves on the Caribbean slopes of the Talamanca Mountains, surviving primarily through subsistence agriculture. These two related groups have managed to retain much of their culture, languages, animistic dances, and shamanistic practices.

The most accessible of the reserves is the Reserva Indígena KeköLdi, spread across 14 sq miles (36 sq km)

→

Surfing across cresting waves off Playa Negra, before the setting sun

in the hills southwest of Puerto Viejo. The reserve's local conservation projects include a farm where green iguanas are bred. The farm lies off the main road near Hone Creek, a half-hour walk from Puerto Viejo.

Farther south, beyond the regional center of Bribri, is the Reserva Indígena Talamanca-Bribri. Centered on Shiroles, 11 miles (18 km) from Bribri, this reserve encompasses the Valle de Talamanca, a broad basin carpeted by plantations of bananas. From Bambú, 6 miles (10 km) west of Bribri, a trip by dug-out canoe down Río Yorkín leads to Reserva Indígena Yorkín, where visitors housed in traditional lodgings gain an appreciation of Indigenous culture.

Another reserve worth visiting in this area is Reserva Indígena Talamanca-Cabécar, reached from Shiroles along rugged dirt roads that push up the valley of Río Coén. This remote settlement of the San José Cabécar is an important center of shamanism and Indigenous culture.

A wide range of guided hikes and overnight visits to the reserves are arranged by Talamanca Association for Ecotourism and Conservation (ATEC), a non-profit organization based in Puerto Viejo de Talamanca, and by the excellent National Ecotourism Network (COOPRENA), which supports local development. Note that the only place where a permit to visit is not required is the iguana farm in the Reserva Indígena KeköLdi.

←

Walkway at the Refugio Nacional de Vida Silvestre Gandoca-Manzanillo

⑭
Puerto Viejo de Talamanca

🗺️ G4 🚗 10 miles (16 km) S of Cahuita 🚌 ℹ️ ATEC; www. ateccr.org

One of the Caribbean coast's best surfing areas, Puerto Viejo de Talamanca is also a must-visit destination for travelers looking to get off the beaten path. Little more than a collection of stilt-legged shacks as recently as the 1990s, it has since expanded rapidly. Although electricity arrived in 1996, later followed by other developments, the village retains an earthy, laid-back quality.

Experienced surfers come here between December and March to test their skills against the notorious reef break La Salsa Brava, where the famously consistent waves can reach heights of up to 21 ft (6.5 m). The palm-fringed black sands of Playa Negra curl north from town.

Inland of the beach, **Finca La Isla Botanical Garden** is an excellent place to explore the coastal rainforest along well-kept trails. Bromeliads are a specialty of this lovely garden, which also has exotic fruits and ornamental plants. A self-guided booklet is available.

Puerto Viejo has some of the best budget accommodation in all of Costa Rica, as well as numerous outstanding eateries. Open-air bars and buzzy dance clubs come alive at night, with revelers spilling onto the sands.

A string of surfing beaches – Playa Cocles, Playa Uva, and Playa Chiquita – runs south from Puerto Viejo to the hamlet of Manzanillo. A paved road lined with lodge-style *cabinas* and hotels lies along the shore, with forested hills rising inland. At Playa Chiquita, the **Jaguar Rescue Center**, where all kinds of animals are rehabilitated, as well as these great cats, is not to be missed.

Finca La Isla Botanical Garden
♿ ⊘ 🚗 1 mile (1.6 km) NW of Puerto Viejo 📞 2750-0046 or 8886-8530 🕐 10am–4pm Fri–Mon

Jaguar Rescue Center
♿ ⊘ 🚗 3 miles (5 km) S of Puerto Viejo 🕐 Entry by guided tours only: 9:30am & 11:30am Mon–Sat (book ahead) 🌐 jaguarrescue.com

---

SHAMANISM

The Indigenous Cabécar and Bribri peoples ascribe to a spirit-filled, animist vision of the world in which the shaman-healer is the central authority in the community. Shamanic tools such as *uLú* (healing canes) and medicinal herbs are used along with ritual song and dance to cure a person who is ill, or to restore harmony within the community.

STONE-CARVED SHAMAN

A small convoy of boats gliding over sun-dappled water, past wildlife-rich banks ↑

A BOAT TOUR
CANAL DE TORTUGUERO

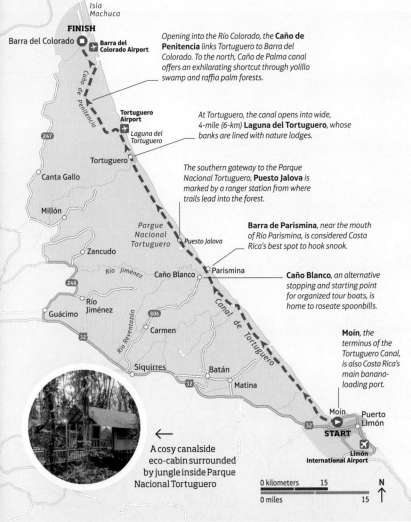

Canal de Tortuguero

THE CARIBBEAN

Locator Map
For more detail see p214

Length 65 miles (105 km) **Stopping-off points** Parismina has fishing lodges and simple restaurants; tour boats will stop on request

Travel along the Caribbean seaboard became possible with the building of the Tortuguero canal system in 1966–74. Four canals make up this 65-mile- (105-km-) long aquatic highway, which connects the port of Moín to Barra del Colorado village, and is lined with rainforest. Narrow in places, when the looming forest seems to close in on the water, the canal offers the chance of fascinating boat trips, with sightings of caimans and river turtles, and birds such as aracaris and kingfishers, all along the way.

Isla Machuca

FINISH
Barra del Colorado

Barra del Colorado Airport

Opening into the Río Colorado, the **Caño de Penitencia** *links Tortuguero to Barra del Colorado. To the north, Caño de Palma canal offers an exhilarating shortcut through yolillo swamp and raffia palm forests.*

Tortuguero Airport

Laguna del Tortuguero

At Tortuguero, the canal opens into wide, 4-mile (6-km) **Laguna del Tortuguero**, *whose banks are lined with nature lodges.*

Tortuguero

Canta Gallo

Millón

The southern gateway to the Parque Nacional Tortuguero, **Puesto Jalova** *is marked by a ranger station from where trails lead into the forest.*

Barra de Parismina, *near the mouth of Río Parismina, is considered Costa Rica's best spot to hook snook.*

Parque Nacional Tortuguero

Puesto Jalova

Zancudo

Río Jiménez

Caño Blanco — Parismina

Caño Blanco, *an alternative stopping and starting point for organized tour boats, is home to roseate spoonbills.*

Río Jiménez

Guácimo

Carmen

Río Reventazón

Moín, *the terminus of the Tortuguero Canal, is also Costa Rica's main banana-loading port.*

Siquirres

Batán

Matina

Moín — Puerto Limón

START

Limón International Airport

← A cosy canalside eco-cabin surrounded by jungle inside Parque Nacional Tortuguero

0 kilometers 15
0 miles 15

N ↑

SOUTHERN ZONE

Costa Rica's southern reaches were first inhabited by the nomadic Chibchas and Diquís peoples, whose relics now lie smothered in dense mainland jungles. These groups vied for territory with the Boruca and Guaymí, whose burial sites have been found on the sacred Isla del Caño. Spanish conquistadors marched into the region in the mid-1500s, meeting fierce resistance from the Boruca, in a vain search for gold; in the end, though the Indigenous populations were nearly decimated, the Spanish remained generally disinterested by their newly acquired land. The coastal area fell into an isolated backwater, neglected by distant colonial rulers, for several centuries. In 1938, the United Fruit Company arrived, and planted bananas across the valleys of the Sierpe and Coto-Colorado Rivers. The subject of protest in the late 20th century, the country's largest indigenous communities now live in isolated mountain retreats in this region.

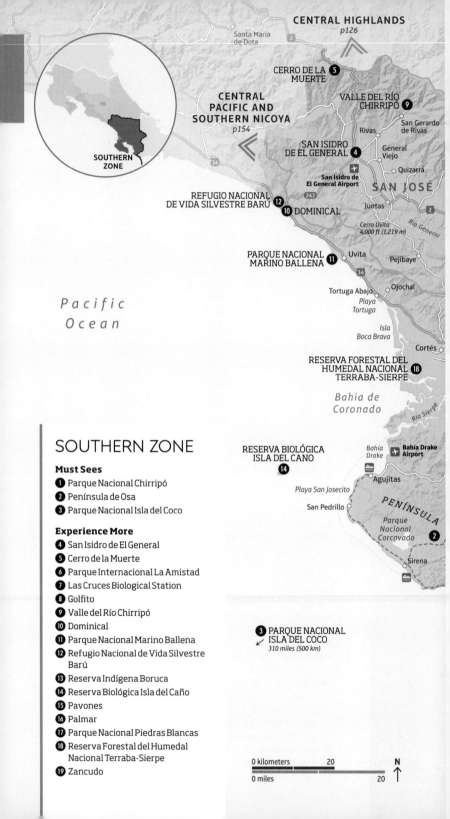

Santa María
de Dota

CERRO DE LA ⑤
MUERTE

VALLE DEL RÍO
CHIRRIPÓ ⑨

CENTRAL
PACIFIC AND
SOUTHERN NICOYA
p154

San Gerardo
de Rivas

Rivas

SAN ISIDRO
DE EL GENERAL ④

General
Viejo

Quizarrá

San Isidro de
El General Airport

SAN JOSÉ

REFUGIO NACIONAL
DE VIDA SILVESTRE BARÚ ⑫
⑩ DOMINICAL

Juntas

Río General

Cerro Uvita
4,000 ft (1,219 m)

PARQUE NACIONAL
MARINO BALLENA ⑪

Uvita

Pejibaye

34

Ojochal

Tortuga Abajo

Playa
Tortuga

Pacific
Ocean

Isla
Boca Brava

Cortés

RESERVA FORESTAL DEL
HUMEDAL NACIONAL ⑱
TERRABA-SIERPE

Bahía de
Coronado

Río Sierpe

RESERVA BIOLÓGICA
ISLA DEL CAÑO
⑭

Bahía
Drake

Bahía Drake
Airport

Agujitas

Playa San Josecito

San Pedrillo

PENÍNSULA

Parque
Nacional
Corcovado ②

Sirena

SOUTHERN ZONE

Must Sees

① Parque Nacional Chirripó

② Península de Osa

③ Parque Nacional Isla del Coco

Experience More

④ San Isidro de El General

⑤ Cerro de la Muerte

⑥ Parque Internacional La Amistad

⑦ Las Cruces Biological Station

⑧ Golfito

⑨ Valle del Río Chirripó

⑩ Dominical

⑪ Parque Nacional Marino Ballena

⑫ Refugio Nacional de Vida Silvestre Barú

⑬ Reserva Indígena Boruca

⑭ Reserva Biológica Isla del Caño

⑮ Pavones

⑯ Palmar

⑰ Parque Nacional Piedras Blancas

⑱ Reserva Forestal del Humedal Nacional Terraba-Sierpe

⑲ Zancudo

③ PARQUE NACIONAL
ISLA DEL COCO
310 miles (500 km)

0 kilometers   20

0 miles   20

N

❶
PARQUE NACIONAL CHIRRIPÓ

🅰F4 🏛12 miles (19 km) NE of San Isidro de El General 📞2742-5083 🚌To San Gerardo de Rivas ranger station, 2 miles (3 km) W of the park 🕐Trail to summit: 3–10am daily (advance registration required) 🌐sinac.go.cr

Costa Rica's highest mountain, Cerro Chirripó (12,530 ft/3,820 m) is enfolded in the 194-sq-mile (502-sq-km) Chirripó National Park. The park is part of the Amistad Biosphere Reserve, protecting three distinct "life zones" in rugged, virgin territory where wildlife flourishes with minimal interference from humans.

Best known for its excellent hiking trails, and for containing as many as 60 percent of all wildlife species in Costa Rica, the park is best visited in spring when the widest array can be seen. Most people come here to see the Los Crestones rock formations in person, and for the challenge of mounting Sendero Termometro and La Cuesta del Agua, two of the steepest sections of the 12-mile (19-km) trail that leads to the summit. The trail winds through a valley of montane forests and an understory of bamboo and ferns, then up sheer hillsides where you can see the top of the canopy. Visitors must register in advance and report to the ranger station in San Gerardo de Rivas before setting out to the summit. Centro Ambientalista El Páramo (2447-7476), the sole lodging on the mountains, rents out sleeping bags, blankets, and stoves.

> **△ GREAT VIEW**
> **From on High**
>
> Climb to the summit on clear days and enjoy staggering 360-degree views of the park, and vistas that stretch from the Pacific Ocean to the Caribbean Sea. The best time to see it is in the light of early morning.

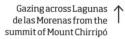

Gazing across Lagunas de las Morenas from the summit of Mount Chirripó ↑

1 A hiker pauses on one of the tree-lined trails at verdant Parque Nacional Chirripó.

2 The dramatic vertical rock formations of Los Crestones were considered a sacred site by pre-Columbian cultures.

3 A tiny margay, one of the six native cat species that can be seen in the park, surveys its territory, on the lookout for predators and prey.

HIKING IN THE PARK

Most visitors take to a well-marked trail that climbs 8,200 ft (2,500 m) from the trailhead, near San Gerardo de Rivas, to ascend the summit. The 20-mile (32-km) hike to the top and back normally takes two days, with an overnight stay near the top of the mountain. Hire guide-porters in San Gerardo. An alternative route is from Herradura via Cerro Uran.

Did You Know?

Páramo alpine savanna can go from freezing to as high as 30° C (86° F) in a single day.

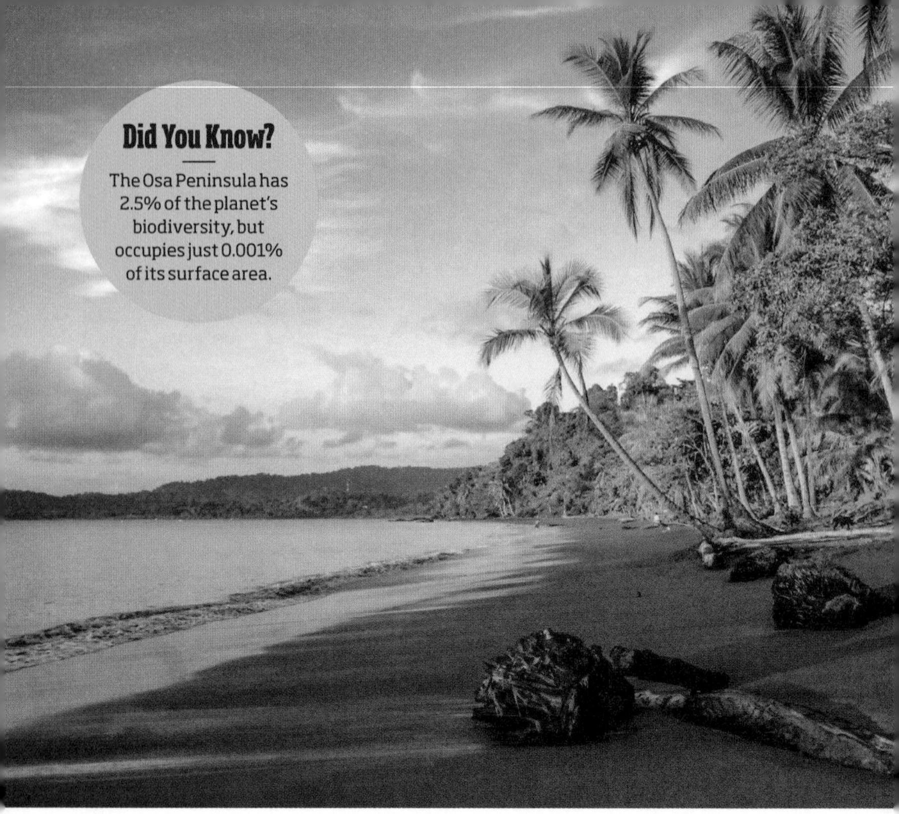

Did You Know?

The Osa Peninsula has 2.5% of the planet's biodiversity, but occupies just 0.001% of its surface area.

2

PENÍNSULA DE OSA

E6-F7 109 miles (175 km) SW of San Isidro de El General Puerto Jiménez, Carate, PN Corcovado, or Bahía Drake To Puerto Jiménez or La Palma To Bahía Drake

Washed on three sides by warm Pacific waters, the isolated, nearly untouched Osa Peninsula curls around the Golfo Dulce, with the lush rainforests of Corcovado lying at its heart. Although tourism has boomed in recent years, travel into the interior is still a challenge. Highway 245 follows the eastern shore and a rugged dirt road links Rincón to Bahía Drake, but the only guaranteed access to the western shores is by boat or small plane.

The peninsula was once a center for the pre-Columbian Diquís culture, whose skill as goldsmiths sent Spanish conquistadors on a futile search for fabled gold mines. Deluged by year-round rains, much of this rugged area remains uninhabited and trackless, and is covered with virgin rainforest. About half of Osa is protected within sprawling Parque Nacional Corcovado, the largest of the parks and reserves that make up the Corcovado Conservation Area, set aside to preserve one of the last original tracts of the Pacific coast's tropical rainforest in Mesoamerica. Those with a taste for adventure are rewarded with wilderness and some of the most spectacular wildlife-viewing in the nation. Wilderness lodges offering a variety of activities line the coast, and tours of the national park with local guides are available from one of the four ranger stations.

INSIDER TIP
The Bug Lady

A nighttime insect tour of the rainforest with biologist Tracie Stice (the "Bug Lady") and naturalist Giancomo Gómez reveals a world unseen by day, with fascinating tidbits from the guides *(www.thenight tour.com).*

GOLD MINING

Oreros (gold panners) had sifted for gold in the rivers of the Osa Peninsula for centuries. When the United Fruit Company pulled out of the region in 1985, unemployed workers flooded the peninsula, leading to a latter-day gold rush. Though short-lived, it caused major damage: trees were felled, river banks dynamited, and exposed soils sluiced. After violent clashes with the authorities, the *oreros* were ousted in 1986. Some still work the outer margins of Corcovado, while others make a living leading gold hunts for tourists.

↑ Ideal for scuba diving and sportfishing, the calm seas of beautiful Bahía Drake

①
Bahía Drake
E6

Rocky cliffs and forested hills provide a compelling setting for this scalloped bay, one of the most inaccessible areas in Costa Rica. The dirt road from Rincón is often impassable, and most visitors arrive by boat from the village of Sierpe. Among the activities available are whale-watching, snorkeling, and kayaking, as well as zipline in the verdant rainforest with **Corcovado Canopy Tours**.

From Agujitas, a coastal trail leads south for 8 miles (13 km) to Parque Nacional Corcovado, passing **Refugio Nacional de Vida Silvestre Punta Río Claro**, both of which teem with wildlife. When canoeing on Laguna Chocouaco, to the east of Augjitas, tapirs and crocodiles are often sighted.

Corcovado Canopy Tour

⌂ Los Planos, 8 miles (14 km) SE of Agujitas ⓦ corcovado canopytour.com

Refugio Nacional de Vida Silvestre Punta Rio Claro

🚲 🛶 🦜 ⌂ Playa Caletas, 4 miles (6 km) S of Agujitas 🕗 8am–6pm daily ⓦ sinac. go.cr

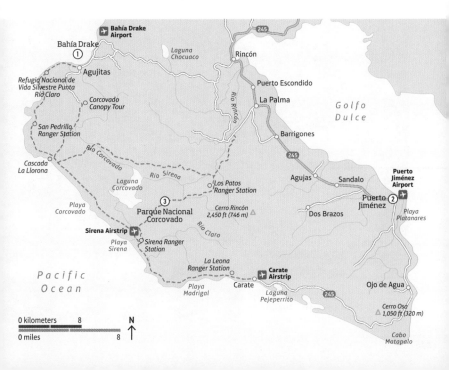

② Puerto Jiménez

A F6 **△** 109 miles (175 km) SW of San Isidro de El General

The main settlement on the peninsula, this dusty village is popular with backpackers. In the 1980s, it briefly blossomed on income from local gold and gained a "Wild West" reputation, where gun carrying was considered a good idea, but today, the town thrives on tourist trade. Various adventure activities are available. Kayakers flock to the east, where mangroves extend along the shore of the Golfo Dulce (Sweet Gulf) to the estuary of the Río Platanares. Home to crocodiles, caimans, freshwater turtles, and river otters, this ecosystem is protected within the 555-acre (225-ha) **Refugio Nacional de Vida Silvestre Preciosa Platanares**. Along the shores of the lovely Playa Platanares, it has a small coral reef that is good for snorkeling. The beach is a nesting site for five species of marine turtles, and a small *vivero* (nursery)

raises hatchlings for release into the jade-green waters.

The shore south of Puerto Jiménez is lined with beaches. Cabo Matapalo, at the tip of the peninsula, and Playa Sombrero offer great surfing.

Refugio Nacional de Vida Silvestre Preciosa Platanares

🕸️ 🐾 👁️ **△** 2 miles (3 km) E of Puerto Jiménez

---

③ Parque Nacional Corcovado

🕸️ 🐾 👁️ **A** E6 **△** 25 miles (40 km) SW of Puerto Jiménez **⊙** Check website; opening hours vary; reservations and a guide are obligatory **w** sinac.go.cr

Considered the crown jewel among the protected regions

> Considered the crown jewel among the protected regions of the humid tropics, this 165-sq-mile (425-sq-km) park was created in 1975 to preserve the largest Pacific coast rainforest in the Americas.

of the humid tropics, this 165-sq-mile (425-sq-km) park was created in 1975 to preserve the largest Pacific coast rainforest in the Americas, as well as 20 sq miles (52 sq km) of marine habitat. Corcovado (meaning "hunchback") has eight distinct zones, including herbaceous swamps, flooded swamp forest, and montane forest. The area receives up to 158 inches (400 cm) of rainfall per year, with torrential rains from April to December.

Wildlife viewing is splendid and among the most diverse in Costa Rica. The park has over 400 species of birds, including the endangered harpy eagle, and the largest population of scarlet macaws in Central America; birdwatchers who make the trek into the park are rewarded with guaranteed sightings. Jaguars are spotted more frequently here than at any

Did You Know?

Corcovado's rivers are home to caimans, crocodiles, and bull sharks.

A narrow stretch of river breaking across a trail in Corcovado National Park ↑

↑ Cyclists taking a well-earned break beside the water in the former gold-rush village of Puerto Jiménez

Interesting attractions close to the Parque Nacional Corcovado include Humedal Lacustrino Laguna Pejeperrito wetlands, 2 miles (3 km) east of Carate, and the 2-sq-mile (3-sq-km) Refugio Nacional de Vida Silvestre Pejeperro, 2 miles (4 km) farther east. They are little visited, but offer good opportunities for birdwatching, as well as for spotting crocodiles.

other park in the nation, as are tapirs. Both species can often be seen on the beaches, especially just before sunset. Corcovado is also known for its large packs of peccaries – wild hogs which look cute but should be avoided. The titi, an endangered squirrel monkey, is also found here. There are in excess of 115 species of amphibians and reptiles. Look out for poison-dart frogs, easily seen in their gaudy livery; the elusive lime-green red-eyed tree frog and tiny Fleischmann's transparent frog are harder to spot. On the beaches, the fortunate might

even witness green, hawksbill, leatherback, or Pacific ridley turtles as they crawl ashore to nest. Unfortunately, the park is understaffed and its wildlife is under threat by poachers.

Although there are hotels and organized tours close by, the park is best suited to self-sufficient hikers who enjoy rugged adventures. There are four official entry points and ranger stations. San Pedrillo, to the west, is linked by a trail from Bahía Drake. In the east, Los Patos can be reached from La Palma, 12 miles (19 km) northwest of Puerto Jiménez. La Leona, to the south, is just 1 mile (1.6 km) west of the airstrip at Carate, a tiny hamlet 25 miles (40 km) west of Puerto Jiménez; visitors must then hike or ride a horse from Carate. Sirena, the main ranger station, is 10 miles (16 km) northwest of La Leona and 16 miles (26 km) southeast of San Pedrillo. Trails connecting the stations are poorly marked, so it is wise to hire a guide.

The two-day coastal San Pedrillo–La Leona trail passes the dramatic 100-ft- (30-m-) high Cascada La Llorona. Be prepared on this hike to ford rivers inhabited by crocodiles. The northern section is open only from December to April. The San Pedrillo–Los Patos trail allows access to Laguna Corcovado, where tapirs and jaguars are often sighted.

There is no scheduled air service to the airstrips near the park, but air-taxis are offered by charter companies.

STAY

Luna Lodge
Zen and eco-awareness go hand-in-hand at this ocean-facing lodge with jaw-dropping views.

🅰F7 🅰Carate
Ⓦlunalodge.com

⑤⑤⑤

Finca Maresia
Unpretentious luxe defines this hilltop boutique hotel with ocean views.

🅰E6 🅰Drake Bay
Ⓦfincamaresia.com

⑤⑤⑤

Iguana Lodge
Delightful hosts, and gourmet organic fare highlight this laid-back beachfront lodge.

🅰F6 🅰Playa Platanares
Ⓦiguanalodge.com

⑤⑤⑤

Lapa Rios
This deluxe rainforest eco-lodge has romantic ridge-top villas and good food.

🅰F7 🅰Cabo Matalpo
Ⓦlaparios.com

⑤⑤⑤

3

PARQUE NACIONAL ISLA DEL COCO

⌂ 310 miles (500 km) SW of mainland 🚢 With dive operators (a 36-hr journey)
ℹ Fundación Amigos de La Isla del Coco: www.cocosisland.org; email ranger station for permit: islacoco@ns.minae.co.cr

The island that inspired *Jurassic Park*, Isla del Coco was named a National Park in 1978 and covers 330 miles (532 km) off the coast of Cabo Blanco. The 9-sq-mile (23-sq-km) island began as a volcano, a part of the Galapagos chain. As the world's largest uninhabited island, it is used as a natural laboratory for evolutionary study; it became a UNESCO World Heritage Site in 1997 to ensure its preservation.

During the 17th and 18th centuries, the island had such a reputation for being a haven for pirates and corsairs it was known as "Treasure Island". Today it holds treasure of a different sort – as a refuge for over 1,000 species of animal and the dense premontane moist forest, which protects endemic fauna such as the Cocos anole, as well as 70 endemic plant species. A highlight of this wildlife trove is the huge colonies of seabirds, including magnificent frigate birds and white terns. Despite the broken topography and torrential rainfall that cause countless waterfalls to cascade into the sea, the crystal-clear waters that surround the island are world-renowned for diving. Visitors to the island need a permit, which can be arranged through dive operators.

↑ A wall of jacks darting away from a scuba diver in the waters around Cocos Island

Colorful market stalls of local farmers and producers in San Isidro de El General

The uninhabited Cocos Island, surrounded by pristine blue seas

TOP 5 SHARKS IN THE SEAS

Hammerhead Sharks
The male hammerhead shark will bite the female until she agrees to mate with him.

Whale Sharks
The largest known living fish, this lengthy creature is a slow-moving filter feeder.

Tiger Sharks
The dark stripes that streak down its body, resembling a tiger's pattern, fade as the shark matures.

White-Tip Reef Sharks
These curious sharks are rarely aggressive towards divers but will swim in for a closer look.

Silky Sharks
Named for the smooth texture of their skin, these toothy beasts trail schools of tuna looking for a bite.

EXPERIENCE MORE

4

San Isidro de El General

🗺 E5 🚗 51 miles (82 km) S of Cartago 🚌 ℹ Selva Mar, Calle 2

The peaceful market town of San Isidro de El General sits at the base of Cerro de la Muerte. For tourists, it serves mainly as a refueling stop and base for exploring the Chirripó and La Amistad national parks. The only sight of interest in town is the modern, concrete cathedral on the east side of the plaza, with stained-glass windows and a simple altar dominated by a mural of San Isidro Labrador, patron saint of San Isidro.

At Quizarrá, 9 miles (14 km) southeast of San Isidro, there's a treat for bird-lovers: Los Cusingos Neotropical Bird Sanctuary. Administered by the Tropical Science Center of Costa Rica, this 1-sq-mile (3-sq-km) refuge for birds was founded by eminent American ornithologist Dr. Alexander Skutch (1904–2004), co-author of the authoritative *Birds of Costa Rica*. More than 300 bird species have been noted in the sanctuary, and Skutch's former home, surrounded by a botanical garden, has been kept and maintained as if he still lived there.

5

Cerro de la Muerte

🗺 E4 🚗 31 miles (50 km) S of Cartago 🚌 San José-San Isidro

Cerro de la Muerte acquired its name – "Mountain of Death" – in remembrance of the people who died of exposure while on the road to San José with their produce before the Pan-Am Highway was built across it. The road passes along boggy grassland below the wind-buffeted summit (11,500 ft/ 3,500 m). When the clouds part, there are superlative views.

🔺 GREAT VIEW
Eyes Down

When driving over Cerro de la Muerte, stop at Km 119, where the view down over Valle de El General from Mirador Vista del Valle is stunning. Linger over a meal at the veranda restaurant here to savor the vista below.

↑ Cute and colorful, a resplendent quetzal at La Amistad park

Parque Internacional La Amistad

A F4 **Q** 66 miles (107 km) SE of San Isidro **C** Estación Altamira HQ: 2730-9846 or 2200-5355 **To** Guácimo, then by jeep-taxi **Q** 8am-4pm daily

Extending into Panama, the International Friendship Park is contiguous with other protected areas that form the sprawling Reserva de la Biosfera La Amistad (Amistad Biosphere Reserve). It spans over 675 sq miles (1,750 sq km) of the rugged Talamanca Mountains, and ranges from elevations of 490 ft (150 m) to 11,650 ft (3,550 m) atop Cerro Kamuk. The diverse wildlife in this enormous park includes five cat species and the bare-necked umbrella-bird. With permits and a

Did You Know?

La Amistad spans eight "life zones," from low montane rainforest to swampy high-altitude grassland.

guide, experienced hikers can cross the Talamancas on a trail that starts from the town of Buenos Aires, 38 miles (61 km) southeast of San Isidro, and leads to the Reserva Indígena Talamanca-Cabécar *(p222)*.

The main ranger station, a hostel, and an ecology exhibition are at Estación Altamira, the recommended entry point north of Guácimo. All the official access points require 4WD.

At **Finca Coffea Diversa**, below Estación Altamira, visitors can wander among rows of flowering shrubs and more than 200 coffee bush species. The rural communities of Carmén, Altamira and Biolley are enlivened with ceramic murals.

Finca Coffea Diversa

Q Altamira, 1 mile (1.6 km) W of Estación Altamira **Q** 8am-5pm daily **w** coffea diversa.net

Las Cruces Biological Station

A G6 **Q** 4 miles (7 km) S of San Vito **San** Vito-Ciudad Neily **Q** 8am-5pm daily **w** tropicalstudies.org

One of the world's leading tropical research and educational centers, Las Cruces is run by the Organization of Tropical Studies (OTS). The center is surrounded by a 1-sq-mile (3-sq-km) mid-elevation forest, in which incredible diversity of birds and mammals can be seen along 15 miles (25 km) of trails. Clouds envelop the reserve, nourishing the many ferns, palms, bromeliads, and orchids laid out in the Wilson Botanical Gardens, designed by distinguished Brazilian landscaper Roberto Burle-Marx. A riot of color in even the rainiest of weather, the collection extends to glass-houses, where tropical plants are propagated.

8

Golfito

A F6 **Q** 48 miles (77 km) SE of Palmar **Q** **golfito** costarica.com

A sportfishing base, port, and administrative center for the southern region, dilapidated Golfito (Small Gulf) unfurls along 4 miles (6 km) of shoreline. Established by the United Fruit Company in 1938, the town's reign as the nation's main banana-shipping port ended when the company pulled out in 1985. The legacy of "Big Fruit" can be seen in the intriguing architecture of Zona Americana, at the north end of town, which has stilt-legged wooden houses. The

EAT

Il Giardino
This family-run Italian restaurant offers tasty pizza and pasta, along with sweeping views of the Golfo Dulce.

A F6 **Q** Puerto Jiménez **C** 2735-5129

**$**$$$

Phat Noodle
Great Thai food and cocktails served from a funky converted school bus to diners at canopied tables.

A E5 **Q** Dominical **w** phatnoodlecosta rica.com

**$**$$$

Citrus
Stylish restaurant with a sophisticated menu of fusion dishes.

A E5 **Q** Ojochal **C** 2786-5175

**$**$$$

small plaza in Pueblo Civíl, the town center, abuts a busy water-taxi wharf. The **Museo Marino** nearby is worth a peek for its corals and seashells.

On weekends and holidays, Golfito is flooded with Ticos drawn to the Depósito Libre (Free Trade Zone) shopping compound created in 1990 to revive the town's fortunes.

The forested hills east and north of town are protected within the Refugio Nacional de Vida Silvestre Golfito.

Museo Marino

🏠 Hotel Centro Turístico Samoa, just N of Pueblo Civíl ☎ 2775-0233 🕐 7am–10pm daily

---

⑨

Valle del Río Chirripó

🅰 E4 🏠 6 miles (10 km) E of San Isidro 🚌 From San Isidro

This valley is scythed from the Talamanca Mountains by the turbulent Río Chirripó. Trout swim in the river's waters, where rapids provide kayaking thrills. A great place to stop in the valley is the fruit-and-coffee *finca* Rancho La Botija, a popular destination

PRE-COLUMBIAN PETROGLYPHS

Costa Rica's pre-Columbian cultures left their legacy etched on boulders. Significant finds include Guayabo National Monument *(p130)*, where jaguars, snakes, frogs, and birds of prey symbolize creation, wealth, and power. Piedra de Los Indios and Rancho La Bojita, both in Valle del Río Chirripó, have interesting petroglyphs, including a crude map of the Talamanca region.

for locals on weekends. Its attractions include an antique sugarcane mill, a restaurant, and cosy rooms. Nearby, the roadside Piedra de los Indios (Rock of the Indians) bears pre-Columbian petroglyphs as well as some modern graffiti.

The scenery grows more dramatic as the road climbs into the mountains to reach San Gerardo de Rivas. Perching over the river gorge, this hamlet is the gateway to the Parque Nacional Chirripó. Close by, the **Museo el Pelicano** is a curiosity for its inspired stone and timber art by coffee farmer Rafael Elizondo Basulta. **Aguas Termales**, nearby, has natural thermal pools popular with local families seeking to counter the chilly mountain air.

A steep track leads past the trailhead to the summit of Cerro Chirripó and ends at the **Chirripó Cloudbridge Reserve**; there are also some good hiking trails.

Museo el Pelicano

🏠 Canaan, 10 miles (16 km) E of San Isidro ☎ 2742-5050 🕐 7–11am daily

Aguas Termales

🏠 1 mile (1.6 km) NW of San Gerardo ☎ 2742-5210 🕐 7am–5pm daily

Chirripó Cloudbridge Reserve

🏠 San Gerardo de Rivas, 12 miles (20 km) E of San Isidro 🕐 6:30am–6:30pm daily 🌐 cloudbridge.org

↑ Water cascading from the mountains down the Valle del Río Chirripó

→ Domenical beach, popular with families, budget travelers, and surfers

⑩
Dominical

Ⓐ E5 **Ⓓ 23 miles (37 km) SW of San Isidro de El General** 🚌

A surfers' paradise, this village thrives on the backpacker trade: the community is a mix of locals and foreign surfers who have settled here. Its long beach extends south to the fishing hamlet of Dominicalito. In town, **Costa Rica Surf Camp** offers a great introduction to the waves. Non-surfers should beware of riptides.

South of Dominical, lie thickly forested mountains, the Fila Costanera, also called Escaleras (Staircase). Tour companies in Dominical offer hikes, plus all-terrain-vehicle trips up its slopes.

Highway 243 winds through the Río Barú valley, connecting Dominical to San Isidro. Tour companies offer trips to **Don Lulo's Nauyaca Waterfalls**, a dramatic, two-tiered waterfall a 4-mile (6-km) jeep ride from the highway. Nearby, **Parque Reptilandia** exhibits dozens of reptile species, including a

komodo dragon and giant turtles. Guided tours offer an insight into reptilian behavior.

Costa Rica Surf Camp
Ⓒ 8am–8pm daily
Ⓦ crsurfschool.com

Don Lulo's Nauyaca Waterfalls
🌐 Ⓓ Platanillo, 6 miles (10 km) E of Dominical
Ⓦ cataratasnauyaca.com

Parque Reptilandia
🌐🌐 Ⓓ Platanillo Ⓒ 9am–4:30pm daily Ⓦ crreptiles.com

TROPICAL FLOWERS
A hothouse of bio-diversity, Costa Rica has over 15,000 known plant species. Each one has evolved to thrive in its ecosystem.

↑ The pollen-covered blue "perch" from where birds reach the strelitzia's nectar

FOR THE BIRDS
Bird-pollinating plants often have elongated flowers that mimic the shape of a bird's beak. The long orangish-red tubular flowers of the firebush are perfect for the curved beak of the hummingbird. Also known as the humming-bird bush, the flowers' sweet-tasting nectar is an additional draw.

OPEN ALL HOURS
Flowers that open at night or in the darkness of predawn, such as those of the endemic Costa Rican sage, ensure that they receive more visits by pollinators, even when their scent starts to fade.

FOUL ODOURS
Several flowers emanate a foul smell to attract pollinators. The "Dutchman's pipe", for example, smells like rotting flesh, to attract flies.

TOP 4

WHALES OFF COSTA RICA

Humpback
These whales will leap out of the water in "super groups" of up to 200.

False Killer
Actually a dolphin, these highly social mammals form pods with as many as 500 members.

Bryde's
Known for their taste for anchovies, these whales snap up shoals at a time.

Pilot
Scientists can't explain why these whales so often beach themselves.

Parque Nacional Marino Ballena

A E5 **⌂** 11 miles (18 km) S of Dominical **🚌** From Dominical **🕐** 8am–4pm daily **W** sinac.go.cr

Created to protect the nation's largest coral reef, Whale Marine National Park stretches for 8 miles (13 km) along the shore of Bahía de Coronado, and extends 9 miles (14 km) out to sea. It is named after the humpback whales that gather in the warm waters at a peculiar whale-tail-shaped point to breed between December and April. Several tour operators offer whale-watching trips. Regulations on operators and the number of whale-spotting boats that can be in the bay at any given time are very strict. The Costa Rican government has over 60 policy points that each licensed tour operator must fulfill before they are allowed to take to the seas.

The park incorporates Las Tres Hermanas and Isla Ballena, which are important nesting sites for frigate birds, brown boobies, and pelicans. Kayaking and scuba diving trips can be arranged.

Refugio Nacional de Vida Silvestre Rancho Merced, to the north, offers city-slickers a chance to play cowhand; it also functions as a wildlife refuge. To the south, sustainably operated La Cusinga Lodge offers great wildlife-spotting opportuties on its trails in the hilltops above pristine beaches. Nearby, the twin hamlets of Tortuga Abajo and Ojochal make a good base for exploring the area; Ojochal has some great restaurants.

Refugio Nacional de Vida Silvestre Rancho Merced

⌖ **⌂** Uvita, 11 miles (18 km) S of Dominical **W** ranchola merced.com

ORCHIDS

Over 1,400 species of orchids grow in Costa Rica. The greatest numbers are found below 6,000 ft (1,830 m). All orchids have three petals and three sepals. Some have evolved features to attract specific pollinators such as markings visible only to insects that can see the ultraviolet spectrum.

The curved, colorful flower heads (bracts) attract birds with a curved beak, such as the violet sabrewing.

The waxy bracts are produced on long panicles.

HELICONIA

The heliconias's huge, narrow stems can grow to a towering 25 ft (8 m).

12 Refugio Nacional de Vida Silvestre Barú

E5 2 miles (3 km) N of Dominical From Dominical to Quepos 6am–6pm daily, with prior reservation only haciendabaru.com

A former cattle ranch and cocoa plantation, the 1-sq-mile (3-sq-km) Hacienda Barú has varied habitats, including 2 miles (3 km) of beach that draw nesting turtles. Here turtle eggs are collected and incubated in a nursery for release. Barú also has more than 310 bird species, and mammals such as the arboreal kinkajou. There are butterfly and orchid gardens, and opportunities for guided tree-climbing, kayak trips through the mangroves, and overnight stays in treetop tents.

13 Reserva Indígena Boruca

F5 22 miles (35 km) S of Buenos Aires From Buenos Aires boruca.org

This is just one of several Indigenous reserves inhabited by the Boruca and Bribri in the mountains that hem the Valle de El General. It is especially known for its Fiesta de los Diablitos, as well as its carved *jícaras* (gourds) and balsa-wood *máscaras* (masks). The women use traditional backstrap looms to weave sturdy cotton purses and blanket-like shawls. Local culture is showcased in the **Museo Comunitario Boruca**.

Flanking the Boruca reserve, the Reserva Indígena Cabagra, home to the Bribri, can be accessed from the town of Brujo, 7 miles (11 km) southeast of Buenos Aires.

Museo Comunitario Boruca

Boruca, 25 miles (40 km) SW of Buenos Aires 2730-5178 9am–4pm daily

14 Reserva Biológica Isla del Caño

E6 14 miles (23 km) W of Bahía Drake Tours from Bahía Drake, Manuel Antonio, & Dominical 8am–3pm daily sinac.go.cr

Thrust up from the sea by tectonic forces, the 1-sq-mile (3-sq-km) uninhabited Isla del

FIESTA DE LOS DIABLITOS

The Boruca gather on December 31 to reenact the war between their ancestors and Spanish conquistadors. At the sound of a conch, men in devil masks pursue a fellow tribesman dressed as a bull. The *diablitos* (devils) drink corn beer and act out scenes recalling tribal events. After three days, the "bull" is mock-"killed," symbolically freeing the tribe.

Caño was named a protected reserve in 1976, along with its pristine surrounding waters. In the past, the island was considered sacred by the pre-Columbian Diquís peoples.

The coral-colored beaches are great for sunbathing. In the shallows, coral reefs teem with lobsters and fish, while dolphins, whales, and manta

→ Ancient stone sphere at Palmar, associated with the local Diquís culture

rays swim in the warm waters farther out. Scuba diving is permitted in designated zones. Compared to the bounty of the seas, terrestrial wildlife is relatively limited, although the lucky hiker might come across opossums, foxes, brown boobies, and ospreys.

Mossy pre-Columbian tombs and mysterious granite *esferas de piedra* (stone spheres) lay scattered along a trail running from the ranger hut on the beachfront to a lookout point.

Overnight stays are not permitted, however lodges in the Bahía Drake area *(p235)* offer day trips.

15
Pavones

⚑F7 **⚑14 miles (23 km) S of Zancudo** **�"** **🚌From Golfito** **🚤Water-taxi from Golfito**

Known in the surfing world for its consistent 1-mile (1.5-km) 3-minute break, this small fishing village has blossomed due to the influx of young surfers. Waves peak offshore between April and October, while all year round coconut palms lean over the beautiful, rocky coastline, and marine turtles nest along the shore.

At Punta Banco, 6 miles (10 km) to the south, the local community participates in the Tiskita Foundation Sea Turtle Restoration Project, which has a nursery to raise baby turtles for release. Nearby, Tiskita Lodge offers fabulous vistas from its hillside perch. This lodge is part of a larger fruit farm that attracts a wealth of bird and animal life. Guided hikes are

← Fabulous corals, a draw for scuba divers at Reserva Biológica Isla del Caño

offered into a private reserve, where waterfalls cascade through majestic rainforest.

16
Palmar

⚑F5 **⚑60 miles (97 km) SE of San Isidro de El General** **�"** **🚌**

Sitting at the foot of the Río Terraba valley, at the inter-section of Costanera Sur and the Pan-Am Highway, Palmar is the service center for the region. The town straddles the Río Terraba, which flows west through the wide Valle de Diquís. Pre-Columbian *esferas* (spheres) and a centenarian steam locomotive are on view in the plaza of Palmar Sur. On the outskirts is **Parque de las Esferas Precolumbino**, a UNESCO World Heritage Site, which displays the pre-Columbian stone spheres. Palmar Norte is the town's modern quarter.

Parque de las Esferas Precolumbino
🅰️🕙 **⚑Finca 6, 5 miles (8 km) S of Palmar** **☎2100-6000** **⚑8am–4pm Tue–Sun**

↑ Forest spreading almost to the shoreline at the Piedras Blancas reserve

19

Zancudo

🅰F6 🅰6 miles (10 km) S of Golfito 30 miles (49 km) 🚌🚢From Golfito

This hamlet on the east shore of Golfo Dulce is known for its stupendously beautiful gray sand beach, caressed by breezes and surf. The 4-mile- (6-km-) long strip of sand is a spit, projecting from the shore. A mangrove swamp inland of the beach is good for spotting crocodiles, caimans, and abundant waterfowl. Sportfishing centers offer superb river-mouth and deepwater fishing, while tarpon and snook can be hooked from the shore.

17

Parque Nacional Piedras Blancas

🅰F6 🅰28 miles (46 km) SE of Palmar 📞2775-2620 🚌From Golfito 🕐8am–4pm daily

Split off from the Parque Nacional Corcovado in 1991, this 55-sq-mile (140-sq-km) park protects the forested mountains to the northeast of Golfo Dulce. In the village of La Gamba, a cooperative runs the Esquinas Rainforest Lodge, which breeds the rodent-like *tepezcuintles* (lowland paca) and offers hikes.

The emerald forests spill over the beaches – Playa Cativo and Playa San Josecito; the latter is home to the botanical garden **Casa Orquídeas**, known for its large collection of orchids and ornamentals. Boat trips, including water-taxi rides, to the two beaches make for pleasant excursions.

Casa Orquídeas

♨♨ 🅰Playa San Josecito, 6 miles (10 km) N of Puerto Jiménez 📞8829-1247 🕐8am–5pm Sat–Thu, by appt only

18

Reserva Forestal del Humedal Nacional Terraba-Sierpe

🅰E6 🅰11 miles (18 km) W of Palmar 📞2788-1212 🚢

Protecting the nation's largest stretch of mangrove forest and swamp, the Terraba-Sierpe National Humid Forest Reserve covers 85 sq miles (220 sq km) between the deltas of the Sierpe and Terraba rivers. Countless channels lace this vitally important ecosystem, which fringes over 25 miles (40 km) of coastline.

A wide array of reptiles, such as basilisk lizards and caimans bask along the shores of these quiet channels, making them easy to spot for kayakers. Monkeys swing through the canopy, while peering though the undergrowth are crab-eating raccoons and coatis. The birding opportunities are also excellent, with herons, egrets, and cotingas among the inhabitants. Guided boat and kayak tours of the reserve are offered from Sierpe, 9 miles (14 km) south of Palmar (*p243*).

STAY

Hacienda Barú
A modest yet comfy ocean-side nature lodge.

🅰E5 🅰Dominical 🌐haciendabaru.com

$$$

Río Chirripó Lodge
Colorful, laid-back, and utterly tranquil.

🅰E4 🅰San Gerardo de Rivas 🌐riochirripo.com

$$$

Flutterby House
Tree-house hammocks and cosy shacks.

🅰E5 🅰Uvita 🌐flutterbyhouse.com

$$$

Tiskita Jungle Lodge
Rustic ecolodge on a forested fruit farm.

🅰F7 🅰Pavones 🌐tiskita.com

$$$

THE MANGROVES OF COASTAL COSTA RICA

Costa Rica's shores contain five of the world's 65 species of mangroves – black, buttonwood, red, tea, and white. Mangroves are woody halophytes – plants able to withstand immersion in saltwater – and form swampy forests in areas inundated by tides.

THE MANGROVE ECOSYSTEM

Mangrove forests are of vital importance to the maritime ecosystem, fostering a wealth of wildlife. They grow up and down Costa Rica's Caribbean coastline thanks to pendulous seed pods that drop and float away at high tide to begin a new colony.

The tangled roots buffer the action of waves, preventing coastal erosion. They also filter out the silt washed down by turbulent rivers. The dense mud leaves little oxygen, and nutrients are supplied by decomposing leaf litter lying close to the surface. As a result, most plants develop interlocking stilt roots that rise above the water to draw in oxygen and food. The nutrient-rich mudflats that form around their roots, creating a food source for marine creatures, while the roots themselves create protective spaces for eggs and young to develop away from predators.

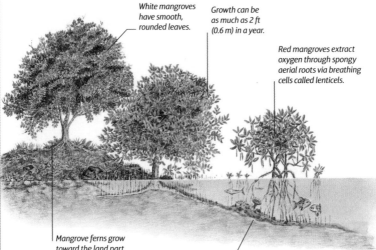

White mangroves have smooth, rounded leaves.

Growth can be as much as 2 ft (0.6 m) in a year.

Red mangroves extract oxygen through spongy aerial roots via breathing cells called lenticels.

Mangrove ferns grow toward the land part of the ecosystem.

The nutrient-rich mudflats provide a vital food source.

THE RICH FAUNA OF THE MANGROVES

In the nutrient-rich muddy beds of coastal mangrove forests, microorganisms flourish. These tiny creatures foster the growth of larger animals such as shrimps and other crustaceans, which in turn attract various species of mammals, reptiles, and birds.

The dense, protective root system acts as an aquatic nursery for oysters, sponges, and other invertebrates, as well as numerous fish species, including sharks and stingrays, which thrive in the murky tannin-stained waters. The roots also protect baby caimans and crocodiles from predators, while at the same time providing them with a plentiful food source. Larger species, such as raccoons, coyotes, snakes, and wading birds forage along the shoreline for small lizards and crabs.

The upper branches of the mangroves provide well-placed roosting spots for many species of birds, especially frigate birds and pelicans, and a number of endemic species including the yellow mangrove warbler.

A curious, vivid little blue heron considering its options in the mangroves

NEED TO KNOW

Fishing off the coast of Guanacaste

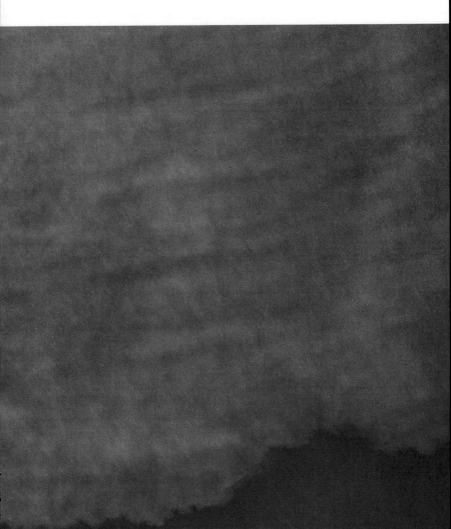

BEFORE
YOU GO

Things change, so plan ahead to make the most of your trip. Be prepared for all eventualities by considering the following points before you travel.

AT A GLANCE

CURRENCY
Colón (CRC) or US dollars ($).

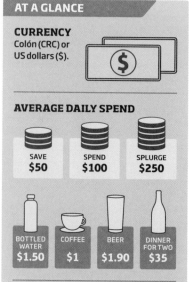

AVERAGE DAILY SPEND

SAVE	SPEND	SPLURGE
$50	$100	$250

BOTTLED WATER	COFFEE	BEER	DINNER FOR TWO
$1.50	$1	$1.90	$35

CLIMATE

There are 12 hours of daylight per day.

Temperatures are relatively consistent between regions, from highs of 81°F (27°C) along the coasts to lows of 70°F (21°C) in the mountains.

The rainy season is from May to November. Annual rainfall is around 100 inches.

ELECTRICITY SUPPLY
Power sockets are type A and B, fitting two- and three-pronged plugs. Standard voltage is 110v.

Passports and Visas

For entry requirements, including visas, consult your nearest Costa Rican embassy or the **Costa Rica Tourism Board** website. EU nationals and citizens of the UK, US, Canada, Australia, and New Zealand do not need a tourist visa for stays of less than 90 days. All visitors need a return or onward ticket. A tourist card will be issued on arrival; valid for 90 days, this can be extended at a *migración* (immigration) office.

If transiting via the US, you must apply for the Electronic System for Travel Authorization (**ESTA**) before traveling.
Costa Rica Tourism Board
W visitcostarica.com
ESTA
W estas.cbp.dhs.gov

Government Advice

Now more than ever, it is important to consult both your and the Costa Rican government's advice before traveling. The **UK Foreign and Commonwealth Office**, the **US Department of State**, the Costa Rica Tourism Board, and the **Australian Department of Foreign Affairs and Trade** offer the latest information on security, health, and local regulations.
Australia
W smarttraveller.gov.au
UK
W gov.uk/foreign-travel-advice
US
W travel.state.gov

Customs Information

You can find information on the laws relating to goods and currency taken in or out of Costa Rica on the Costa Rica Tourism Board website.

Insurance

We recommend that you take out a comprehensive insurance policy covering theft, loss of belongings, medical care, cancellations and delays, and read the small print carefully.

Vaccinations

It is recommended that you are inoculated against tetanus, typhoid, and hepatitis A and B. Bring mosquito repellent, especially if you are traveling during the wet season. For information regarding COVID-19 vaccination requirements, consult government advice *(p248)*.

Booking Accommodation

In the dry season, hotels fill up fast, and prices become inflated. Costa Rica excels in wilderness nature lodges, usually located close to, or within, national parks. It is possible to camp in some national parks. **Hostelling International Costa Rica** can help make reservations for hostels.

Costa Rica has adopted the Certificate for Sustainable Tourism (CST) system, which grades hotels by their cultural and ecological sensitivity.

Hostelling International Costa Rica
w hihostels.com

Money

The official Costa Rican currency is the colón, but US dollars are used for most tourist transactions. This book gives prices in US dollars. Most establishments accept American Express, Visa, and MasterCard, but it is always a good idea to carry some cash in colónes for bus tickets and smaller items. Tipping is not expected at restaurants unless you see the statement *impuestos no incluidos* (taxes not included), when a tip of 10 percent of the total bill is customary. Hotel porters and housekeeping will expect a tip of $1 per bag or day, but it is not usual to tip taxi drivers.

Travelers with Specific Requirements

Historic buildings do not tend to have wheelchair access or lifts, but most modern hotels provide toilets and other amenities for wheelchair users. In San José, buses comply with government requirements for accessibility. **Taxis Alfaro** has wheelchair-friendly vans in the city.

While most national parks and outdoor attractions are unsuitable for those with limited mobility, Parque Nacional Volcán Poás and Parque Nacional Santa Rosa both have well-tended trails, and the Rainforest Aerial Tram has wheelchair-friendly tram cars. **Responsible Travel** offers customized tours to Costa Rica for travelers with specific needs.

Responsible Travel
w responsibletravel.com
Taxis Alfaro
w taxialfaro.com

Language

The official language of Costa Rica is Spanish, but many Costa Ricans speak English, as well as other languages. In rural areas, however, the level of English and other foreign languages can be limited. Locals appreciate visitors' efforts to speak Spanish, even if only a few words.

Opening Hours

> **COVID-19** Increased rates of infection may result in temporary opening hours and/or closures. Always check ahead before visiting museums, attractions and hospitality venues.

Lunchtime Most offices and many museums close for one hour or longer in mid-day.
Monday Many museums close for the day.
Sunday Most museums have shorter hours.
Public holidays Shops, offices, and many museums close early or for the entire day.

PUBLIC HOLIDAYS

1 Jan	New Year's Day
11 Apr	Juan Santamaría Day
18 Apr	Maundy Thursday
Mar/Apr	Good Friday
1 May	Labor Day
25 Jul	Guanacaste Day
2 Aug	Virgin of Los Angeles Day
15 Aug	Mother's Day
15 Sep	Independence Day
12 Oct	National Cultures Day
25 Dec	Christmas Day

GETTING AROUND

Whether you are visiting for a beachy break or eco-lodge retreat, discover how best to reach your destination and travel like a pro.

AT A GLANCE

TRANSPORTATION COSTS

SAN JOSÉ TO LIBERIA

$125

One-way airplane

SAN JOSÉ TO LIMÓN

$80

One-way airplane

SAN JOSÉ TO PUERTO JIMÉNEZ

$140

One-way airoplane

TOP TIP
Book bus fares for long journeys a day ahead to ensure you get a seat.

SPEED LIMIT

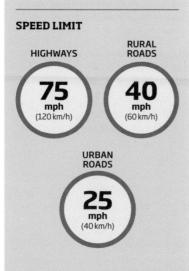

HIGHWAYS

75 mph (120 km/h)

RURAL ROADS

40 mph (60 km/h)

URBAN ROADS

25 mph (40 km/h)

Arriving by Air

Juan Santamaría International Airport is Costa Rica's main airport. International flights also arrive at Daniel Oduber International Airport. The latter is preferred for destinations on the Nicoya Peninsula. US, Canadian, and European airlines fly to these airports, as does **Avianca Costa Rica** (formerly Lacsa), Costa Rica's national airline. **Sansa Airlines** runs internal flights within the country.

There are regular bus services from various terminals in San José. For information on getting between San José and Juan Santamaría International Airport, see the table opposite.
Avianca Costa Rica
W avianca.com
Sansa Airlines
W flysansa.com

Train Travel

A commuter service runs between San José and Heredia, and San José and Cartago. There are also tentative plans to restore the line between San José and Puntarenas.

Long-Distance Bus Travel

Several companies operate modern bus services from San José to every part of the country. Departure points are scattered around San José. The Costa Rica Tourism Board website *(p248)* keeps an up-to-date timetable. Fares rarely exceed $25. Buses are either *directo* (express) or *colectivo* (with many scheduled stops). They are often crowded and luggage space is limited. Watch your luggage at stops, as theft does occur. **Costa Rica Shuttle**, **Grayline**, and **Interbus** are among the many companies that offer scheduled shuttle buses to the most popular destinations, by reservation.
Costa Rica Shuttle
W costaricashuttle.com
Grayline
W graylinecostarica.com
Interbus
W interbusonline.com

GETTING TO AND FROM THE AIRPORT

Airport	Distance to city	Taxi fare	Journey time
San José (Juan Santamaría)	9 miles (15 km)	$25-35	30 min
Liberia (Daniel Oduber)	7 miles (12 km)	$20-30	25 min
Bahía Drake (Puerto Jiménez)	11 miles (18 km)	$25-35	33 min

JOURNEY PLANNER

Plotting the main driving routes according to journey time, this map is a handy reference for traveling between Costa Rica's main towns and tourist destinations by car. The times given reflect the fastest and most direct routes available.

Liberia
La Fortuna
Puerto Viejo de Sarapiquí
Tamarindo
Monteverde
Nicoya
Sarchí
San José
Limón
Puntarenas
Cartago
Cahuita
Sámara
Jacó
Quepos
San Isidro
Puerto Viejo de Talamanca
Dominical

••• Direct bus routes

Puerto Jiménez

San José to Cahuita	3.75 hrs
San José to Cartago	45 mins
San José to Jacó	2 hrs
San José to La Fortuna	3 hrs
San José to Liberia	4 hrs
San José to Limón	3 hrs
San José to Monteverde	3.25 hrs
San José to Puerto Viejo de Sarapiquí	2.5 hrs
San José to Puerto Viejo de Talamanca	4.25 hrs
San José to Puntarenas	2 hrs
San José to Sarchí	1.25 hrs
San José to San Isidro	4.5 hrs
Dominical to Puerto Jiménez	3 hrs

Jacó to Quepos	1.25 hrs
La Fortuna to Monteverde	4.5 hrs
Liberia to Tamarindo	1.5 hrs
Liberia to Nicoya	1.75 hrs
Nicoya to Sámara	1 hr
Quepos to Dominical	45 mins
San Isidro to Dominical	1.25 hrs
Tamarindo to Sámara	3 hrs

Public Transportation

All towns operate multiple transportation servces including buses and taxis.

Buses

Local in-town bus services serve San José and larger towns, including Alajuela, Heredia, Puerto Limón, Golfito, and Puntarenas. Buses have their destination displayed on the windshield. Many city buses also have the fare displayed, as well as the name of the bus company, so look for that to make sure it's the correct bus. All fares are paid in colónes.

Most private companies use modern, air-conditioned *guaguas* – pronounced *wahg-wahs* (coaches), with reclining seats, but smaller people carriers also provide services. They pick up at signed stops along scheduled routes. Shorter trips between smaller towns and villages are typically serviced by older, more basic second-class buses. The Costa Rica Tourism Board (*p248*) publishes a bus schedule. Rural buses can be waved down at *paradas* (bus stops) along their routes.

In most towns, the bus terminal is close to the main plaza. Some towns have more than one; for example, there are two large bus terminals in San José, with additional bus stations all around downtown. Buses to the Caribbean leave from Gran Terminal Caribe, and those to most other parts of the country from a series of bus stops concentrated in an area called "Coca Cola", which is located west of downtown.

Taxis

Taxis are common throughout the country and can be found around the central plazas in most towns. In San José, you can also call one of several taxi companies such as **Coopetico**, which is one of the bigger operators. Licensed taxis are red (though airport taxis are orange), with a white triangle on the front door showing the license number. For journeys under 8 miles (12 km), drivers are required to use their *marias* (meters), but many will make an excuse not to do so in order to be able to charge more. The rates for longer journeys are negotiable. Outside the capital, fares are usually negotiated with the driver before setting off.

Jeep-taxis serve many communities that are difficult to reach due to mountainous terrain or poorly maintained roads and are the main means of public transportation for locals. The most remote communities and tourist destinations are also served by *colectivos*, usually open-bed pickup trucks with seats and awnings. Like *colectivo* buses, they follow fixed routes and can be flagged down anywhere along the route. *Colectivo* taxis normally charge a flat fee, regardless of distance, typically the

equivalent of £1. Carry small bills and change, as few drivers will be able to change a large bill.

Uber also operates in San José, as do other freelance (licensed) *porteadores* (private taxis); it is recommended to use a local SIM card in your phone to communicate with your driver. **EasyTaxi** is a local alternative that works exclusively with official red taxis, permitting you to call a taxi on a mobile app.

Taxis Aeropuertos are licensed to run to and from the airport only, but can take you anywhere in the country. They can be called for pickup anywhere in San José.

Coopetico
🆆 coopetico.co.cr

Easy Taxi
🆆 easytaxi.com

Taxis Aeropuertos
🆆 taxiaeropuerto.com

Boats and Ferries

Naviera Tambor car-and-passenger ferries connect Puntarenas to Paquera (serving Tambor, Montezuma, and Malpaís) and Naranjo (serving Nicoya and beach resorts), on the Nicoya Peninsula. They operate on a first-come, first-served basis, but it's best to buy your ticket in advance through **QuickPayCR**.

Lanchas (water-taxis) operate throughout Golfo Dulce from Golfito and Puerto Jiménez and will run you to whatever destination you wish, including to Pavones and Zancudo.

Naviera Tambor
🆆 navieratambor.com

QuickPayCR
🆆 quickpaycr.com

Driving

Renting a car provides the greatest travel flexibility, especially when visiting Costa Rica's more remote areas.

Costa Rica has an extensive network of paved roads, but beyond the capital many roads are unpaved or unmaintained, and a 4WD is recommended. Costa Rican drivers have a poor reputation for speeding, running stop signs and red lights, and failing to indicate when turning. Make sure you are familiar with the rules of the road and have all the necessary documentation. *Tránsitos* (traffic police) patrol the highways, using radar guns to catch speeders. They are not allowed to collect money. Fines should be paid at a bank or at the rental company.

A *toll autopista* (freeway) links San José to Puntarenas and Jacó; and portions of the Pan-American Highway (Carretera 1) have toll booths. Many mountain roads, such as that linking San José to the Caribbean via Parque Nacional Braulio Carrillo, are subject to fog and landslides, and roads in the Central Highlands are convoluted. A GPS is virtually essential for finding your way, as away from main roads signage is limited.

The unpaved roads to Bahía Drake and Parque Nacional Corcovado, on the Peninsula de Osa, and those along the Pacific shore of Nicoya between Tamarindo and Playa Santa Teresa, have unbridged rivers that require fording. Use extreme caution, especially in rainy season. Ask locals about current conditions and for the best route to follow. Note that damage incurred while fording is not insured by the car rental company.

Car Rental

To rent a car in Costa Rica you must be over 21, but many car rental agencies ask that drivers be at least 25 years old. You will need a valid driver's license or International Driver's Permit (IDP) and a credit card for a deposit. Check with your local automobile association about obtaining an IDP. If you wish to stay for more than three months, you will need a domestic driver's license.

Many well-established car rental agencies operate in Costa Rica as franchises. Smaller local agencies may offer better rates. It's wise to make reservations well in advance, especially in high season, and in mid-summer when Tico families take their vacations en masse.

Prices are generally lower during the wet season, and unlimited-mileage options tend to work out the cheapest. Discounts apply for rentals of a week or longer. Manual shift is typically cheaper than automatic.

International insurance coverage is valid in Costa Rica; check to see if your credit card insurance covers travel in Costa Rica. Purchasing a limited Collision Damage Waiver (CDW) or fully comprehensive insurance is an alternative. If you waive insurance, you'll have to pay a significantly higher deposit.

Most companies are represented at the two international airports and offer shuttles to their nearby facilities. Two companies to consider are **Adobe** and **Europcar**.

Adobe
w adobecar.com
Europcar
w europcar.co.cr

Rules of the Road

Drive on the right, use the left lane only for passing, and yield to traffic from the right.

Seat belts are required for all passengers. A strict drink-drive policy is enforced, and it is wise to avoid all alcohol if intending to drive. It is illegal to use a mobile phone while driving, unless it's a hands-free device.

In the event of an accident or breakdown, switch on your hazard warning lights and place a warning triangle or small branches 55 yd (50 m) behind your vehicle. In case of accident, do not move the vehicle. Contact your car rental company, and in the event of an injury, your embassy immediately.

Costa Rica has a strict limit of 0.50 grams per liter, or 0.05 BAC (blood alcohol content) for drivers; at 0.75 grams (0.075 BAC), it becomes a criminal offense. Drivers who cause an accident and are found to have a BAC in excess of 0.075 are likely to be given a prison sentence.

Gas Stations

Unleaded gas, or *gasolina*, is sold as either super or regular; the latter is lower-octane and less expensive. Diesel is cheaper still. *Gasolineras* (gas stations) are plentiful in towns, but much scarcer in rural areas, especially in Nicoya. It is wise to refill whenever the tank drops to half-full. In remote areas, gasoline is usually available at *pulperías* (grocery stores), where it may cost twice as much as at gas stations.

Gas stations are typically open from 6am to midnight. They are not self-service, and most will accept credit cards.

Cycling and Motorbiking

Although Costa Ricans are passionate about cycle racing and mountain biking, bicycling is not well-established in towns, and very few Costa Ricans risk riding bicycles in San José. However, mountain biking is a great way of exploring the countryside. Several reputable companies offer guided bicycle tours, including **Backroads** and **Bike Arenal**. Mountain bikes can be rented in tourist towns for around US$10 to US$20 per day; some may require a deposit, but they do not typically supply helmets or repair kits. If you bring your own bike, wearing a helmet and carrying a sturdy lock are essential. Bicycle mechanics can be found in most towns.

Motorcycling is also popular and a thrilling way to explore. **Costa Rican Trails** specializes in organized tours; **Wild Rider** rents bikes.

Backroads
w backroads.com
Bike Arenal
w bikearenal.com
Costa Rican Trails
w costaricantrails.com
Wild Rider
w wild-rider.com

Walking

Costa Rica is a walker's paradise, with a large network of hiking trails running through its national parks, wildlife refuges, and cloud forests. Remember that this is a mountainous country so the terrain is often hilly. The most rewarding way to get around the cities is on foot where many sights are only a short distance apart.

PRACTICAL INFORMATION

A little local know-how goes a long way in Costa Rica. Here you will find all the essential advice and information you will need during your stay.

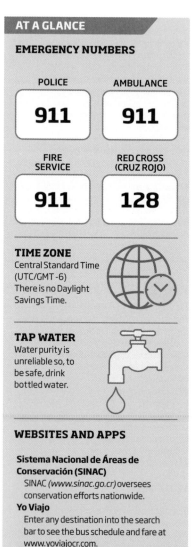

AT A GLANCE

EMERGENCY NUMBERS

POLICE	AMBULANCE
911	**911**

FIRE SERVICE	RED CROSS (CRUZ ROJO)
911	**128**

TIME ZONE
Central Standard Time (UTC/GMT -6) There is no Daylight Savings Time.

TAP WATER
Water purity is unreliable so, to be safe, drink bottled water.

WEBSITES AND APPS

Sistema Nacional de Áreas de Conservación (SINAC)
SINAC (www.sinac.go.cr) oversees conservation efforts nationwide.

Yo Viajo
Enter any destination into the search bar to see the bus schedule and fare at www.yoviajocr.com.

Maps.me
Select the maps that you want from this app before arriving in Costa Rica.

Personal Security

Costa Rica is relatively safe, and most of the country's dangers are nature-related, such as riptides, earthquakes, and volcanoes. National parks surrounding active volcanos may close depending on volcanc activity.

Petty theft does occur, so avoid placing cameras and other valuables where you can't see them, or carrying them loose on your shoulder. Luggage sometimes "goes missing" at stops during long-distance bus journeys. It is best to keep all of your valuables in sight at all times. Be wary of pickpockets on public transportation and in crowded city centers. San José's Coca Cola terminal has a reputation for pickpockets and muggings, so be on your guard in this area. Never get in an unlicensed private taxi, known locally as *piratas* – some tourists have been robbed by the drivers or their accomplices. If you have anything stolen, report the crime within 24 hours to the nearest police station and take your passport with you. If you need to make an insurance claim, get a copy of the *denuncia* (crime report). Contact your embassy if you have a passport stolen, or in the event of a serious crime or accident.

Costa Rica is a culturally diverse country and, as a rule, Costa Ricans are accepting of all people. Costa Rica recognized the right to legally change your gender in 2018 and in 2020 it became the first Central American country to legalize same-sex marriage. While cities and towns such as San José, Quepos, and Manuel Antonio in particular, have a thriving LGBT+ scene, smaller towns and some rural areas are more conservative in their views, and overt displays of affection might attract unwanted attention. **Gay Manuel Antonio** lists LGBT+ events, attractions, bars, restaurants, and tours in the town.
Gay Manuel Antonio
w gaymanuelantonio.com

Health

Costa Rica has world-class healthcare. There is both a government-run public healthcare system (Caja Costarricense de Seguro Social)

and private healthcare. Emergency medical care for visitors is given at public clinics and hospitals. You will need to show your medical insurance documents. A nominal fee may be charged for treatment you receive, which you may be able to claim back later. As such, it is important to arrange comprehensive medical insurance before traveling (p248).

Pharmacies (farmacias) are a good source of advice – pharmacists can diagnose minor ailments and suggest appropriate treatment.

There is a low risk of malaria in the wet season and in the southern region of the Caribbean. Outbreaks of dengue fever also sometimes occur there. Consult your doctor about taking antimalarial drugs.

Smoking, Alcohol, and Drugs

Smoking is banned in all enclosed public spaces, including restaurants. In 2012 a law was passed to make drinking alcohol in public places such as beaches, parks, and streets illegal but the police almost always turn a blind eye. Costa Rica has zero tolerance of possession and use of illegal drugs and this could result in a prison sentence.

ID

By law you must carry passport identification at all times in Costa Rica. A photocopy of your passport photo page should suffice. If you are stopped by the police you may need to present your original passport within 24 hours.

Sustainable Tourism

A pioneer in sustainability, Costa Rica has put in place many environmental protection measures to maintain its rich biodiversity, from renewable energy sources to reforestation programs. With the aim of making the country completely carbon neutral by 2050, the tourism board has launched the **Pura Vida Pledge**, which encourages visitors to stay in eco-lodges and to offset their carbon footprint by making a donation to be invested in local environmental projects. The scheme also promotes volunteering at wildlife rescue centers and supporting local communities.

Pura Vida Pledge
w puravidapledge.co.uk

Local Customs

Costa Ricans are very courteous and avoid confrontation. The country is Catholic and religious values are respected. When visiting churches, dress codes apply: cover your torso and upper arms, and ensure shorts and skirts cover your knees. Shoes must be worn. Topless or nude bathing are offenses and can incur a fine.

Mobile Phones and Wi-Fi

It is worth buying a local SIM card with airtime and a data bundle to allow you to make local calls, send texts, and use data cheaply. SIM cards can be purchased from shops selling mobile phones for any of the three companies (**Claro**, **Kolbi**, and **Movistar**) that provide mobile phone services in Costa Rica. Wi-Fi is available throughout most of the country but coverage in more remote areas can be patchy. Many restaurants, cafés, and hotels allow free use of their Wi-Fi, and free Wi-Fi hotspots can be found in public parks and shopping centers.

Claro
w claro.cr
Kolbi
w kolbi.cr
Movistar
w movistar.cr

Post

Estampillas (stamps) are sold at post offices, and prepaid postcards to anywhere in the world are sold at many souvenir stalls. Letters and post-cards sent through **Correos de Costa Rica**, Costa Rica's postal service, can take two weeks or longer to arrive. There are also private courier companies such as **DHL**.

Correos de Costa Rica
w correos.go.cr
DHL
w dhl.co.cr

Taxes

A sales tax of 13 percent applies on all purchases except food and medicines. There is a departure tax of $29; check with your airline whether this has already been included in the cost of your flight before paying at the tax counter.

National Parks and Wildlife Refuges

Arranging a wildlife tour is fairly straightforward. The biggest hurdles at the planning stage will be choosing between a self-guided adventure or an organized tour and deciding which national parks and refuges to visit – with the diversity of Costa Rica's national parks and wildlife reserves, visitors are spoilt for choice. If you're opting for the DIY approach, it's easy to book everything online – the National System of Conservation Areas (**SINAC**) website is very user-friendly; other refuges and reserves are privately run. If your itinerary includes visits to more than one park, it may be worth investing in an **Amigos de los Parques Nacionales (Friends of the National Parks)** card, which allows entry to up to 12 national parks. Most parks can be visited by car, although many can be reached only with a jeep-taxi, and others are accessible only by hiking or by boat, such as the Terraba-Sierpe International Humid Forest Reserve (*p244*).

For those preferring to join a tour, there are plenty of reputable tour operators in Costa Rica and elsewhere to offer specialist guidance and to set transportation and accommodation arrangements in place. It is best to choose a company that is recognized by the Costa Rica Tourism Board (*p248*).

Amigos de los Parques Nacionales (Friends of the National Parks)
w proparques.org
SINAC
w sinac.go.cr

Wildlife Spotting

Costa Rica is a year-round destination, but ideal conditions for wildlife viewing vary from region to region. Guanacaste is best visited in the dry season (December to April), when animals gather at water holes. This is also the best time for birding: migrants flock in from colder climates and waterbirds fill the wetlands. Because this is peak season, the most popular parks can be overrun with visitors.

Wet season (May to November) sees high rainfall throughout the country, and the landscape turns green and lush. Many trails become muddy, and accessibility to some areas may be restricted. Wetlands such as Caño Negro Wildlife Refuge flood, granting greater accessibility by boat. The wide availability of water also leads to a higher threat of malaria in risk areas.

Early morning and late afternoon are the best times to see wildlife. Come dusk, many animals such as monkeys bed down, and a variety of noctural creatures emerge, including bats, kinkajous, frogs, and cats. The nighttime exploration of lagoons and wetlands by boat reveals crocodiles and nocturnal birds, such as owls and the boat-billed heron. Bring a field guide and a pair of binoculars. Insect repellent, sunblock, sunglasses, and a flashlight (at night) are also essential.

Always keep a safe distance from all animals, which can become aggressive if startled or if they feel threatened. Never feed animals, as this disrupts their natural behavior and increases the possibility of you being bitten. If you are bitten, stay calm, move slowly, and seek medical assistance at once. Crocodiles are present in lowland rivers, so do not swim there. Be aware of snakes – look down while walking trails, and never place your hand on or under a surface without looking.

Self-Guided Tours

Most of the national parks and wildlife reserves can be explored without being accompanied by a local, trained guide. Self-guiding booklets can be purchased when visiting Mistico Arenal Hanging Bridges Park and La Selva Biological Station. Other national parks, such as Parque Nacional Cahuita, have an information hut at the entrance to the park, which leads to well-marked, well-maintained trails

Guided Tours

National parks close before dusk, but lodging is available at Parque Nacional Chirripó; and several private reserves with lodgings offer night tours. Multi-day treks and white-water rafting can be arranged by many tour operators. Nocturnal hikes can also be booked via many tour operators and guides. Generally you will see more wildlife on a guided tour than on a self-guided one.

INDEX

PHRASE BOOK

Costa Rican Spanish is essentially the same as the Castilian spoken in Spain, with some differences in vocabulary and pronunciation. The most noticeable difference is the pronunciation of the soft "c" and the letter "z" as "s" rather than "th".

IN AN EMERGENCY

Help!	¡Socorro!	soh-**koh**-roh
Stop!	¡Pare!	pah-reh
Call a doctor!	¡Llame a un médico!	yah-meh ah oon meh-dee-koh
Fire!	¡Fuego!	foo-**eh**-goh
Could you help me?	¿Me podría ayudar?	meh poh-**dree**-yah ah-yoo-**dahr**
policeman	policía	poh-lee-**see**-ah

COMMUNICATION ESSENTIALS

Yes	Sí	see
No	No	noh
Please	Por favor	pohr fah-**vohr**
Thank you	Gracias	**grah**-see-ahs
Excuse me	Perdone	pehr-**doh**-neh
Hello	Hola	oh-lah
Good morning	Buenos días	bweh-nohs dee-ahs
Good afternoon	Buenas tardes	bweh-nahs **tahr**-dehs
Good night	Buenas noches	bweh-nahs **noh**-chehs
Bye (casual)	Chao	cha-oh
Goodbye	Adiós	ah-dee-**ohs**
See you later	Hasta luego	ah-**stah** loo-**weh**-goh
Morning	La mañana	lah mah-**nyah**-nah
Afternoon	La tarde	lah tahr-deh
Night	La noche	lah **noh**-cheh
Yesterday	Ayer	ah-**yehr**
Today	Hoy	oy
Tomorrow	Mañana	mah-**nyah**-nah
Here	Aquí	ah-**kee**
There	Allá	ah-**yah**
What?	¿Qué?	keh
When?	¿Cuándo?	kwahn-doh
Why?	¿Por qué?	pohr-keh
Where?	¿Dónde?	dohn-deh
How are you?	¿Cómo está usted?	koh-moh ehs-tah oos-**tehd**
Very well, thank you	Muy bien, gracias	mwee-byehn-**ehn grah**-see-ahs
Pleased to meet you	Mucho gusto	moo-**choh goo**-stoh
I'm sorry	Lo siento	loh see-**ehn**-toh

USEFUL PHRASES

That's fine	Está bien	ehs-**tah** bee-ehn
Great/fantastic!	¡Qué bien!	keh bee-ehn
Where does this road go?	¿Adónde va esta calle?	ah-**dohn**-deh bah ehs-tah kah-yeh
Do you speak English?	¿Habla inglés?	ah-blah een-**glehs**
I don't understand	No comprendo	noh kohm-**prehn**-doh
I want	Quiero	kee-**yehr**-oh

USEFUL WORDS

big	grande	**grahn**-deh
small	pequeño/a	peh-**keh**-nyoh/nyah
hot	caliente	kah-lee-**ehn**-teh
cold	frío/a	**free**-oh/ah
good	bueno/a	**bweh**-noh/nah
bad	malo/a	**mah**-loh/lah
open	abierto/a	ah-bee-**ehr**-toh/tah
closed	cerrado/a	sehr-**rah**-doh/dah
left	izquierda	ees-key-**ehr**-dah
right	derecha	deh-**reh**-chah
near	cerca	**sehr**-kah
far	lejos	**leh**-hohs
up	arriba	ah-**ree**-bah
down	abajo	ah-**bah**-hoh
early	temprano	tehm-**prah**-noh
late	tarde	**tahr**-deh
now/very soon	ahora/ahorita	ah-**ohr**-ah/ah-ohr-**ee**-tah
more	más	mahs
less	menos	**meh**-nohs
very	muy	mwee
a little	(un) poco	(oon) poh-koh
opposite	frente a	**frehn**-teh ah
below/above	abajo/arriba	ah-**bah**-hoh/ ah-**ree**-bah
entrance	entrada	ehn-**trah**-dah
exit	salida	sah-**lee**-dah
stairs	escaleras	ehs-kah-**leh**-rahs
elevator	el ascensor	ehl ah-sehn-**sohr**
toilets	baños/servicios sanitarios	**bah**-nyohs/sehr-**vee**-see-yohs sah-nee-**tah**-ree-ohs
women's	de damas	deh **dah**-mahs
men's	de caballeros	deh kah-bah-**yeh**-rohs
sanitary napkins	toallas sanitarias	toh-**ah**-yahs sah-nee-**tah**-ree-yahs
tampons	tampones	tahm-**poh**-nehs
condoms	condones	kohn-**doh**-nehs
toilet paper	papel higiénico	pah-**pehl** hee-**hyen**-ee-koh
(non-)smoking area	área de (no) fumar	**ah**-ree-ah deh (noh) foo-**mahr**
camera (a roll of) film	la cámara (un rollo de) película	lah **kah**-mah-rah (oon roh-yoh deh) peh-**lee**-koo-lah
batteries	las pilas	lahs **pee**-lahs
passport	pasaporte	pah-sah-**pohr**-teh
visa	visa	**vee**-sah

POST OFFICES AND BANKS

post office	oficina de correos	oh-fee-**see**-nah deh kohr-**reh**-ohs
stamps	estampillas	ehs-tahm-**pee**-yahs
postcard	una postal	oo-nah pohs-**tahl**
postbox	apartado	ah-pahr-**tah**-doh
cashier	cajero	kah-**heh**-roh
ATM	cajero automático	kah-heh-roh ahw-toh-**mah**-tee-koh
bank	banco	**bahn**-koh
What is the dollar rate?	¿A cómo está el dolar?	ah koh-moh ehs-tah ehl doh-**lahr**

SHOPPING

How much does... this cost?	¿Cuánto cuesta... esto?	**Kwahn**-toh... kwehs-tah ehs-toh
Do you have?	¿Tienen?	tee-**yeh**-nehn
Do you take credit cards/ traveler's checks?	¿Aceptan tarjetas de crédito/ cheques de viajero?	ahk-**sehp**-tahn tahr-**heh**-tahs deh kreh-dee-toh/cheh-kehs deh vee-ah-**heh**-roh
discount	un descuento	oon dehs-koo-**ehn**-toh
expensive	caro	**kahr**-oh
cheap	barato	bah-**rah**-toh
clothes	la ropa	lah **roh**-pah
size, clothes	talla	**tah**-yah

size, shoes	número	noo-*mehr*-oh
bakery	panadería	pah-nah-deh-*ree*-ah
bookstore	librería	lee-breh-*ree*-ah
grocer's	pulpería	pool-peh-*ree*-ah
market	mercado	mehr-*kah*-doh
shoe store	la zapatería	lah sah-pah-teh-*ree*-ah
supermarket	el supermercado	ehl soo-pehr-mehr-*kah*-doh
travel agency	la agencia de viajes	lah ah-*hehn*-see-ah deh vee-*ah*-hehs

SIGHTSEEING

bay	bahía	bah-*ee*-ah
beach	playa	*plah*-yah
building	edificio	eh-dee-*fee*-see-oh
cathedral	catedral	kah-teh-**drahl**
church	iglesia	ee-**gleh**-see-ah
farm	finca	*feehn*-kah
forest	bosque/selva	bohs-keh/sehl-bah
garden	jardín	hahr-**deen**
lake	lago/laguna	lah-goh/lah-goo-nah
mangrove	manglar	mahn-**glahr**
mountain peak	cerro	**seh**-roh
mountain range	cordillera	kohr-dee-**yeh**-rah
museum	museo	moo-**seh**-oh
neighborhood	barrio	**bah**-ree-oh
port	puerto	poo-**her**-toh
ranger station	puesto de guardia	**poo**-ehs-toh deh goo-**ahr**-dee-ah
river	río	*ree*-oh
trail	sendero	sehn-**deh**-roh
theater	teatro	teh-**ah**-troh
tourist information office	oficina de turismo	oh-fee-**see**-nah deh too-**rees**-moh
viewpoint	mirador	mee-rah-**dohr**
ticket	el boleto/la entrada	ehl boh-**leh**-toh lah ehn-**trah**-dah
guide (person)	el/la guía	ehl/lah **gee**-ah
guide (book)	la guía	lah **gee**-ah
guided tour	una visita guiada	oo-nah vee-**see**-tah gee-**ah**-dah
map	el mapa	ehl **mah**-pah

HEALTH

I feel ill	Me siento mal	meh seh-**ehn**-toh mahl
We need a doctor	Necesitamos un médico	neh-seh-see-**tah**-mohs oon meh-dee-koh
drug store	farmacia	fahr-**mah**-see-ah
medicine	medicina	meh-dee-**see**-nah
ambulance	ambulancia	ahm-boo-**lahn**-see-ah
mosquito coils	espirales	ehs-pee-**rah**-lehs

TRANSPORTATION

When does the... leave?	¿A qué hora sale el...?	ah keh oh-*rah* sah-leh ehl...?
Is there a bus to...?	¿Hay un bus a...?	eye oon boohs ah...?
bus station	la estación de autobuses	lah ehs-tah-see-**ohn** deh ow-toh-**boo**-sehs
ticket office	la boletería	lah boh-leh-teh-**ree**-ah
airport	aeropuerto	ah-ehr-oh-poo-**ehr**-toh
customs	la aduana	lah ah-doo-**ah**-nah
taxi stand/rank	la parada de taxis	lah pah-**rah**-dah deh **tahk**-sees
car rental	rent a car	**rehn**-tah cahr
motorcycle	la moto(cicleta)	lah moh-toh-(see-**kleh**-tah)
4WD	doble tracción	**doh**-bleh trahk-**siohn**
bicycle	la bicicleta	lah bee-see-**kleh**-tah

water-taxi	una panga/un bote	oo-nah **pahn**-gah/oon **boh**-teh
aerial tram	teleférico	teh-leh-**feh**-ree-koh
insurance	los seguros	lohs seh-**goo**-rohs
gas station	gasolinera	gah-soh-leen-**ehr**-ah
garage	taller de mecánica	tah-**yehr** deh meh-**kahn**-ee-kah
I have a flat tire	Se me ponchó la llanta	seh meh pohn-**shoh** lah yahn-tah

STAYING IN A HOTEL

I have a reservation	Tengo una reservación	tehn-goh **oo**-nah reh-sehr-vah-see-ohn
Do you have a vacant room?	¿Tienen una habitación libre?	tee-**eh**-nehn oo-nah ah-bee-tah-see-**ohn**lee-breh
double room	habitación doble	ah-bee-tah-see-ohn doh-bleh
single room	habitación sencilla	ah-bee-tah-see-ohn sehn-see-yah
room with a bath	habitación con baño	ah-bee-tah-see-ohn kohn bah-nyoh
shower	la ducha	lah doo-chah
The ... is not working	No funciona el/la...	noh foon-see-oh-nah ehl/lah...
Where is the dining-room/bar?	¿Dónde está el restaurante/el bar?	**dohn**-deh ehs-**tah** ehl rehs-toh-rahn-teh/ehl bahr
hot/cold water	agua caliente/fría	**ah**-goo-ah kah-lee-**ehn**-teh/**free**-ah
soap	el jabón	ehl hah-**bohn**
towel	la toalla	lah toh-**ah**-yah
key	la llave	lah **yah**-veh

EATING OUT

Have you got a table for ...?	¿Tienen mesa para...?	tee-**eh**-nehn meh-sah pah-**rah**...?
I want to reserve a table	Quiero reservar una mesa	kee-eh-roh reh-sehr-**vahr** oo-nah **meh**-sah
The bill, please	La cuenta, por favor	lah **kwehn**-tah pohr fah-**vohr**
I am a vegetarian	Soy vegetariano/a	soy veh-heh-tah-ree-**ah**-no/na
waiter/waitress	mesero/a	meh-**seh**-roh/rah
menu	la carta	lah **kahr**-tah
fixed-price menu	menú del día	meh-**noo** dehl **dee**-ah
wine list	la carta de vinos	lah **kahr**-tah deh **vee**-nohs
glass	un vaso	oon vah-soh
bottle	una botella	oo-nah boh-**teh**-yah
knife	un cuchillo	oon koo-chee-yoh
fork	un tenedor	oon teh-neh-**dohr**
spoon	una cuchara	oo-nah koo-**chah**-rah
napkin	la servilleta	lah sehr-vee-**yeh**-tah
breakfast	el desayuno	ehl deh-sah-**yoo**-noh
lunch	almuerzo	ahl-moo-**ehr**-soh
dinner	la cena	lah **seh**-nah
main course	el plato fuerte	ehl **plah**-toh foo-**ehr**-teh
starters	las entradas	lahs ehn-**trah**-das
dish of the day	el plato del día	ehl **plat**-toh dehl **dee**-ah
rare	término rojo	**tehr**-mee-noh **roh**-hoh
medium	término medio	**tehr**-mee-noh meh-**dee**-oh
well done	bien cocido	bee-**ehn** koh-**see**-doh
chair	la silla	lah **see**-yah

Is service included?	¿El servicio está incluido?	*ehl sehr-**vee**-see-oh ehs-**tah** een-kloo-**ee**-doh*
ashtray	cenicero	*seh-nee-**seh**-roh*
cigarettes	los cigarros	*lohs see-**gah**-rohs*
food stall	una soda	*oo-nah **soh**-dah*
neighborhood bar	una cantina/ un bar	*oo-nah kahn-tee-nah/oon bahr*

MENU DECODER

el aceite	*ah-see-**eh**-teh*	oil
las aceitunas	*ah-seh-toon-ahs*	olives
el agua mineral	*ah-gwa mee-neh-**rahl***	mineral water
el arroz	*ahr-rohs*	rice
el azúcar	*ah-**soo**-kahr*	sugar
una bebida	*beh-**bee**-dah*	drink
boca	*boh-kah*	snack
el café	*kah-**feh***	coffee
la carne	*kahr-neh*	meat
el cerdo	*sehr-doh*	pork
la cerveza	*sehr-**veh**-sah*	beer
el chocolate	*choh-koh-**lah**-teh*	chocolate
la ensalada	*ehn-sah-**lah**-dah*	salad
la fruta	*froo-tah*	fruit
el helado	*eh-**lah**-doh*	ice cream
el huevo	*oo-**eh**-voh*	egg
el jugo	*hoo-goh*	juice
la leche	*leh-cheh*	milk
la mantequilla	*mahn-teh-**kee**-yah*	butter
los mariscos	*mah-**rees**-kohs*	seafood
el pan	*pahn*	bread
las papas	*pah-pahs*	potatoes
las papas a la francesa	*pah-pahs ah lah frahn-**seh**-sah*	French fries
las papas fritas	*pah-pahs **free**-tahs*	potato chips
el pastel	*pahs-**tehl***	cake
el pescado	*pehs-**kah**-doh*	fish
picante	*pee-kahn-teh*	spicy
la pimienta	*pee-mee-yehn-tah*	pepper
el pollo	*poh-yoh*	chicken
el postre	*pohs-treh*	dessert
el queso	*keh-soh*	cheese
el refresco	*reh-**frehs**-koh*	soft drink/soda
la sal	*sahl*	salt
la sopa	*soh-pah*	soup
el sánguche	*sahn-goo-she*	sandwich
el té negro	*teh neh-groh*	tea
la torta	*tohr-tah*	burger
las tostadas	*tohs-tah-dahs*	toast
el vino blanco	*vee-noh blahn-koh*	white wine
el vino tinto	*vee-noh teen-toh*	red wine

CULTURE AND SOCIETY

campesino	*cahm-peh-**see**-noh*	subsistence farmer
cantón	*cahn-tohn*	county
carreta	*cah-reh-tah*	oxcart
cumbia	*coom-bee-ah*	Columbian music
Josefino	*hoh-seh-**fee**-noh*	resident of San José
marimba	*mah-**reem**-bah*	kind of xylophone
merengue	*meh-**rehn**-geh*	fast-paced Dominican music
sabanero	*sah-bah-**neh**-roh*	cowboy
salsa	*sahl-sah*	Cuban dance music
Tico/ costarricense	*tee-coh/**cohs**-tah-ree-**sehn**-seh*	Costa Rican

NUMBERS

0	cero	*seh-roh*
1	uno	*oo-noh*
2	dos	*dohs*
3	tres	*trehs*
4	cuatro	*kwa-troh*
5	cinco	*seen-koh*
6	seis	*says*
7	siete	*see-eh-teh*
8	ocho	*oh-choh*
9	nueve	*nweh-veh*
10	diez	*dee-ehs*
11	once	*ohn-seh*
12	doce	*doh-seh*
13	trece	*treh-seh*
14	catorce	*kah-tohr-seh*
15	quince	*keen-seh*
16	dieciséis	*dee-eh-see-**seh**-ees*
17	diecisiete	*dee-eh-see-see-eh-teh*
18	dieciocho	*dee-eh-see-oh-choh*
19	diecinueve	*dee-eh-see-nweh-veh*
20	veinte	*veh-een-teh*
30	treinta	*treh-een-tah*
40	cuarenta	*kwah-**rehn**-tah*
50	cincuenta	*seen-**kwehn**-tah*
60	sesenta	*seh-**sehn**-tah*
70	setenta	*seh-**tehn**-tah*
80	ochenta	*oh-**chehn**-tah*
90	noventa	*noh-**vehn**-tah*
100	cien	*see-ehn*
500	quinientos	*khee-nee-**ehn**-tohs*
1,000	mil	*meel*
1,001	mil uno	*meel oo-noh*
5,000	cinco mil	*seen-koh meel*

TIME

one minute	un minuto	*oon mee-noo-toh*
one hour	una hora	*oo-nah oh-rah*
Monday	lunes	*loo-nehs*
Tuesday	martes	*mahr-tehs*
Wednesday	miércoles	*mee-ehr-koh-lehs*
Thursday	jueves	*hoo-weh-vehs*
Friday	viernes	*vee-ehr-nehs*
Saturday	sábado	*sah-bah-doh*
Sunday	domingo	*doh-meen-goh*
January	enero	*eh-neh-roh*
February	febrero	*feh-breh-roh*
March	marzo	*mahr-soh*
April	abril	*ah-breel*
May	mayo	*mah-yoh*
June	junio	*hoo-nee-oh*
July	julio	*hoo-lee-oh*
August	agosto	*ah-gohs-toh*
September	setiembre	*seh-tee-**ehm**-breh*
October	octubre	*ohk-**too**-breh*
November	noviembre	*noh-vee-**ehm**-breh*
December	diciembre	*dee-see-**ehm**-breh*

DK would like to thank the following for their contribution to the previous edition: Christoper Baker, Adrian Hepworth, Derek Harvey

The publisher would like to thank the following for their kind permission to reproduce their photographs:

Key: a-above; b-below/bottom; c-centre; f-far; l-left; r-right; t-top

123RF.com: Blueseacz 85tr; Simon Dannhauer 11t, 222bl; Jiri Hrebicek 85cr; Ondrej Prosicky 94br; Gioia Speer 94tl; Kevin Wells 22-3t; Charles Wollertz 71tr, 187bl; Ekachai Wongsakul 58-9ca.

4Corners: Pietro Canali 17bl, 154-5.

Adrian Hepworth: 100-1, 230-1b, 231tr.

Alamy Stock Photo: age fotostock 24crb, 235tl, / Alvaro Leiva 164bl, 182tl; Amar and Isabelle Guillen - Guillen Photo LLC 22-3ca, 74tr, 97crb; shams faraz amir 185cr; Antiqua Print Gallery 51tl; ARCTIC IMAGES / Ragnar Th Sigurdsson 218t; Arterra Picture Library / Clement Philippe 181br; Artokoloro Quint Lox Limited 116br, / liszt collection 139br; Avalon / Bruce Coleman Inc 98b, / Photoshot License 63cra, 74crb, 161bl; Stephen Bay 119t; Elizabeth Bennett 50crb; Georg Berg 10clb, 132bc; Bildagentur-online / Schickert 107tr, 113tl; Billberryphotography / YAY Media AS 143b; Biosphoto 94cra, / Jean-Francois Noblet 209br; Sabena Jane Blackbird 137cra, 239tr; Eduardo Blanco 140-1t, 142tl; Blickwinkel 70crb, 75cra, 94crb; Steve Bly 12cl, 33br; Jurate Buiviene 46tc; Carlos Villoch - MagicSea.com 12t; CarverMostardi 163t, 167bl; Cavan Images 225bl; Chronicle 51cla; ClassicStock / A. Littlejohn 138tr; Thornton Cohen 13cr, 30tl, 42bl, 48cla, 208bl; Helmut Corneli 83cra; Jan A. Csernoch 131tl; Yaacov Dagan 19t, 212-3; David R. Frazier Photolibrary, Inc. 142bc; Design Pics Inc / Deddeda / Destinations 162b; Oscar Dominguez 123tl; Michael Dwyer 125cra, 223br; Eagle Visions Photography / Craig Lovell 141br; Patrick J. Endres 165t; Lindsay Fendt 49tr, 49cr, 242tr; S. Forster 209t; Chris Fredriksson 207tc; Roberto Fumagalli 158clb; Gabbro 39bl, 200br; Gaertner 144bl; George Karbus Photography 80-1; hemis.fr 20cr, 32tl, 42-3t, 174tl, 237tr, / Gardel Bertrand 8-9b, 20t, 107cra, 186br, 240t, / Gregory Gerault 244tl, / Franck Guiziou 117cl; adrian hepworth 28tl, 77br, 177b, 189br, 231cra; Historic Collection 52crb; Zach Holmes 60cla; Claude Huot 44-5t; imageBROKER 74br, 79crb, 107br, / Oliver Gerhard 162cra, 185fcra, / Sonja Jordan 204br, / Peter Schickert 115b, / Siepmann 180tr; ImageSync Ltd 211tr; Jon Arnold Images Ltd 24t; Philip Jones 88cr; juniors@ wildlife / Poelzer; W. 167fcra; John Keates 24cr, 224; Dave Keightley 95cra; Cara Koch 48clb; Russell Kord 17t, 126-7; Ivan Kuzmin 74cra; Natalia Kuzmina 91tr; Larry

Larsen 219tr; Keith Levit 46br; Look 200t; Look / Konrad Wothe 148tl; Luis Louro 99cra; Mario Humberto Morales Rubí 185crb; Mauritius Images Gmbh 23tr; mauritius images GmbH / Reinhard Dirscherl 167cra; Neil McAllister 20crb, 26bl, 124bl, 135tr, 137tl, 243tr; Media Drum World 82tr; Megapress 34-5t; Christopher Milligan 96tr; John Mitchell 52bc; Josep Moreno 60-1ca; Mostardi Photography 43bl; MShieldsPhotos 39cr; Juan Carlos Muñoz 37tl, 37cl, 51tr; My Lit'l Eye 192t; Nature Picture Library 82cra; Nature Picture Library / Chris & Monique Fallows 167crb, / Doug Perrine 167cr; Newscom / BJ Warnick 53br; M. Timothy O'Keefe 84b; ONEWORLD PICTURE / Stefan Oberhauser 118bl; Oyvind Martinsen-Panama Wildlife 238tl; Stefano Paterna 35br, 111bc, 146crb, 146b; M L Pearson 191tr; Anthony Pierce 82br; Francesco Puntiroli 221cb; Rana Royalty free 45cl; Sergi Reboredo 203bl; Whit Richardson 239b; robertharding 11cr, 18cb, 22cla, 194-5, 199crb; robertharding Rob Francis 186t, 188t, 190-1b, / R H Productions 190tl; Juan Carlos Muñoz Robredo 28br; Stefan Rosengren 97cra; Marcin Roszkowski 185tr; Jeff Rotman 47br; Bert de Ruiter 184t; Kevin Schafer 149tc; Peter Schickert 134b, 219bl; Martin Shields 44b; Kumar Sriskandan 42tc, 53tr; Stephen Frink Collection 29tr; Steve Bloom Images 177t; Martin Strmiska 31cb; 83tr; SuperStock / MOCA Jacksonville 192bc; ticopix 111ca; travelib prime 183br; Universal Images Group North America LLC / Education Images 210tl; UtCon Collection 52tl; Rosa Isabel Vazquez 203cla; Margus Vilbas 121cra; VWPics / Kobby Dagan 160-1t; WaterFrame 242b, / gno 189tc, / mus 167br; Maximilian Weinzierl 241r; Corey Wise 193bl; Xinhua / Kent Gilbert 13br, 48cl, 48cr; Galyna Andrushko 151cla, / Lev Kropotov 185cra, / S.Schnepf 122bl.

AWL Images: John Coletti 114tl, 130clb.

Bridgeman Images: University of Miami / Collection of the Lowe Art Museum, U / Gift of Sylvia Coppersmith in memory of Dora Coppersmith 50bc; Private Collection / © Look and Learn 51cb.

Centro Costarricense De Ciencias Y Cultura: 111tl, 111cra, 111crb.

Christopher Baker: 109cra, 131tr.

Coffea Diversa S.A.: 139t.

Costa Rica Piano Festival: 49cl.

Depositphotos Inc: wollertz 201b.

Dreamstime.com: Alfredohr2000 185b; Ammit 175bl; Galyna Andrushko 8cl; Andrey Armyagov 79cra; Damian Olivera Bergallo 240bl; Bobhilscher 96br; Brizardh 178cl; Harry Collins 92-3; Kobby Dagan 24bl; Louis Michel

Penguin
Random
House

This edition updated by
Contributor Shafik Meghji
Senior Editor Alison McGill
Senior Designers Stuti Tiwari Bhatia,
Tania Gomes
Project Editors Dipika Dasgupta, Rada Radojičić
Project Art Editor Bharti Karakoti
Editor Anuroop Sanwalia
Picture Research Coordinator
Sumita Khatwani
Assistant Picture Research Administrator
Vagisha Pushp
Jacket Coordinator Bella Talbot
Jacket Designer Ben Hinks
Senior Cartographic Editor Casper Morris
Cartography Manager Suresh Kumar
DTP Designer Tanveer Zaidi
Senior Production Editor Jason Little
Production Controller Rebecca Parton
Deputy Managing Editor Beverly Smart
Managing Editors Shikha Kulkarni,
Hollie Teague
Managing Art Editor Bess Daly
Senior Managing Art Editor Priyanka Thakur
Art Director Maxine Pedliham
Publishing Director Georgina Dee

First edition 2005

Published in Great Britain by Dorling Kindersley Limited,
DK, One Embassy Gardens, 8 Viaduct Gardens,
London SW11 7BW

The authorised representative in the EEA is
Dorling Kindersley Verlag GmbH. Arnulfstr.
124, 80636 Munich, Germany

Published in the United States by DK Publishing,
1450 Broadway, Suite 801, New York, NY 10018

A CIP catalog record for this book
is available from the British Library.

A catalog record for this book is available
from the Library of Congress.

ISSN: 1542 1554
ISBN: 978 0 2415 4251 4

Printed and bound in China.

www.dk.com

A NOTE FROM DK EYEWITNESS
The rapid rate at which the world is changing is
constantly keeping the DK Eyewitness team on our toes.
While we've worked hard to ensure that this edition of
Costa Rica is accurate and up-to-date, we know that
opening hours alter, standards shift, prices fluctuate,
places close and new ones pop up in their stead.
So, if you notice we've got something wrong or
left something out, we want to hear about it.
Please get in touch at travelguides@dk.com